FROM THE MIND
INTO THE BODY

FROM THE MIND INTO THE BODY

——

The Cultural Origins of Psychosomatic Symptoms

Edward Shorter

THE FREE PRESS
A Division of Macmillan, Inc.
NEW YORK

Maxwell Macmillan Canada
TORONTO

Maxwell Macmillan International
NEW YORK   OXFORD   SINGAPORE   SYDNEY

The Free Press
A Division of Macmillan, Inc.
866 Third Avenue, New York, N.Y. 10022

Maxwell Macmillan Canada, Inc.
1200 Eglinton Avenue East
Suite 200
Don Mills, Ontario M3C 3N1

Macmillan, Inc. is part of the Maxwell Communication Group of Companies.

Printed in the United States of America

printing number
1   2   3   4   5   6   7   8   9   10

Library of Congress Cataloging-in-Publication Data

Shorter, Edward.
  From the mind into the body : the cultural origins of
psychosomatic symptoms / Edward Shorter.
    p.   cm.
  Includes index.
  ISBN 0-02-928666-2
  1. Medicine, Psychosomatic—Cross-cultural studies—
History. I. Title.
RC49.S354 1994
616'.001'9—dc20   93-5430
                                                       CIP

For my dearest Anne Marie, again

Contents

Preface

IN THE WORLD OF ILLNESS some people suffer more frequently than others. It does not surprise us, for example, that cancer strikes smokers more often than nonsmokers or that heart disease fells the aged more than the young. We understand the social causes of these differences.

But what about conditions that affect the mind? And within the huge province of psychiatry, what about psychosomatic illness in particular, defined as the perception of physical symptoms for which the patient seeks medical help and for which there is no organic cause? Whom does it strike? And why? This book looks at people who suffer the symptoms of illness without disease. Do such illnesses affect the rich more than the poor? Women more than men? The young more than the old?

And to what extent, if any, does biology play a role in determining the victims of psychosomatic illness? Not only stress or misfortune can make us ill. Our genes may do so as well. In psychosomatic illness there seem to be underlying biological or constitutional circumstances, evidently genetic in nature, that cause some people to come down with psychosomatic illnesses more often than others. Understanding such symptoms means coming to grips with elements of biology as well as of culture.

This book suggests that the process of becoming ill without being organically sick occurs as an interaction between the genetically driven brain and the socially conditioned mind. It is committed to the notion that psychosomatic illness has a biological as

well as a cultural basis. Scholars have long known about some of
the social circumstances involved in psychosomatic illness. And in
my previous book, *From Paralysis to Fatigue: A History of
Psychosomatic Illness in the Modern Era* (Free Press, 1992), I discussed changes in psychosomatic illness from century to century,
principally as a result of physicians' changing views of what they
considered to be legitimate disease.

Here I focus on such social circumstances as gender, social
class, ethnic group, and age—also seen historically—and how they
have helped to construct illness. Looking at symptoms in this way
confers a longer perspective on both biology and society. When
symptoms change, is it because social life has become more stressful, because the biological basis of illness has altered, or because
the culture enveloping us has started sending different messages?
Thoughtful people may ask these questions, and a historical view
gives enough information about change actually to answer some of
them.

Although this book ventures a few tentative answers, it would
nonetheless be pretentious to think that historical evidence gets us
much beyond the tentative, for so much of the material is anecdotal in nature—gathered from manuscript patient histories and
medical periodicals scattered in archives and libraries throughout
Europe and North America. The kinds of systemic surveys that
one needs to pin down the factors that matter statistically—and
those that do not—were not done in the past. We shall never have
that information. But one does get a sense of patterns, and of differences from group to group, by studying thoroughly the anecdotal sources of the time. These are very rich, and I am confident
that the historical conclusions I draw are based on evidence that is
representative of its day.

I am not claiming to have cracked a riddle as vast as that of psychosomatic illness. Still, a historical view may offer some fresh insights. Humanists and social scientists who have grown up in the
tradition that only nurture—and not nature—determines human
behavior may encounter a surprise or two in these pages, for psychiatric illness, of which psychosomatic symptoms are a part, has
an uncontestable biological and genetic basis. Clinicians accustomed to seeing their patients' psychosomatic symptoms in the

context of a life history of stress or anxiety may be surprised to see certain groups of symptoms characterize certain social classes or ethnic groups, for symptoms have a social as much as an individual stamp. Patients themselves may find some encouragement in these pages, for individuals who have psychosomatic illnesses often, to their detriment, tend to cling to the belief of organicity, seeing their symptoms as evidence of actual physical disease. They may therefore find it enlightening to discover themselves to be part of larger patterns of behavior, of which previously they had little understanding.

The book is based on the premise that biology and culture interact in the production of psychosomatic symptoms. But the interesting question is *how* they interact, for it is notions of social class, gender, ethnicity, and age that help us sort out their interplay. Both social disposition and the biological element are active principles: Genetics counts for a good deal, but so does culture.

I would like to thank the Social Science and Humanities Research Council of Canada and the Hannah Institute for the History of Medicine for helping with the many expenses incurred in doing this research. The dedication of the staff of the Science and Medicine Library of the University of Toronto made it possible for me to read very widely across the sources. And my research assistants Kaia Toop and Erika Steffer helped me assemble the evidence in order to achieve this look at doctors and patients across the centuries. I also would like to acknowledge the fine work of my secretary Andrea Clark. Dr. Gary Remington had the kindness to look over some of my conclusions, and I am thankful again in this volume, as in the last, for the careful criticism of Dr. Walter Vandereycken, who with his comprehensive knowledge of the history of psychiatry suggested numerous additions and corrections. Finally, I am grateful for Susan Llewellyn's fine work as copy editor, and for the great good sense of Joyce Seltzer, my friend and my editor at The Free Press.

FROM THE MIND
INTO THE BODY

1

——

The Play of Biology and Culture

IT GOES VERY MUCH against the grain to think of ourselves as driven by any force other than our own sweet intelligence. Yet it is clear that in both health and illness much human behavior has a biological basis animated by our genes—by the very substance of our physical beings—rather than rationally determined by our minds. Humanists, defending our ability to reason, usually rail at assertions of biologically conditioned behavior because of their terrifying and potentially destructive social and political implications. And they are not wrong to do so. The fact that culture plays a major role alongside biology in the genesis of psychiatric illness in particular makes psychiatry different from many other fields of medicine: The patients' problems are determined by their life stories and social situations, not just by disorders in the physical fiber of their bodies. Nevertheless biology matters.

In the world of psychiatry psychosomatic illness offers a special challenge to people interested in the play of biology and culture because psychosomatic symptoms are so convincing to the patient as evidence of real organic disease. But by definition in psychosomatic illness, the problem arises in the mind; it is psychogenic; there is no physical lesion (unless it is a genetic one). And yet, at the level of perception and sensation, the cognitive dimension of our cultural life, the evidence of disease seems to those afflicted to be so undeniable. How can this be "all in our minds"? patients ask. But then the news for patients may be even worse: Not only are they given to understand, if they are told the truth, that their problems are psychogenic. If the doctor goes on to say all that is on his or her mind, the patient learns that in addition to being nonorganic, the problem may well be genetic. Although most patients are likely to take this home as alarming and bewildering news, it goes without saying that in the real world few physicians would ever couch the news in such terms.

But we, together in this book, do not have a doctor-patient relationship. Rather we have that of author and potentially skeptical readers. I am trying to convince you that what seems improbable and unacceptable to many is in fact true. Even the most privately perceived physical experiences, which appear to be so intimately derived from our personhood, are in fact determined partly by biology (meaning genetics) and partly by such categories as gender, social class, and age, the larger organizing principles of the social world. In the whole domain of the mind-body relationship there can be no more interesting problem than the untangling of genes and perceptions: When we perceive physical symptoms that we take for evidence of organic illness and for which we seek medical help, what is the role of genes and what is that of culture? And how do genes and culture affect each other?

The Evidence of Biology

So elemental is the biological nature of much mental illness that physicians have always been aware of it, though often able to articulate it only in the most impressionistic manner. The experience of hearing, day after day across years of practice, patients tell of close relatives who also have psychiatric problems convinced many doctors in the past that psychiatric illness was in part inherited. In 1787 the English physician William Perfect had gathered twenty years of experience in boarding mentally ill patients at his home in Westmalling in Kent. He deplored the tendency to attribute "insanity" either to some change in the blood vessels of the brain or to the influence of sudden passions. "I must ever be of opinion that, were we oftener to extend our enquiries by tracing them back in a lineal direction to the progenitors of the maniacal patients, we should generally adopt the maxim, that the much greater number of mankind who become insane upon any particular change in the constitution have an hereditary predisposition to madness." Perfect had kept "an exact genealogical register, to demonstrate the force of my enquiries" and gave the example of a patient who "spoke with surliness and ill-nature, suspected everyone of sinister views and nefarious intentions, even those in whom, but a few days before, he had reposed an implicit confidence." Perfect's patient "seemed anxious to avoid all conversation, to fly from the society of mankind, and the very appearance of the human species filled him with scorn and disgust; if he was spoken to, he would frown and look contumeliously, turn away with silent scorn, or mutter malice and dislike." As the patient entered Perfect's home, "he would not eat a morsel of anything unless it was left in his room by [Perfect]." "Upon inquiry," said Perfect, to prove his point about ancestry, "I discovered that the grandfather of this unfortunate man was afflicted with a similar species of insanity for three years before his death."[1] The case illustrates the tendency across the ages of highly experienced physicians to implicate heredity in mental illness.

Similarly, diffuse apprehensiveness about heredity seeps out of the body of medical writing before World War I. To Ewald Hecker, among the first psychiatrists to describe schizophrenia and in the 1880s director of a nerve sanatorium on the Rhine, it was clear that his patients often had a familial disease: "The insight developed very early in psychiatry that psychoses have a pronounced tendency to be hereditary." What was more, neurotic and psychosomatic illnesses passed themselves from generation to generation, including "Hysteria, hypochondria, epilepsy, neuralgia, migraine [Hemikranie]. . . ." To save families from the nightmare of nervous illness turning into insanity, Hecker counseled early treatment in establishments such as his own.[2]

In the course of the nineteenth century such scattered insights became structured into dogmatic constructions about heredity and degeneration. French psychiatrist Jacques Moreau de Tours, who in the early 1850s worked at a private asylum outside Paris, popularized the notion that mental illness was organic in nature and hereditary in origin. His colleague Bénédict-Augustin Morel, a psychiatrist at a state asylum in Rouen, went on to elaborate the concept of degeneration: that psychiatric illness worsened as it was passed from generation to generation, leaving at the end of the line a population of degenerates.[3] In the 1880s Valentin Magnan, the third French member of this organicist triad and chief psychiatrist of the Sainte-Anne asylum in Paris, anchored the doctrine of degeneration as a horror of bad blood in the consciousness of European culture.[4]

The flirtation of psychiatry itself with degeneration was relatively brief. Yet by the turn of the twentieth century the notion had spread far beyond medicine and was being applied by racialist and conservative social thinkers to matters of race and class. The doctrine of degeneration became infamous as one of the "justifications" for Hitler's persecution of the Jews, and as a foundation of the eugenics movement.[5] Hitched to these twin causes, degeneration became odious in the eyes of liberal social thinkers and was condemned as rubbish. It went completely out of style in the 1930s and 1940s and in its passing dragged organically oriented psychiatry down with it.

Simultaneously with the doctrine of degeneration in France came the development of much more scientifically based neuroscience in Germany. In the second half of the nineteenth century, a whole series of German asylum psychiatrists and professors of psychiatry in medical schools were undertaking fundamental research in the anatomy of the brain, particularly its microscopic structure. They were looking for the causes of mental illness but found very little, with the exception of the rather special case of neurosyphilis. Yet by 1900 such researchers as Franz Nissl and Aloys Alzheimer at Heidelberg (who in 1907 first described the form of dementia named for him) and Ludwig Edinger in Frankfurt, had charted the fine structure of the brain, an undeniable scientific accomplishment. These German psychiatrists also believed that mental illness was inheritable, though they cared less about degeneration than did the French.[6] These two schools together, the French degenerationists and the German neuroanatomists, might be called the first biological psychiatry.

With the rise of psychoanalysis in the first half of the twentieth century, however, hereditary notions seemed headed for the ash heap. Psychoanalytic doctrine insisted on the psychogenesis—that is, the mental origin (as opposed to the neurogenesis, or brain-based origin)—of psychiatric illness. Psychoanalysis implicated styles of parenting in the first line, and larger social and cultural patterns in the second, as the basic causes of neurosis and even psychosis. Although Freud remained circumspect about the applications of his doctrine to major psychiatric diseases, his epigones showed less reticence. In the view of the analysts who came after Freud, both neurosis and psychosis were caused by anomalies of early childhood socialization. For example, in 1948 Frieda Fromm-Reichmann, a German emigré psychoanalyst who practiced at Chestnut Lodge, a private nervous clinic near Washington, implicated the neurotic mother as the main cause of schizophrenia in the child, coining the phrase the "schizophrenogenic mother."[7] In these years organicist and hereditarian ideas in psychiatry were scorned as evidence that one had not caught up with contemporary theory and practice.[8]

The revival of genetic ideas in psychiatry, the second biological psychiatry, began with large-scale surveys that demonstrated on the basis of thousands of cases the clustering of mental illness in families. The English geneticist Lionel Penrose conducted a survey in 1945 in Ontario, Canada, based on more than five thousand pairs of relatives in whom some major mental illness had occurred. Penrose found that schizophrenia and depression tended to cluster in the same families, and that psychotic illness generally (meaning schizophrenia and depression together) tended much more often than would be expected at random to be passed from mother to daughter and especially from father to son. The implication of this sex-linked transmission was that a gene causing the illness might be located somewhere along the sex chromosomes.[9] Yet possible social explanations for the findings of this and other surveys came to mind as well: If mental illness seemed to run in families, perhaps it was because of the style of child rearing in that family rather than because of heredity. The finding of clustering did not constitute proof of genetic causality.

Biological psychiatry received a more powerful impetus from the field of pharmacology than from the results of survey research.

In 1950 a chemist at the Rhône-Poulenc Laboratories in France discovered that a drug named chlorpromazine possessed interesting sedative properties. In 1952 Pierre Deniker and Jean-Paul-Louis Delay at the Sainte-Anne asylum in Paris requested samples of chlorpromazine, and between May and July of that year gave it systematically to patients with serious psychotic illness. The results were astonishing: No drug in the history of psychiatry had calmed the agitation of psychotic patients and abolished their delusions and hallucinations as chlorpromazine had. In 1953 the Philadelphia drug firm Smith Kline & French brought it to the United States and, with the aid of Deniker himself, marketed chlorpromazine from mental hospital to mental hospital. Although the psychoanalysts turned up their noses at it as a "glorified sedative," the desperate asylum physicians presiding over the back wards of the state hospitals leapt on chlorpromazine.[10] The drug clearly worked. A new chapter in the history of psychiatry had been opened: If a drug affected mental illness so dramatically, the seat of that illness must be in the brain itself rather than merely in the distressed mind. The schizophrenogenic mother had been exculpated.

Nevertheless the discovery that mental illness had a pharmacology of its own did not necessarily mean that it had its own genetics. Only the identification of specific chemical pathways causing those mental illnesses that run in families—or the location of specific genes—would constitute definitive proof that heredity played a strong role in mental disorder. The first psychiatric disease whose genetic mechanism was revealed was a rare familial pediatric condition in which, among other features, children behaved with extreme hostility and gnawed uncontrollably at their lower lips and finger tips, shredding them bloody. In 1964 Michael Lesch of Johns Hopkins and William Nyhan of the University of Miami established that this disorder was caused by an excess of uric acid in the blood, owing to the absence of a single strategic enzyme. Because the disorder was inheritable, the mechanism causing this excess must be genetic.[11] The disorder became known as the Lesch-Nyhan syndrome. From this point on, genetic arguments in psychiatry would begin to regain ground: Genetic disease had been shown to affect human behavior.

In psychiatry the 1970s and 1980s saw the explosive growth of "molecular biology," using techniques of DNA analysis in an attempt to locate specific disease-causing genes on the chromosomes. Researchers would take cell samples from families or isolated groups in the population subject to, say, manic-depressive illness and then use molecular analysis to determine which patterns in the genetic material seemed to recur among these affected individuals. In this manner the noose started to close around manic-depressive illness, some forms of major depression, and schizophrenia as genetic disorders.[12]

Meanwhile studies of illnesses running in families or recurring in twins would provide a statistical presumption in favor of genetic transmission. By the late 1980s it had become clear that first-degree relatives (meaning parents, sibs, children) of patients with depression, schizophrenia, panic disorder, and the like stood far higher chances of becoming ill than did the population as a whole. In manic-depressive illness (renamed bipolar affective disorder in 1980) family members were said to be "at least 24 times more likely" to develop the illness than were relatives of control subjects. The risk in families of schizophrenics was eighteen times greater, in families of alcoholics ten times, and in families of patients with panic disorder nine times.[13] Whereas the population as a whole stands a less than 1 percent chance of developing schizophrenia (0.86 percent), the children of a schizophrenic parent have a 12 percent chance of getting the disease, and a 37 percent chance if both parents are schizophrenic.[14]

Twin studies provided even more dramatic findings. When, for example, a schizophrenic mother gives birth to twins who grow from one ovum (monozygotic), the chances that both of the twins will become schizophrenic are forty to sixty times greater than in the population as a whole. The assumption is that both twins share all the same genes and that the mother has transmitted the disease to them in her DNA.[15] Other researchers found a large overlap between diseases traditionally considered as neurological—meaning of demonstrable organicity—and psychiatric disorders. For example, there is a much greater incidence of depression in families in which one member suffers from Huntington's disease—a fatal degenerative neurological condition—than in the population as a whole. Was it just that everyone was depressed about the ill relative? No, the onset of the affective disorder often preceded the appearance of neurological symptoms. In families of patients with Tourette's syndrome, a neurological illness marked by uncontrollable tics, compulsive swearing, and the shouting out of strange words, the incidence of obsessive-compulsive disorder is much higher than one would expect. It is also higher in the patients themselves. Tourettism is almost certainly inherited, and in many cases obsessive-compulsive disorder may be inherited as well.[16]

A capital advance in pinning down the role of genes in schizophrenia occurred between 1988 and 1991 as several genes that are implicated in the chemistry of schizophrenia were identified ("cloned"). Schizophrenia seems to be caused by an excess of a neurotransmitter called dopamine (too little dopamine causes Parkinson's disease). The dopamine molecules lock onto receptors on the walls of the brain cells (neurons), triggering changes inside the neurons that ultimately lead to the symptoms of schizophrenia. The D4 receptor in particular, cloned in 1991, had a special affinity for a drug called clozapine. Clozapine blocks the receptor so that the dopamine molecules can't attach themselves, reducing the patient's symptoms. Thus the circle is being drawn ever tighter around possible genetic sources of schizophrenia: the location of genes that regulate several different dopamine receptors was established, and one particular receptor was closely associated—via clozapine—with schizophrenia. If this work continues, it should be possible to identify the genetic basis of schizophrenia itself.[17]

The evidence of a genetic component in many psychiatric disorders is now so clear that it cannot be dismissed for ideological reasons. These are solid, scientific findings that may not simply be brushed from the table on the grounds that they are inconvenient. Indeed, it is incumbent upon a whole generation of humanist scholars who learned that "only nurture, not nature" determines human behavior to reassess their position. One still encounters commonly among humanists this ostrichlike posture, as for example in 1992 an English historian, reviewing a book on the history of hereditarian thought, deplored "the current resurgence of hereditarian ideas in psychological medicine," as though such ideas were mainly a matter of opinion.[18] One is reminded of the rejoinder of the young German psychiatrist Albrecht Bethe, who around 1904 was giving a lecture on brain anatomy that Adolf Strümpell attended. Strümpell was then in his early fifties and the dean of Central European neurology. "At an unexpected assertion," noted an American physician present at the session, "Strümpell shook his head skeptically. Whereupon Bethe stopped and introjected, 'Even if you shake your head, Herr von Strümpell, it's still true!' "[19]

Psychosomatic Illness: A Biological Basis?

What about psychosomatic illness? Is it driven by biology in the same way as the major psychiatric illnesses? Here the evidence is much less firm, partly because so little research has been done, partly because the concept of psychosomatic embraces everyone from the person who has a stomachache before an important meeting to the grand valetudinarian who lies abed for decades. But short-lived twinges do seem to be different in kind from long-term disability, and it is likely that the chronic form of psychosomatic illness does have some element of genetic component.

Physicians have always suspected that, as with major psychiatric illness, the phenomenon of symptoms without disease was passed on from generation to generation. The first work to go beyond mere prejudices about womb hysteria and to use quantitative data was that of Paris psychiatrist Pierre Briquet, a staff physician at the Charité Hospital in the 1840s and 1850s. He understood the term *hysteria* to mean mainly physical symptoms such as fits or paralyses without an obvious organic cause. He asked his female patients systematically about these phenomena in their own first-degree relatives and then accumulated a comparison group of 167 female patients over the age of twenty-five who did not have hysteria or any other nervous disease in order to see what was distinctive about the hysteria patients. Of Briquet's 351 female hysteria patients for whom a family history could be elicited:

- 2 percent had fathers with hysteria
- 32 percent had mothers with hysteria
- 30 percent had sisters with hysteria
- 3 percent had brothers with hysteria

Among the control group, by contrast, there was virtually no hysteria in first-degree relatives. At most 4 percent had hysterical mothers (and none of the fathers or brothers were said to have hysteria). Briquet concluded, "Among the relatives of our hysteria patients, there is twelve times more hysteria than among those of the non-hysteria patients. This figure obviously establishes the role of heredity."[20] Because Briquet probably included some of his female patients as much on the basis of their "hysterical" personality characteristics as on their physical symptoms, his hysteria may not be exactly identical with psychosomatic illness. Nonetheless psychosomatic symptoms were at the core of the phenomenon he was describing. His research stands as an early statistical demonstration of familial factors in the production of somatic symptoms.

Other historical data exist as well. Lennart Ljungberg examined the records of 381 patients admitted for "hysteria" over the years 1931–45 to Stockholm hospitals, conducting interviews with almost 3,000 of their relatives. He found that 7 percent of the female relatives of female hysteria patients also had hysteria, as opposed to one half of 1 percent of the population as a whole. The author concluded: "The uniform morbidity risks throughout several generations support the hypothesis of genetical factors in the production of hysterical reactions."[21]

At the anecdotal level there is no shortage of medical opinion that patients inherit chronic psychosomatic illness, as opposed to acquiring it as a result of stress or unhappiness. Just to sample this voluminous body, in 1903 psychiatrist Pierre Janet, writing of a neurotic and heavily psychosomatic condition that he called psychasthenia, thought the basic problem was a biological one: "cerebral impotence." This impotence Janet deemed "hereditary in nature, completely a result of constitution."[22] In 1912 Paris society nerve doctor Paul Hartenberg assigned to those neurasthenics who were "incurable" a "constitutional taint [*tare constitu-*

tionnelle]," the patients having been ill in one form or another since childhood.[23] Here is Walter Alvarez, an internist at the Mayo Clinic in Rochester, Minnesota, describing in 1943 a large part of his practice:

> The main trouble with many of the patients I see every day is that they are always weak and tired and full of pain, and always getting sick in one way or another. Many have been operated on several times, but still they aren't well, and they cannot get about and have fun as other people do. Some of the men cannot earn a living, and many of the women complain that they haven't strength and "pep" enough to be a satisfactory wife or mother. They drag around; they cannot do their housework, and they haven't the energy to go out anywhere with husband.

What was the matter with these patients? Alvarez said their problems were hereditary. He urged his colleagues not to satisfy themselves with such diagnoses as "chronic nervous exhaustion" or "neurasthenia," but to "apply a label—constitutional inadequacy—which will keep reminding us that we are dealing with an inborn and essentially ineradicable disease. As I say to these patients, 'The only way in which I could hope to really cure you would be to start with another set of grandparents.' "[24]

In those days such opinions did not necessarily count as conservative prejudices. In 1954 Stephen Taylor of London, a physician and prominent Labour spokesman, described his practice as filled with "multiple-ailment 'heavy burden' patients": "It almost appears that these people are made of poor stuff, both mental and physical. They begin with an excessive liability to physical ailments; they top this off with a mental incapacity to grin and bear it. They are best thought of as 'weaker brethren,' travelling through life with a double handicap."[25] If being made of "poor stuff" existed as a condition, it would be a genetic one.

That doctors have held all these opinions, often filled with gender and class prejudice, over the ages does not make them correct. It merely establishes the source of the impetus, after World War II, to look closely at the relationship between chronic psychosomatic illness and heredity.

In 1951 three researchers at Tufts Medical School and Harvard

Medical School did a landmark investigation. They compared fifty women who had been diagnosed with hysteria in Boston-area hospitals with various control groups, including fifty healthy working women. By hysteria was meant mainly chronic physical symptoms. (94 percent had headaches, 78 percent loss of appetite, 74 percent a lump in the throat, and so forth.) Although the three authors did not investigate the patients' family histories, they did establish that hysteria itself tended to be a chronic, early-onset disorder. Thirty-eight percent of the hysteria patients, for example, had trouble with school, as opposed to none of the healthy control group. Fifty-six percent experienced vomiting in pregnancy after the third month (compared to 8 percent of the healthy group). Seventy-two percent of the hysteria patients had had an appendectomy, versus 28 percent of the healthy controls (this at a time when surgeons were still operating for "chronic appendicitis" in order to cure vague abdominal pains and other physical complaints). In 48 percent there was a welter of symptoms, such as: "I am sore all over. Can't explain it. I have been sick all my life." Or: "This is my seventy-sixth hospitalization."[26]

A young psychiatrist at Washington University in Saint Louis, named Samuel Guze, became intrigued with these findings. Guze had received his M.D. in Saint Louis in 1945 and stayed on, first as an intern at Barnes Hospital and then as an instructor in the psychiatry department. Guze's particular interest in what he was still calling hysteria was triggered in 1961, when Eliot Slater, a distinguished British psychiatrist, wrote an article pooh-poohing the whole notion of hysteria (having found in a follow-up study many "hysteria" patients to have mental illnesses or organic brain disease).[27] In an exchange of letters, Slater encouraged Guze to press forward with his own research.[28] Guze and his colleagues in Saint Louis therefore conducted a series of studies of chronic psychosomatic illness.

In 1963 Guze published the first of his "family studies" of hysteria. Investigating thirty-nine Saint Louis women who had been diagnosed hysteric, he found that, among female relatives, hysteria was ten times more frequent than among a control group. And he found an increased frequency of antisocial personality and of alcoholism among first-degree male relatives.[29] This study established the interpretation by "the Saint Louis school" of hysteria as a familial disease. The mechanism of familial transmission, whether genetic or socialization, was as yet unclear, but that so many of the male relatives should be sociopaths spoke to some kind of genetic influence, expressing itself differently in male members than in females. In 1970 the Saint Louis group formally rebaptized hysteria "Briquet's syndrome," after Pierre Briquet.[30] In 1975 they published the results of their first two-generation study. Looking at forty-six families of convicted felons, they found that "the daughters of sociopathic fathers had a significantly higher prevalence of hysteria than did the daughters of other fathers."[31] Thus again, there seemed to be some kind of underlying genetic influence that presented itself in men as a tendency to bar fights and criminality and in women as multiple, chronic physical symptoms. After 1975 the number of studies demonstrating an interaction between familial and environmental influences in chronic neurosis continued to grow.[32]

Today it still has not been definitively established that chronic psychosomatic illness has a major genetic component, and certainly no gene has yet been found. But the presumption of heredity makes sense, given that psychosis and psychosomatic illness both involve widespread disturbances of the mind-body relationship. Just as melancholic patients complain of manifold physical pains, psychosomatic patients often are subject to additional psychiatric problems, such as anxiety or personality disorders.[33] Disturbances of the mind-body relationship reach, just as other mental illnesses do, across a wide range of brain activity. Today it still remains to be established that such generalized disruption might have a genetic cause.

The Play of Culture

Not even the most ardent somaticist would insist that genetically predisposed patients will inevitably develop psychiatric illness. The argument is merely that if one does not have the gene that causes something like schizophrenia, one will not become schizophrenic regardless of the stress and unhappiness to which one is subject. Yet having the gene does not necessarily mean that one will become schizophrenic either. The social situation and personal development of individuals, molded perhaps by the mores of their social class or their ethnic group, must somehow lead them down the pathway to illness. This is the other half of the equation: the "nurture," without which "nature" will remain silent and unexpressed.[34]

The role of culture in the production of nervous illness, just like that of heredity, has always been recognized. For example, Wilhelm Erb, the famous Heidelberg neurologist, spoke in 1893 of "the growing nervosity of our own time." He described how nervous illness had changed over the years: First there was the nervous upheaval of the Napoleonic years, then the quiet years between 1815 and 1848 "in which the nervous system could recover somewhat." After 1848 commenced not just war and revolution "but cultural upheavals, great discoveries and inventions that exercised a powerful influence on the whole world of culture and therewith on the nervous system itself."[35] So for Erb it was clear: Nervous illness came heavily from nurture as well as nature.

How might the surrounding culture impose a psychosomatic illness? Changing notions of what is proper behavior for people or what constitutes legitimate disease may alter individuals' perception of their bodies and patterns of illness. For example, among the most exasperating problems for pediatricians today are children who present symptoms of "allergies." When, upon examination, the child's immune system is found to be entirely normal, many of these allergies tax the physicians' patience. Further inquiry reveals parents who have implanted in the child's mind the notion that he or she is "allergic." Persuasive suggestion and authority testify to nurture at work.

A typical case was that of young Maurice, who appeared before the family doctor in Manchester, England, supposedly beset by allergies for which he was taking medication. His mother and father also believed they had allergies, and the household was a beehive of allergy chatter. Although Maurice had apparently demonstrated some physical symptoms (which an obliging private-clinic physician had diagnosed as "allergies"), his problems mainly manifested themselves in his "being nasty and rude to his mother." On the day of the visit to the family doctor, Maurice was wearing "a large and extraordinary facial mask designed to reduce his inhalation of car exhaust fumes to which, it seemed, he had lately been shown to be allergic."

The family doctor referred Maurice to a psychiatric clinic. But Maurice's mother rejected the referral because "the clinic was bound to be full of allergens such as hairsprays and disinfectants. In circumstances like that, the mother 'could not be responsible for what the boy might do.' "

So Maurice was brought to the university pediatric clinic. When "firmly challenged to bring the boy into the building, the mother used the neutralizing drops, priced at £25 per phial, to counter the putative allergens."

When Maurice came into the clinic he said to his mother, "Now I'm here why don't you fuck off!"

The mother said, "There! Now I knew he'd be allergic!"

The only people in this story who believed in Maurice's allergies were his father and mother, her fears foisted on her by fashionable physicians and an alarmist press. For example, following a newspaper story headed "Rain makes boy a monster," she feared that "a single drop of rain [could] turn Maurice into a violent maniac." The mother thought that a wide variety of dietary indiscretions would produce allergic reactions in her, and the father believed that he himself had a "potato allergy." There was apparently nothing organically wrong with anybody in the family, yet all the members attributed their physical sensations to the phantom "allergies."[36]

Maurice's story may end there. But if Maurice himself goes on—and his children after him—in his mother's and father's footsteps, to a lifetime of hypochondriacal behavior, then perhaps one could begin to talk about the interaction of nature and nurture in the making of psychosomatic illness.

A historical example similarly shows how culture can suggest individuals into illness, in this case the family culture of the household of Charles Darwin. Among Darwin's several psychological problems was his preoccupation with his body and his chronic tendency to somatize, in the form of giddiness, nausea, and headaches. Periodically Darwin would seek relief by taking the healing waters of the spa at Malvern. Sometime before going there he wrote to a friend, "I believe I have not had one whole day or rather night without my stomach having been grossly disordered during the last three years and most days great prostration of strength; thank you for your kindness; many of my friends, I believe, think me a hypochondriac."[37] In the four months that Darwin first spent at Malvern in 1849, he felt that the various frictions and packings did great good for his ailments, which he situated in his "head or top of spinal cord." "At present," wrote Darwin to a friend, "I am heated by spirit lamp till I *stream* with perspiration, and am then suddenly rubbed violently with towels dripping with cold water: have two cold feet-baths, and wear a wet compress all day on my stomach." He assured his correspondent, "I feel certain that the water cure is no quackery." And indeed this therapy did give Darwin momentary relief from his symptoms, almost certainly psychosomatic in nature.[38]

It is interesting that Darwin's daughter Henrietta also suffered from chronic hypochondriacal complaints. "She had been an invalid all her life," as Gwen Raverat, Darwin's granddaughter, recalled of Henrietta ("Aunt Etty") in the early 1950s, "but I don't know what (if anything) had originally been the matter with her." Apparently Henrietta had been told by a doctor at age thirteen that, after a "low fever," she should "have breakfast in bed for a time. She never got up to breakfast again in all her life."

The problem was that in the Darwin house "it was a distinction and a mournful pleasure to be ill. This was partly because my grandfather [Charles Darwin] was always ill, and his children adored him and were inclined to imitate him; and partly because it was so delightful to be pitied and nursed by my grandmother." The letters between Mrs. Darwin and her daughter Henrietta were chockablock with "dangerously sympathetic references to the ill health of one, or several, of the family."

Aunt Etty's psychosomatic illness was in part culturally determined. "Unfortunately," said Ms. Raverat, "Aunt Etty, being a lady, had no real work to do; she had not even any children to bring up. . . . As it was, ill health became her profession and absorbing interest."[39] In line with the passive social position of women in late–Victorian England, Aunt Etty might well have registered some subterranean discontent with her life by taking on medical symptoms that required of her physical passivity, long bed rest, and immobility. In addition she had clearly learned the role of the invalid while growing up in Charles Darwin's household, her father having socialized her into it. Yet Darwin himself, no slouch at teasing out the role of biology, felt that his own problems were in part a result of heredity, and those of his children also.[40] In the case of the Darwin family it is impossible to sort out the role of nature versus nurture. Probably both played a role, which is exactly the point: Biology and culture interact in the production of psychosomatic symptoms.

But how? Genes and culture can affect one another in several different ways to elicit in individuals psychiatric symptoms in general and the phantom feeling of organic illness in particular.[41]

One way is additive—simply totaling the number of defective genes and the number of sources of stress and unhappiness and calling their sum the link between biology and society. A group of individuals genetically at risk for psychiatric illness, once subjected to a stressful environment, will probably develop dizziness and headaches in addition to more overt psychiatric symptoms. In the nineteenth century such individuals were probably at greater risk of contracting a hysterical paralysis than they would have been or, in the eighteenth century and before, of experiencing convulsions. In this approach what changes historically is the level of stress and the nature of the cultural models themselves for presenting underlying illness—the eighteenth-century legitimating fits; the nineteenth, paralysis; and so forth. However, the genetic diposition is there to be activated. The more stressful the environment, the more psychosomatic illness occurs, and the culture of the time determines the form it will assume.

A second approach says there might be genes that are sensitive to stress rather than genes for psychosomatic illness as such. These explanations emphasize sensitivity. One might argue for the existence of a gene that makes some people more vulnerable to stress than others. Here again the interesting question is changes in levels of stress, for these levels determine whether the gene will switch itself on. (In the language of genetics, stress levels provide "the environmental control of gene expression.") If an increasing number of genetically sensitive people come into contact with stress (or if the level of stress rises), the level of psychosomatic illness will rise. In this approach genetic sensitivity to social factors is at issue.

It is not so farfetched to imagine the existence of a gene making one sensitive to stress. There seems to be, for example, a kind of salt-sensitivity gene, making some people more vulnerable to developing high blood pressure than others, given equal amounts of salt in the diet. A stress-sensitivity gene may help explain why, at equal levels of stress, some people are more likely to become depressed than others.[42] Thus it is conceivable that a stress-sensitivity gene of this nature equips some better than others to deal with change. Historically, therefore, a protective environment would reduce levels of psychosomatic illness; a predisposing environment would increase them. Did a subpopulation of Victorian housewives, those with a stress-sensitivity gene, encounter such a predisposing environment and become bedridden with psychosomatic fatigue and weakness? And how did Victorian males with the stress-sensitivity gene react?

Finally, genes and social factors influence each other by modifying exposure to stress. We know, for example, that there is great variability in human personality, some of which is probably under genetic control.[43] Perhaps certain personality types are drawn to situations that are unhealthy for them. For example, individuals with mistrustful personalities seem more likely to put credence in the impersonal media than they do in a flesh-and-blood physician sitting before them.[44] Such individuals would be exposed more to media alarmism about disease-of-the-month syndrome, and—unlikely to be reassured by a physician's findings—be more at risk of falling ill with such media-spawned plagues as fibrositis or chronic fatigue syndrome.[45] Our personalities determine our susceptibility to environmental factors, and genes help shape our personalities.

In this third scenario there is an analogy to depressive illness. Individuals with impulsive personalities and a low tolerance for frustration might change jobs more frequently and become depressed in consequence of their instability of employment. Here a personality gene would be responsible for their depression, not a depression gene. The personality gene puts them in depressing situations. Analogizing back to psychosomatic illness, there might be a personality gene that influences life events and brings the individual in contact with media-generated illness, rather than there being a specific gene for psychosomatic illness.

These speculations are designed to reinforce the point that one should avoid reductionism of either kind in inquiring into the effects of mind and body in psychosomatic illness. Biological reductionism makes us seem to be creatures of our genes, limiting the scope of culture and human determination. Cultural reductionism creates the impression that we, as individuals, are fully in control of our bodies and the interpretation of the signals they give off. Genetic research into other kinds of psychiatric illnesses establishes the untruth of this notion, and there is little reason to think it might be true in psychosomatic illness. In reality, contracting such an illness is the result of interaction between genes and environment, between biology and culture.

CHAPTER

2

―――

Chronic Illness in the Comfortable Classes

HOW ARE PEOPLE CHANNELED into illness? One way is the social class to which they belong. Historically speaking, middle-class people have developed quite different illness patterns from working-class people, sometimes just in being the first to take on a new symptom or sometimes in being the only social class to manifest a given symptom. We do not know if membership in a given class has a biology of its own, a different genetics, as eugenists once believed. But it is clear that culture, in the form of social class, does have the ability to mold subjective personal sensations into a specific presentation of illness. This molding is all the more intriguing because those affected have little awareness of its influence. What the sufferers conceive to be genuine organic disease often comes from illness models self-consciously suggested to them by the class to which they belong.

The distinctive feature of the middle classes is the leisure they have always enjoyed. Symptoms characteristic of middle-class life could not have arisen in the absence of leisure, for the symptom that flourishes best in its midst is invalidism. Among historical patients with psychosomatic illnesses, few are more striking than the middle-class nineteenth-century women who took to their beds, there to remain literally for years or decades. In the first half of the twentieth century this generation of patients gave way to another, again largely female and middle class, who to be sure were no longer bedridden but who instead underwent unnecessary abdominal operations. After many operations they would end up with "battlefield abdomens," whose scars recalled a battlefield. Both the bed cases and the battlefield abdomens were class-specific expressions of chronic neurosis. Occurring primarily in the middle classes they raised the question of cultural shaping as opposed to a genetic factor associated with class.

Psychosomatic Illness and Social Class

It would be a mistake to imagine that the middle classes are more at risk for psychosomatic illness than the working classes. Historically the working classes have shouldered an equal burden of "hysteria" and its companions, although the middle classes have traditionally been more anxious to interpret physical sensations as evidence of disease and to seek help for them.[1] Many physicians in the past believed that both classes shared an equal burden. Bénédict-Augustin Morel, for example, director of an asylum at Saint-Yon outside of Rouen, said in 1866 that psychiatric delusions *(délire émotif)* seemed equally distributed in all classes. Then he added, "The same is true for hysteria and hypochondria, which are not the exclusive monopoly of certain social classes . . . as was once believed. These neuroses are found today among all social groups, rich or poor, educated or not."[2] Although Pierre Briquet saw mainly working-class females with hysteria at the Charité Hospital in Paris, he asked his colleagues in private practice how commonly they encountered it among the middle classes. The result was that, while only one out of seven middle-class patients had hysterical fits, one of five working-class patients did so.[3] In 1909 Thomas Savill, a London neurologist who had been superintendent of the working-class Paddington Infirmary and also practiced among the middle classes, was able to find virtually no difference in rates of hysteria between rich and poor: The rate of hysteria among patients "in easy circumstances, not obliged to work," was sixty-seven per one thousand patients; the rate among "those who are destitute" was sixty per one thousand (and among "those who work for their living," fifty-three per one thousand, so there was no trend).[4]

Contemporary studies suggest that psychosomatic illness is actually commoner among the poor today. After seeing one hundred psychiatric patients with persistent pain in the early 1960s in Sunderland and Sheffield, England, psychiatrist Harold Merskey concluded that hysterical pain "tends to appear most often in women who are semiskilled and unskilled workers or married to men in comparable occupations," although he conceded there was plenty of psychogenic pain among the higher classes as well: "Patients of this type are often known as 'thick-folder' patients, their hospital records bulging uncomfortably and weighing much more than the average."[5] A study in the mid-1960s of more than seventeen hundred adults in the Washington Heights district of New York City concluded, "There is a distinct tendency on the part of lower-class groups to express psychological distress in physiological terms."[6] And a study of Monroe County, New York, over the period 1960–69 found that the poorer you were, the more likely you were to have a psychosomatic illness. The rate of "hysterical neurosis" was only eighteen per one hundred thousand population for the highest class and forty-four for the lowest, and it increased steadily as one went from high to low.[7] I am aware of no study showing that the rich are more hysterical than the poor.

What gives psychosomatic illness its particular middle-class stamp is the kinds—not the quantity—of symptoms the middle classes present.

Chronic Illness

Chronic illness has always been something of a code word for symptoms in the absence of medical disease, drawn out over years and decades. The term *invalid* was often used interchangeably. To be an invalid once meant, practically speaking, having a chronic psychosomatic illness. Before World War II, small towns in the American South were familiar with the figure of the invalid, the female variety "occupying converted front rooms of old homes" (to which clung the characteristic odor of unguents and liniments), going about in a bathrobe, and often remaining unmarried; the male variety sitting "in rockers in front of the local hotel" and complaining of "locked bowels" and being "all tore up inside." In these little southern towns the male invalids tended to be married to schoolteachers and librarians, making it unnecessary for the men to work.[8] In American and European life this sort of chronic illness has always characterized middle-class individuals, for only they had the leisure to permit themselves lives bonded to self-absorption.

People whose lives are organized about illness have been familiar to doctors for centuries. "Nothing is more characteristic of [nervous] disease than a constant dread of death," wrote William Buchan in 1769. "This renders those unhappy persons who labour under it peevish, fickle, impatient, and apt to run from one physician to another, which is one reason why they seldom reap any benefit from medicine. . . . They are likewise apt to imagine that they labour under diseases from which they are quite free, and are very angry if any one attempts to set them right, or laugh them out of their ridiculous notions."[9]

In one of the first modern descriptions of "hypochondria," in 1799 the Irishman James Sims, then physician to the General Dispensary in London, described sufferers whose minds were "almost entirely taken up with the state of their health, which they imagine to be infinitely worse than it is, constantly auguring death, or the most dreadful consequences from even the most trifling ailments." "Hypochondriac persons," he continued, were not just apprehensive of falling ill but highly symptomatic, with "a number of bodily complaints which are real and serious, although the dejected state of their spirits makes them exaggerate them very much." What complaints? "The first, and indeed the most permanent symptoms of hypochondriacism, are those of indigestion. The patients complain of a heat and pain along the course of the esophagus . . . called heartburn." They have windy bowels, belch, and are constipated. "There are frequent flushing and flying heats of the face, and even over the whole body, at other times the face is pale. Headaches are frequent, followed by great giddiness. Their eyes are dim at times, and they complain of a sounding in their ears. In short there is no part of their frame that does not seem indisposed."[10] Sims's account stands as a classic description of chronic somatization or chronic neurosis.

It was among the comfortable classes that one of the characteristics of chronic illness first became manifest: doctor-shopping. Only the well-to-do can afford to go from doctor to doctor until they find a diagnosis that suits them. Charles Cowan, a physician in Reading, England, said of the chronic cases he had seen there in the year 1840, "The great majority of applicants have already consulted a surgeon. Many, after having for years been seeking relief from a succession of medical men, are attracted by a fresh name, and from renewed hopes are often for a time benefited, until the novelty wears off."[11] And from his fifty years of practice in Fort Covington, New York, William Macartney recalled one nervous patient who said to him in the course of general conversation, "Yes, of course, I know that a doctor must sometimes get very tired, but when I wear one doctor out, I simply get another."

"After that remark," said Macartney, "I saw to it that she never got a chance to wear *me* out."[12]

Paradoxically, in view of the fact that they were dealing with a well-heeled clientele, physicians tended to loathe chronic illness. Knowing they were not facing organic disease, organically oriented physicians tensed up whenever they encountered chronic somatizers. And doctors' accounts of this condition make apparent their distaste. In 1806 Joseph Schneider, a physician in the little court city of Fulda, Germany, wrote:

"I can think of no greater misery for a husband, no grimmer fate, than having a hysterical wife. The whole year long he and the doctor who is treating her are plagued with misery. And after she has been doctored through every imaginable illness that her imagination can devise, and told husband and doctor about them all, she runs through it all again from scratch. If I am called to a hysterical patient, I have to arm myself in advance with every conceivable bit of patience, and then as the doctor I at least have the good fortune of sitting through it all for only a half hour. But just think of her husband and family who have to endure this the whole day, and, I have to say, sometimes the whole night too.[13]

Patience with psychological cases was not exactly the strong point of Dr. Schneider's bedside manner.

As the number of physicians—the "nerve doctors"—who treated explicitly psychosomatic cases grew in the nineteenth century, the medical profession's empathy for this variety of patient diminished correspondingly. Jules-Joseph Dejerine, who had a unit for psychoneurotic patients at the Salpêtrière Hospital in Paris, despised the population of "pseudo-gastropaths, pseudo-enteropaths, pseudo-cardiopaths, pseudo-genital cases, pseudo-neurological and pseudo-brain cases, who often present quite grave symptoms, the origin of which is entirely psychic and who day in and day out are treated for organic disease. The result of this is to fix even more in their minds the idea of a disease localized in the organ of which they are complaining. Of these patients, I have seen thousands."[14]

Dejerine was actually not an unsympathetic physician. He had much influenced the English psychiatrist Thomas Ross, director of the Cassel Hospital for Functional Nervous Disorders at Penshurst, who had the reputation of being a humane physician. Ross's description in 1929 of "patients who go in and out of illness over a long period" showed how short his own patience with this kind of individual had become. "The neurotic is immensely interested in his illness and takes the utmost care of it. If he has palpitation he is sure to think he has grave heart disease, and will accept and better any instructions he may receive about resting his heart," in contrast to the true heart patient, who is likely to "go about his business with edema up to his knees." Ross described a population of sufferers who had "failed with unusual frequency to meet the ordinary difficulties of life in an adequate way." Ross had in mind soldiers unable to go into battle after receiving a bit of sunstroke and the like. "Oh, no, it was not your fault," the chronic neurotic wished to hear from listeners. "And always that wretched health of his was giving way at critical times." Ross, who made his living from such patients, clearly was unsympathetic to them and given his druthers would have reminded them of the call of "duty."[15]

Texts and advice manuals written for other physicians indicate that this contempt for chronic illness of psychogenic origin was not just a private and personal reaction but a professional norm. An American psychiatry textbook published in 1905 scorned the "parasitic existence" of the chronically ill, or the "hysterics," who were said "to be a burden on relatives, employers, the government, to live on a pension and do no work."[16] Stanley Sykes, who had graduated in 1921 in medicine from Cambridge, wrote an advice manual for general practitioners six years after beginning his own practice in a small town near Leeds: "The worst of all are the neurotics who delight in being ill, whose whole universe is full of their ailments, who weep with self-pity when you ask them how they are, and take it as a personal insult if you tell them they are looking better. They lack the will to get well, and personally my sympathies are with the unfortunate relatives."

Sykes recalled a vexatious patient, "an exceedingly healthy-looking woman of fifty-four," who "complained of pain after food." Tests revealed nothing. "She had a constant flow of symptoms, fresh each day, and talked incessantly of her ailments and how bad she was. It was quite impossible to checkmate her. As soon as examination showed no cause for one pain, its place was promptly taken by another." They finally did an exploratory operation, which revealed nothing. Then she had a stroke of good fortune, he said: She fell down the stairs. "This was a heaven-sent opportunity for her. She developed a violent pain in the back, in describing which she showed the fertile imagination of the neurasthenic. At one time her back was opening and shutting, at another she was sure it had collapsed." She took to her bed, "whence it was impossible to dislodge her. She insisted that she could not walk."[17] Whether this patient could walk is really beside the point. Dr. Sykes and his colleagues hated chronically somatizing patients, and the patients, sensing this dislike, took every recourse to convince the doctor of the organicity of their complaints. It is indeed this desire to please the doctor that helps the chronic bed cases seize on operations as a final hope of proving "organicity."

A final characteristic of chronic illness among the comfortable classes was the commitment to a way of life that it implied—a career of invalidism that mainly the well-to-do could contemplate. It is remarkable how many nineteenth-century women would really never be well again after menstruation had begun. Anton Theobald Brück, the spa doctor who treated the well-heeled in Bad Driburg, called his pattern "the chlorosis of puberty," and from it might emerge "catalepsy, chorea and somnambulism." Brück elaborated:

> Those suffering such major disorders in the springtime of life have lost, if I may say so, the innocence of health [*die Unschuld der Gesundheit*] and will never again achieve the pure freshness of youth. You need only follow the lives of those apparently recovered cataleptics, chlorotics and so forth, as they give birth and nurse and in general encounter later suffering and disease. You will immediately realize you are dealing with a constitution damaged early in life, one that never entirely emerged from reconvalescence.[18]

Paul Dubois, the Swiss neurologist who at the beginning of the twentieth century popularized "rational persuasion" as a method of psychotherapy, said that many of the patients at his exclusive private clinic had begun at puberty to fixate on their bodily sensations. "It is often at this age that the tachycardias [accelerated heart rates], the feelings of globus [lump in throat] and of constriction of the throat begin. The pain of ovarian congestion lingers on and ends up in interminable ovarialgias ["ovarian" pains]."[19] Dubois's patients at this chic private clinic were individuals who devoted their lives to their symptoms, beginning illness behavior early and never being healthy again.

We are not dealing here with a disease of early childhood, such as measles, but with a chronic, relapsing disorder extending over decades. For example, of 3,587 consecutive general medical patients originally seen between 1932 and 1934 at New York Hospital, a private institution, 14 percent had been diagnosed as "psychoneurotic." Of these psychoneurotic patients, fifty-seven percent had nervous symptoms such as weakness, fatigue, insomnia, or numbness. Forty-one percent had gastrointestinal complaints, and so on. What happened to these individuals over the years? In 1939 Constance Friess and Marjory Nelson attempted to follow them up, finding information on slightly more than half, or 269 of them. Of the 269, the two doctors were able to reexamine 177.

The two physicians learned that the prognosis of the psychoneurotics was poor: 66 percent still had the same complaint eight years later; a further 16 percent had the same complaint plus a new complaint; 12 percent had all new complaints; and only 6 percent were symptom-free. Noting how many patients had retained their original symptoms, the authors concluded, "This fixity of the complaint is but one manifestation of the basic changelessness of the psychoneurotic patient, and probably represents his most outstanding characteristic."[20] (Despite the doctors' use of the masculine pronoun, 59 percent of the patients were women.)

Individuals who turned up in the offices of a general practitioner were probably less ill than these hospital outpatients. Yet even in the world of ordinary private practice, a years- and decades-long commitment to neurosis was very much a medical reality. John Fry did a follow-up study of 551 "neurotic" patients seen in 1956 in a general practice in the London suburb of Beckenham. Of these 551, 39 percent were still being treated three years later (27 percent of the male patients, 43 percent of the female).[21] In another study of the same area for the years 1957–63, the authors found that a fifth of the men and a third of the women treated for psychiatric problems failed to get better (and that the psychiatric cases represented more than one-third of the total caseload of the general practice in question).[22]

Yet this fixity of symptoms could be influenced by fashion. Over long periods of time the middle classes have tended to abandon presentations of illness that have become unfashionable, conforming instead to the modish diagnoses of a new era. Middle-class people are probably more attuned to the media than the working classes, and more exposed to news about fashionable new diagnoses. A study conducted in the 1960s at the university psychiatric clinic in Lausanne, Switzerland, attempted to follow 159 patients born between 1872 and 1897 who had initially been seen for hysteria. The group is a bit special because two-thirds of them had died by the time of the study, and the survivors may not have been typical of the other hysterics of the day. Their average age was thirty-nine when they were initially examined, seventy-three when reexamined.

The study found much change among the hysterics over this very long period: Of the thirty-eight patients who could be found, 60 percent had taken on new psychiatric pathology. Of these, half had become depressed; others had developed, sometimes in addition to depression, various additional psychosomatic complaints as well as a slew of anxieties, phobias, nightmares, and "hypochondria." Thus most of the original hysteria patients really did not recover. They merely exchanged whatever symptoms they had presented in the 1930s for the kinds of symptoms, such as "depression," that were more favorably received after World War II.[23]

The above-cited studies are not immediately comparable, for their definitions of neurosis, hysteria, and the like are too diverse. But they do suggest that among individuals receiving an initial diagnosis of neurosis or psychosomatic illness, there was a core of chronic patients who would remain ill throughout their lives.

Whether this core of illness sprang from a cultural source or a genetic burden is unclear. People hand down in their genes the shape of their jaw and their propensity to early hair loss. Why not a tendency to chronic illness as well? Yet such illnesses, called "valetudinarianism" in the language of the day, transsected the entire cosseted culture of middle-class life, not just selected hypochondriacal families. Here surely nurture triumphed over nature.

Wealthy Invalids

Wealthy invalids moved in a special world, in which money spun for them in the great spas and resorts of the Continent a cocooned life-style of silver napkin rings at breakfast and special quarters in the private nervous clinics for their own servants. From this world came the bed cases—people who wintered in Merano and Nice and summered in Baden-Baden and on the Semmering near Vienna— blanket-covered valetudinarians longing daily for "openings" (bowel movements) and prodding their health along as though it were a recalcitrant child. In this world illness was a way of life.

Merano! Surrounded by mountains in the South Tirol, this little jewel of a town is today part of Italy and virtually unknown to Anglo-Saxons. It was once the headquarters of the international elite of hypochondriacs. Although Merano had previously been known for its tuberculosis sanatoriums, by 1900 the indications for admission to its many private establishments had shifted to nervous illness, and the physicians of the town were offering a get-in-control-of-your-life-style approach (called physical-dietetic therapy) for "metabolic" complaints, cases of "convalescence," and the other code words for psychosomatic illness. In March 1900, for example, the spa welcomed Archdukes Otto and Ferdinand of Austria and Duke Philipp of Württemberg and his wife, Duchess Maria Theresia, the latter attended by one lady companion, an imperial major, and seven servants. Lesser mortals, such as Emmanuel B., a merchant from Breslau, would take the cure at the Stefanie Sanatorium, or Countess B. from Munich at the Martinsbrunn Sanatorium.[24] Merano had beautiful walks along a tumbling mountain stream, and the wealthy merchants and nobility would nod and bow to each in their morning constitutionals. What was the matter with these patients that they needed treatment? Mainly constipation, plus a riot of lesser bodily sensations that attentive invalids were ever ready to interpret as illness.[25]

Wealthy nervous patients would consult from spa to spa, and from nerve doctor to nerve doctor. Some of these pilgrimages were picturesque or ludicrous (others profoundly sad, for one of the "nervous" diseases for which women consulted persistently was multiple sclerosis; for men, neurosyphilis). Here, for example is Stockholm nerve doctor Otto Wetterstrand thanking Zurich psychiatrist August Forel in 1898 for the referral of "Herr K.," an obviously wealthy individual who lived in Tsarskoe-Selo, the country residence of the czars not far from Saint Petersburg. Wetterstrand had traveled there the previous October to examine Herr K.

Never in my life have I seen such a strange patient. He was a man of forty-nine, almost unable to walk, and could take on only fluid nourishment with a tube. He couldn't chew for fear of evoking attacks of facial pain. Moreover he was getting daily injections of morphine. Sleep poor. . . .

He had a true furor [for consultation], and had seen over forty prominent physicians all over Europe. Of course the diagnoses were quite various. Charcot assumed multiple sclerosis, so did [Wilhelm] Erb. [Karl] Westphal and [Ernst von] Leyden said syringomyelia. [Friedrich Albrecht] Erlenmeyer diagnosed a brain tumor, and various Russian physicians such as [Michael] Lachtin thought he had syphilis. [Richard von] Krafft-Ebing, Tomaschensky and I were of the opinion that he was suffering from hystero-neurasthenia. As I said, I've never seen such a difficult case. He understood everything, had read everything there was about his illness (he subscribed to eight medical journals), and still believed he could find some powder that would free him from his suffering.[26]

This was a chronic neurosis on the grand international scale: Herr K. had progressed from Paris (Charcot); to Heidelberg and Berlin (Erb, Westphal, and Leyden); to Bendorf on the Rhine, where Erlenmeyer's exclusive private clinic was located; to Moscow, where Lachtin ran a private clinic; to Vienna, where Krafft-Ebing was a professor of psychiatry.

New York nerve doctor Charles Dana had the Herr K.'s of this world in mind when in 1904 he jestingly urged his colleagues to think twice about abolishing the label *neurasthenia:* "The removal of the term neurasthenia from the list of easy diagnoses will have its most tragic effect on the European professors whom our wandering plutocracy consults; and by whom the diagnosis of the 'American Disease' [as neurasthenia was also known] is usually made as the patient is announced."[27] With easy ocean travel, this migratory elite of somatizers had become well known to physicians by 1900 and would be passed on from specialist to specialist, and from clinic to clinic, seeking relief from symptoms that never really turned into organic disease but never improved either.

Such patients were still a presence in the 1920s and 1930s. As Swiss psychiatrist Max Müller, chief physician at an asylum in Münsingen, recalled:

Among some of the people who themselves sought me out in Münsingen, I experienced something I had not previously encountered. There were actually individuals—who naturally had a lot of money—who for years had done nothing other than travel around the world, either for themselves or on behalf of someone else, from one "great man" [*Kapazität*] to another. Their only purpose was to note exactly the diagnostic and prognostic judgment of each physician, to compare it with those already obtained, and to determine with satisfaction that there was no unanimity. Thus one of Freud's patients in Vienna came to me, and then next day travelled on to [Henri] Claude in Paris. And these people were always either hopelessly ill with some organic disease and already treated countless times, or inveterate hypochondriacs. With time, I learned quickly to see through this kind of client and to get rid of them as quickly as possible.[28]

Müller was being especially noble, for many physicians saw the international hypochondriacal elite as their bread and butter. As George Bernard Shaw noted in his 1911 preface to *The Doctor's Dilemma,* "Every hypochondriacal rich lady or gentleman who can be persuaded that he or she is a lifelong invalid means anything from fifty to five hundred pounds a year for the doctor."[29]

The hypochondriasis of the rich breathed nurture rather than nature. It was a cultural posture, lightly taken on in aid of conspicuous consumption, and lightly cast aside as, in the 1920s, the drawing rooms resonated to cries of "Tennis, anyone?" The caricature of the dowager would cede to the equally caricatural "little old lady in white tennis shoes." But, along the same lines, wealthy invalidism had yet another cultural characteristic to offer: It was from its ranks that women sought the shelter of their beds.

The Bed Cases

Unlike the population of chronic neurotics as a whole, the bed cases were almost all women. In the long passage between biology and culture, there are few more interesting way stations. Why was taking to one's bed for much of adult life confined to one gender?

And why did it occur in such a specific historical period, the second half of the nineteenth century?

The first references with which I am familiar—doubtless there are earlier ones in the vast case literature—come from the 1860s. The New York physician Charles Taylor had opened his "New York Orthopedic Dispensary" in 1866, specializing in nervous patients immobilized by backache and the like. He had become known as a specialist in prostrate females, such as Henry James's valetudinarian sister Alice. In 1864 he described a group of women bedridden by an "over-wrought nervous system. . . . I have seen those who could neither see, nor hear, nor touch, much less perform the various active bodily functions without exquisite agony." It was "a class of patients, the most intelligent and worthy of all our young women, who are ruined—yes, literally ruined at school; and New England, for obvious reasons, has probably the most victims. Nearly all the bed-ridden cases, and most of the worst cases of back-ache . . . admit that they have studied excessively at some time, from which they generally date the first symptoms of their disorder."

In June 1857 Taylor saw Miss C., a patient of the gynecologist James Marion Sims. While at college she had got her skirts "drabbled in a new snow then on the ground, and her feet wet, and took a cold which suspended the catamenia [menses], and threw her into a state of extreme prostration." After a number of months she saw Sims, who became convinced that "it was utterly impossible for her to get up. Fainting, followed by great prostration, was always the result of every effort." When Miss C. reached Taylor, "She looked bright, was cheerful, but possessed no ability to get out of the recumbent position." Taylor managed to restore her with a placebolike form of physical therapy.

In June 1860 Taylor was called to another young woman, the daughter of a farmer who was trying to pass her county teachers' exams. "On the last day of the term she fainted and showed other signs of complete exhaustion, but rallied, went through her part in the exercises of the examination . . . went home and to bed, from which she had never got up when I saw her." She had at that point been prostrate for a year, intolerant of light and sound, "and the greatest care had to be taken in speaking and walking even in distant parts of the house." In an adjoining room an elder sister had lain for twelve years.[30]

In the decades to come, such prototypical cases turned into full-blast invalidism, an invalidism that would become almost a mannered response to stress. So accepted was it for women to take to their beds that Mary Jacobi, a New York physician and early feminist, could write in 1895, "today stoicism has vanished from education, as asceticism from creeds; it is considered natural and almost laudable to break down under all conceivable varieties of strain—a winter dissipation, a houseful of servants, a quarrel with a female friend, not to speak of more legitimate reasons. Women who expect to go to bed at every menstrual period expect to collapse if by chance they find themselves on their feet for a few hours during such a crisis."[31] Among the patients who consulted Mary Jacobi, going to bed had—just like certain forms of hysterical paralysis—become a class-specific symptom.

This response was not merely some late-nineteenth-century-American aberration but was found in every country in Western society. In 1869 Samuel Wilks, then a senior physician at Guy's Hospital in London, described a quintessential young female patient: "She has taken to her bed as if for the remainder of her days, and all is arranged accordingly—the stitching, the embroidery, the religious books where they can be comfortably reached, and she generally receives more sympathy from the clergyman and the lady visitors than do cases of real illness."[32] Although Wilks diagnosed such patients as having hysterical paraplegia, he was describing young women getting set for careers of invalidism.

In France, Julia Daudet, wife of writer Alphonse Daudet and herself said to be chronically nervous, referred to some romantic novel as "a book for bed cases" (un livre pour femmes à chaise-longue).[33] Jules Chéron, head of gynecology at the Saint-Lazare Hospital in Paris, described in the 1880s women who had taken to bed, requiring injections of his "artificial serum" to get them going again. One woman, thirty-two, had been weakly for six years:

Her head continually heavy [alourdie], the only thing she wants is to remain in bed. Any activity causes her the greatest fatigue.

In the months preceding my first visit she had renounced all activity, and normally did not leave the bed at all. She said that
her illness had begun with a great sense of weariness in the
head, followed almost immediately by great muscular fatigue.
Since that time she has been irritable, and her stomach has
ceased functioning. "All this," she says, "is just my chlorosis
coming back. I tell all the doctors that but no one wants to believe me."[34]

Chéron's student Jules Batuaud made a specialty of such cases,
referring to them as "la clinomanie neurasthénique," or the
neurasthenic compulsion to lie down. These were women who
"spend a more or less great part of their life in bed or recumbent
upon a chaise-longue," without necessarily being paralyzed.
When called upon to do so they could even walk for a few minutes, or at least attempt a few steps. One patient of Batuaud's
might have a little mechanical cart with the aid of which she could
navigate from room to room. Another, while remaining bedbound, might have a piano brought into the room in order to
"watch personally over the piano lessons of her daughters."[35]
What is so striking in all these cases is the aura of ease that envelops them, a phenomenon primarily—but not entirely—of
upper-middle-class women.
  In fact, there is evidence that the bed cases seeped considerably
down the social scale, affecting such socially middle-of-the-road
patients as Pierre Janet's at the Salpêtrière. Janet's psychological
demonstrations for the medical students, which offered every psychoneurosis imaginable, also featured bed cases. Mme. F., forty-
one, had been hypochondriacal since childhood. All corporeal
acts, such as stool, menses, and eating, were freighted with emotion for her. "She cannot even take an enema without injuring
herself." After a postpartum infection at age twenty-seven, she developed a series of tics, involving especially the facial muscles.
Then, around thirty-five, amid anxiety over sudden death and
choking, she developed a huge phobia about swallowing and had
worked out a complex ritual about breathing as she swallowed.
This state had now lasted for six years. When Janet saw her, she
was "stretched out upon a chaise-longue that she was scarcely able

to leave on account of her extreme weakness. She spends her days trying to take a bit of nourishment. . . . With a tiny spoon she swallows drop by drop some egg yolk, dissolved in a bit of beef juice, spending five or six hours in consuming the yolks of two or three eggs."[36] If Janet's experience is generalizable, the *femme à chaise-longue* languished in many a bedroom of the upper middle classes.

There are several puzzles in these bed cases. Even though they blossomed in the heyday of hysterical paralysis, they were not necessarily a subtype of that sort of paralysis.[37] Most of the patients were not "paralyzed" but rather claimed tiredness or a general inability to cope with life beyond bed. Nor had they assumed their symptoms as a result of medical suggestion, for few doctors believed they had organic disease or even "functional" disease within the nervous system. It is also curious that they were limited largely to the upper crust, or perhaps not so curious, given that a requirement for the maintenance of the symptom was a staff of servants, little mechanical carts, and women with sufficient leisure to spend six hours swallowing two egg yolks. Still, there was relatively little trickle-down to the lower classes, in contrast to hysterical paralyses, in which women with little time to be "paralyzed" nonetheless became so.

In contrast to some of the rather transient hysterical paralyses, women who had transformed themselves into bed cases were often profoundly symptomatic and subjectively experienced great suffering. Miss X., a single woman of forty-five, bedridden for eight years, wrote around 1881 to London society gynecologist William Playfair, "I can hardly tell you what a deep sufferer and how prostrate I have been. For years I have led a completely sedentary life, always lying. It is the position I am easiest in. My back aches sorely. I am peculiarly sensitive to pain. I spend very restless nights. The pain is often then very bad. I have always a sense of great weariness." When Playfair examined her, he found a pale and "very wasted" patient with little appetite. She had a small uterine fibroid tumor that of itself could not have been the cause of such suffering. She was taking almost four hundred milligrams (six grains) of solid morphine a day, injected by her maid.[38] It was precisely such patients, whose suffering, though acute, seemed without organic cause, that the surgeon's knife would come to aid twenty years later.

Others had not even a uterine fibroid, merely shock, grief, or some adolescent upset to justify the sofa. Virginia Woolf's aunt Caroline Emelia was said to be "an intelligent woman who fell, nevertheless, into the role of the imbecile Victorian female. She fell in love with a student and had some reason to suppose that her affection was returned; but the young man never declared his feelings. He went to India and nothing more was heard of him. Her heart was broken and her health was ruined; at the age of twenty-three she settled down to become an invalid and an old maid."[39] In 1840 the poet Elizabeth Barrett, at thirty-four already in bed for a year, was plunged definitively into what sounds like nervous invalidism—but may have been tuberculosis—when at the Cornish resort of Torquay she received news of the death of her brother Sam. (She died twenty-one years later, apparently of TB.[40]) In 1866, at the age of eighteen, Alice James began to develop nervous troubles and went from Boston down to New York to consult with Charles Taylor, who had just opened his Dispensary (though she stayed at his home next door). Another nervous attack two years later then prostrated her, and she, "the sweetest and most patient of all invalids," remained in bed for most of the rest of her life. Nobody could ever figure out what was the matter with her, and she removed to England, which was said to offer "a more congenial setting than Boston for a career of invalidism."[41]

If English society was heavily sown with sofa cases, middle-class life in the 1800s and 1890s in the United States was no less so. The term *bed cases* was, in fact, popularized by Silas Weir Mitchell, the Philadephia neurologist, who said in 1881, "These are the 'bed cases,' the broken down and exhausted women, the pests of many households, who constitute the despair of physicians, and who furnish those annoying examples of despotic selfishness, which wreck the constitutions of nurses and devoted relatives, and in unconscious or half-conscious self-indulgence destroy the comfort of every one about them." Mitchell went on, "There must be in every country thousands of these unhappy people," whom he described as "weak, pallid, flabby, disfigured by acne, or at least with rough and coarse skins; poor eaters; digesting ill; incapable of exercise. . . . They lie in bed, or on sofas, hopeless and helpless, and exhibit every conceivable variety of hysteria."[42] Mitchell's sympathies in the affair were more on the side of the nurses than the patients—for these wealthy families would hire minders to administer Mitchell's rest cure. "I ought to say that the care of these invalids is, even to the well-trained and thoughtful nurse, one of the most severe of moral and physical trials, and that, in the effort to satisfy the cravings of these sick people, I have seen the best nurses crumble as it were in health, and at last give up, worn out and disheartened."[43] Mitchell's account, though unsympathetic, suggests that he must have encountered these cases often in his upper-middle-class Philadelphia practice.

The American richness in this category of patient also became manifest in the proliferation of diagnostic terms for it. William Basil Neftel, born in Riga and educated at Saint Petersburg, who settled in New York in 1865, at the age of thirty-five, had a society practice based on electrotherapy. When Neftel's patients had taken to their beds, he diagnosed "atremia," by which he meant the inability to stand up and walk, in addition to the inability to bear excitement, plus bizarre skin sensations. Like fellow society physician Charles Taylor, he accepted referrals from the gynecologist James Marion Sims. It is interesting to watch Neftel in action because, like Sims, Taylor, and the New York electrotherapists Alphonso Rockwell and George Beard, he made his living from the chronically ill middle-class women of the Eastern Seaboard.

Mrs. J., for example, age thirty, had been an invalid since her first delivery eight years earlier. Her mother had been an invalid too. "She complains," said Neftel, "of every possible strange sensation in her head, back, chest, throat, abdomen—especially in the area of the left ovary, also in the genitals, and in the rectum. There is actually no part where she does not on occasion experience various paresthesias." When Neftel saw her on October 1, 1881, he said, "The patient is almost always in bed, because the slightest exertion, especially walking, greatly worsens her condition, whereby she experiences diarrhea, loss of appetite and sleepless nights." His electrotherapy in New York effected momentary improvement, but she relapsed as soon as she returned home.

Another of Neftel's patients, a woman of fifty-four, had spent most of her adult life drifting in and out of "paralysis," taking definitively to her bed at forty-eight. "For the last six years she has been bedridden, can neither walk nor stand nor sit, although there is no motor paralysis." Any effort to talk produced fainting, vomiting, diarrhea, and so forth. "I feel as if my head could not bear it any longer, and I must lie down," she said. She was now completely isolated and spent the day lying in a darkened room with her eyes shut. With no friends left, she kept thinking about her illness. Every time she saw Neftel she would explain her symptoms to him in great detail. At the end of this recitation, when asked to sit up, she always replied, "But you must realize that this is impossible, with my best will. . . ."[44] If Neftel's experience of these women, flat on their backs in darkened rooms and unable to bear the company of anyone but a servant and their husbands, is at all typical, the number of such patients must have been quite substantial.

For Robert Edes, a physician at the Adams Nervine Asylum in Boston, such cases represented a subtype—"the limp neurasthenic"—of a larger nervous phenomenon that he called "the New England invalid." The patient "talks of being tired" and "lies quiet [so as] not to strain her muscles. She is apt to say that 'all she wants is rest,' and yet she may have been doing nothing but rest for years." Edes could scarcely have given a less sympathetic account of the chronically somatizing female patient:

> The New England invalid is with us all. The old doctor has carried her all his professional life, and yet she is ready to bestow the care of herself upon the young man just making his reputation and proud to be trusted where so many have failed. . . . You see her occasionally. You must go, to be sure, when you know there is nothing to be done and you have not the time to do it. You must listen to the thrice-told tale of symptoms which you are as morally sure have nothing to do with any tangible lesion as if you had the patient upon the dissecting table.[45]

Thus the diagnostic terms for chronic invalidism proliferated, each new specialist proposing his own label for a phenomenon that was clinically inchoate aside from the helplessness and disability of the languishing patients. Yale's John Foster, a tuberculosis specialist who saw a number of chronic neurotics as well, seized the essence of these women's lives. He called them "members of the 'shut in' society." A fifty-four-year-old female patient of his, with a long history of "rheumatism" and a "highly sensitive nervous organization," had haunted the private clinics of the United States. "When this patient came under my care she had finally given up hope of relief from rheumatism and was confined absolutely to her room, most of the time an intense sufferer." Foster became convinced

> that the rheumatism was a thing of the past and that all the symptoms were due to neurasthenia, following prolonged illness. At the time of which I write, the patient had not been out of her house for three years and had not been down stairs for sixteen months. I tried to convince her by argument that she could walk down stairs, and she made several attempts to do so, but after she had taken one step down she screamed with pain and was lifted back onto her bedroom floor.

He cured her by forcibly repeating the view several times that she would soon be up and walking about.[46]

With the outbreak of World War I, references to shut-ins, invalids, bed cases, and the like became much fewer in number. In 1947 Richard Asher, a physician in Essex, regarded patients who "went to bed" as akin to an extinct species. He described one he had seen at some point in the late 1930s, "a lady who had been in bed for seventeen years with a diagnosis of nervous debility and whitlow [a subcutaneous abscess]. She had survived this remarkable hibernation with little damage, and though she was very upset when I ordered her up she became a different person when she was fully ambulant." "Look at the patient lying long in bed," Asher apostrophized. "What a pathetic picture he makes! The blood clotting in his veins, the lime draining from his bones, the scybala [little fecal lumps] stacking up in his colon, the flesh rotting from his seat, the urine leaking from his distended bladder, and the spirit evaporating from his soul."[47]

What had happened to reduce the number of such bed cases in the twentieth century?

Battlefield Abdomen

If women abandoned the chaise longue of the invalid, it was, I believe, because they had found relief in the surgeon's knife. Invoking surgery gave them an active strategy for escaping the passivity of the sofa. It is to be emphasized that most of those—men and women alike—who sought out surgeons in the late nineteenth century belonged to the middle classes. For in the days before private and national health insurance, only well-to-do people could opt for what was essentially elective surgery: the voluntary decision to have various abdominal organs removed in the hope of achieving peace of mind (in contrast to emergency surgery for inflammation and perforation). The organs of choice were the appendix and the large bowel.

Abdominal surgery among the well-to-do had commenced on a large scale with the ovaries in the 1860s. Operations on other, technically more challenging organs dated only from the 1880s, by which time antiseptic and aseptic surgical routines had also diffused, making operations much safer.[48] By 1900 abdominal surgery had become commonplace. The riot of surgery that began in these years gave rise to the sobriquet, used among general surgeons and gastroenterologists in their coffee-room conversation, "battlefield abdomen"—the aspect of a belly that has been opened numerous times.[49]

Battlefield abdomen represented the partial democratizing of therapies for nervousness. Treatments such as the rest cure had been available only to the handful of wealthy people able to afford a private clinic, and staying in bed was the luxury of those who had servants. The growth of surgery now meant that valetudinarians well down the social ladder, though still not poor, would be able to harvest the imagined benefits of an operation for their symptoms. Well-off private patients could now insist on care that was personalized, if highly inappropriate. The collusion between doctor and patient was perfect: The surgeons, mesmerized by scientific rubbish and by their avidity for gain, were willing to operate on request; the patients, eager to distinguish themselves from the riffraff who could not afford private operations, were willing to see themselves mutilated in the interest of modish diagnoses.

This blizzard of unnecessary operations had two sources, appendectomy in "chronic appendicitis" and colectomy in patients whose main problem was constipation. Surgeons who would never have operated on uterus or ovaries for hysteria had no compunction about performing needless appendectomies and colectomies for such symptoms as exhaustion.

Chronic appendicitis, like spinal irritation and ovarian reflex neurosis, belongs to the treasury book of diagnoses that no longer exist. Described for the first time in 1827, it acquired a lively medical following between the 1880s, when appendectomies in general started to be performed, and the 1930s, when the great medical authorities decreed it a nondisease. Said one New England surgeon in 1932:

> There was a time, not so long ago, when every patient with a long-continued or periodically recurring discomfort in the right abdomen [where the appendix is]; or with troublesome gas in the bowels, especially with constipation; or with indefinite abdominal symptoms called indigestion; in fact every patient with abdominal symptoms which could not be readily accounted for by something else, must have his appendix out on a diagnosis of chronic appendicitis.[50]

Another surgeon at the same meeting agreed. "I still see almost every week a patient carrying one, two or three abdominal scars. The first one is almost sure to be that of a so-called chronic appendix."[51]

Behind these useless operations, in which a normal appendix was almost always found, lay the surgeons' readiness to link abdominal discomfort to organic disease and the patients' attachment to organicity as an explanation of subjective sensations. In 1913, for example, Clarence McWilliams, a surgeon at Presbyterian Hospital in New York City, saw a thirty-year-old barber who had been experiencing for four years "sudden attacks of diarrhea when he stood up by his chair." The man had no physical findings, no pain over the appendix, no past history of pain or obstruction, just diarrhea from time to time as he cut his clients' hair. "By exclusion it was considered probable that the appendix was at fault, so in November

1913 I removed that organ." The appendix was essentially normal. McWilliams also tidied up a "kink" in the bowel. "News from this patient, eleven months after the operation, shows that he was cured by the appendectomy. He has had no diarrhea since, and follows his occupation, which requires standing all day, without discomfort."[52] Surgeon and patient were tacitly in agreement that fainting and nervousness were caused by chronic appendicitis. In fact, the removal of a healthy organ responsible for a nondisease had cured psychogenic symptoms.

McWilliams operated even more cavalierly on female patients, such as "H. S., 21. Began to have headaches at 14. She wakes up with intense pain over right eye. There is nausea and she vomits food eaten the previous night. She feels prostrated for the remainder of the day. Three years ago she was put upon a milk diet and was free from headaches for three months, until she returned to solids. Bowels very constipated." As she had some pain in her lower abdomen, McWilliams removed her appendix. "Two and a half years after the operation, the patient considers herself well. She has an occasional mild headache on getting tired."[53] Again McWilliams had treated an absolutely quotidian collection of psychosomatic symptoms with an appendectomy; again the patient concurred in his diagnosis and believed herself cured after the operation.

It was not merely these American surgeons, with their historic record of scientific laggardness,[54] who embraced chronic appendicitis. A number of internationally known European authorities did so as well. In 1923 Julius Mannaberg, a distinguished Viennese professor of medicine, recommended the diagnosis to his colleagues: "Irregularity of stool and loss of appetite often give way at a single blow, in an absolutely magical way, to the feeling of good health, demonstrating the success of the operation."[55]

In the 1920s appendectomy for chronic appendicitis became a common procedure, propelled by doctors' objective reports and patients' subjective ones of success. Robert Hutchison, a physician at the London Hospital, said in 1923 that the appendix had become "the scapegoat of the abdomen." Often these "abdominal" people had already been appendectomized by the time Hutchison saw them:

The subject of the chronic abdomen is usually a woman, generally a spinster, or, if married, childless, and belonging to what are commonly termed—rather ironically nowadays—the 'comfortable' classes. To such a degree, moreover, do her abdominal troubles colour her life and personality that we may conveniently speak of her as an 'abdominal woman.' An abdominal man, on the other hand, is by comparison a rare bird, and when caught has a way of turning out to be a Jew—or a doctor.[56]

The comment about Jews and doctors is exquisite, implicating both ethnicity and class. Hutchison believed Jews to be more hypochondriacal, and it was the families of physicians who could afford such procedures—or by professional courtesy could request them free of charge.

Class and ethnicity help us explain the demand side, or patients' willingness to seek operations out. Surgical greed helps explain the supply side, or willingness to cajole the patients into operations. There was a pecuniary element in this proliferation of appendectomies for vague, nonspecific indications. In 1932 Edward Young, a surgeon at Massachusetts General Hospital in Boston, quoted some anonymous authority to the effect that "there were two kinds of appendicitis, 'acute appendicitis and appendicitis for revenue only.' "[57] Without doubt surgeons did use the latter sort of diagnosis to augment their incomes. Walter Alvarez recalled the fudging of medical records in appendix and gallbladder operations. "At one hospital in which I worked in my youth, many an appendix was removed supposedly to cure the 'vapors' of a neurotic woman. When it appeared normal to the pathologist who examined it with his microscope, he would write, 'chronic appendicitis, grade 1.' He did this partly for legal reasons, and partly so that the surgeon would not have him fired."[58]

While investigating health costs in New York City in the late 1930s, Gladys Swackhamer interviewed a fifty-two-year-old woman who had had "gastritis" for the last twenty-three years:

She was constantly seeking relief in clinics and when a new private clinic opened in her neighborhood she promptly looked in. A doctor there persuaded her to "see a professor" in a private hospital for which the clinic was a feeder. The "professor" played on her fears by telling her she had "chronic appendicitis" and needed an immediate operation. He asked her how much money she had in the bank and when he learned she had $200 he sent her to the bank in a taxi with his assistant to draw it out.

The woman later said she "felt as though she had been hypnotized." The surgeon operated that same day. "The pains in her stomach were not relieved by the operation."[59] So it was not always lofty but incorrect medical ideas, such as reflex theory, that pushed physicians and surgeons to act. In this orgy of intervention lay the profit motive as well, the patients rendered the more helpless in the face of this white-coated venality by their respect for "medical science."

By the mid-1920s chronic appendicitis was starting to pass from mainline medicine. However long it may have lingered in the small towns and community hospitals of the periphery, it became shaken at the center. As Frank Hathaway, a surgeon at the King Edward VII Hospital in Windsor (Edward VII had almost died of a real appendicitis, two days before his scheduled coronation), said in 1926 apropos pain on the lower right side of the abdomen:

> We have all had this same experience until we learnt our lesson. The patient is called "a chronic appendix" and on operation the appendix is removed and found normal or sharing in a mild inflammatory process with the caecum [the part of the bowel to which the appendix is attached]. Our patients, usually girls— but not necessarily so—are of the nervous type. For six months they are better, then all their symptoms return and they are labelled "adhesions." Another operation perhaps is done with the result that "the last state is worse than the first."[60]

In the United States as well, academically oriented doctors began to distance themselves from the chronic appendix, a structure which for reasons of its immunology *always* looks a bit inflamed under the microscope. As John Carnett, professor of surgery at the Jefferson Medical College in Philadelphia, said in 1934, "In common with many other surgeons, I no longer operate for chronic appendicitis."[61]

In the interwar years a whole generation of American internists became committed to the doctrine of "the patient as a person." The essence of this clinical tendency was situating disease in the context of the patient's whole life, and sympathetic physicians remembered William Osler's dictum: "The good physician treats the disease but the great physician treats the patient who has the disease"[62] This generation would put to rest the reflex ideas of the nineteenth century—which maintained that irritation from the ovaries and uterus affected the brain—finding them dehumanizing to the patient. Among such sympathetic doctors in the generation following Osler (who left Johns Hopkins for Oxford in 1905), few were more influential than Walter Alvarez.

Alvarez had little use for the diagnosis of chronic appendicitis. In 1940 he reanalyzed the histories of 385 appendectomized patients, concluding that the procedure had been terribly abused. Of 255 of these patients who had no history of no acute appendicitis, the presenting complaints had been in 15 percent of them "neurosis and nervousness," in 13 percent "constitutional inadequacy," in 10 percent "pseudo-appendicitis" (meaning that the operation did not help the pain), in 9 percent "psychopathic troubles," and so forth. Three patients had been operated on because they "insisted on it."

These surgeons' haste to operate confirmed every apprehension about the state of American medicine. Alvarez said:

> A college girl was rushed to the operating table so fast that she hadn't a chance to impress the surgeon with the fact that she had just been on the type of "walnut fudge bust" which always gave her a violent stomach ache. Another young woman couldn't convince the surgeon that she always got an alarming stomach ache when she ate onions. One patient had an acute duodenal ulcer which was not helped by the appendectomy. . . . Another had just had a violent argument with his wife; several school teachers were worn out with fatigue at the end of the school term, and one girl had simply vomited her dinner.[63]

The unnecessary appendectomy was a direct lineal descendant of the mutilating operations, such as surgical excision of the clitoris or the ovaries, on young women that had flourished in the nineteenth century and provided a great impetus in the early twentieth century to "battlefield abdomen." Although all patients were at risk of being appendectomized, those with chronic symptoms were probably at greatest risk, enduring further surgical derring-do for inconsequential adhesions. It is emphasized that the locus of all this chronicity—the surgeons' target group—was the middle class, for only they could afford these fee-for-service operators. The appendectomy accordingly represented the first wave in the gratuitous assault on the abdomen.

In the second wave came operations for autointoxication, the theory that toxins supposedly leaked from the colon into the rest of the body of a constipated patient. In such fears medicine around 1900 remained in direct continuity with the humoral tradition, which had always insisted on getting those bad humors out. Here was the updated version, taking on a portentous scientific tone: At a medical meeting in 1911, Charles Bonifield, an obstetrician from Cincinnati, Ohio, said that he gave purgatives to patients with "congested pelvic organs." He expressed the view: "It is necessary for the majority of people to have one evacuation of the bowels every twenty-four hours, and most people would be better off if they had more frequent evacuations."[64] John Janvier Black, at the end of a forty-year obstetrical practice in New Castle, Delaware, detailed in 1900 the problems that "auto-intoxications of intestinal origin could cause . . . among them vertigo, dizziness, headaches, disturbances of sight, etc. Many are hypochondriacal. Among the insane are many sufferers." Further, "We may have reflex symptoms arising and expressed in bronchial attacks, local and general convulsions, spasm of the glottis, circulatory irregularities, with skin troubles and rashes of different kinds."[65] Just as with traditional medicine, it was imperative for turn-of-the-century physicians to get those poisons out of there. The difference was that by 1900 doctors had acquired the ability to intervene surgically. Constipation and autointoxication could now be repaired with the knife.

It was the Scotsman William ("Willie") Arbuthnot Lane who introduced colectomy, or removal of portions of the colon, for constipation.[66] At Guy's Hospital in London in one capacity or another since he began his medical studies in 1873, he discovered the menace of the sluggish bowel around the turn of the century. Lane was at the time under the influence of the Russian biologist Élie Metchnikoff, the discoverer in the 1890s of a fundamental mechanism of inflammation. Metchnikoff then occupied himself with the bacteria of the intestine, coming to the erroneous conclusion that the large intestine was "useless." It was actually quite fateful that Metchnikoff published a book in 1903 containing these and other musings, for the English translation fell into Lane's hands.[67]

In 1903 Lane acquired the conviction that a constipated large bowel—a "cesspool," as he put it—could systematically poison patients by giving off "ptomaines." Such constipated patients acquired a characteristic "dirty colour."[68] His writing on this subject has an obsessional quality, pervaded by the delusive belief that feces were leaking from the constipated colon and infiltrating other bodily tissues. (In fact the feces do not leave the colon unless it is perforated, which in Lane's otherwise healthy young female patients it was not).

Lane might comment on the dark-hued skin of a patient or on a fecal odor about the person. Overpowered by the belief that "we suffer and die through the defects that arise in our sewerage and drainage system," in 1903 Lane started freeing up part of the colon surgically by cutting supposed "adhesions" about it.[69] In that year as well he started actually rearranging the plumbing of the large bowel, describing his procedure in a book published in 1904.[70] The operation entailed splitting the downstream portion of the small bowel (the ileum) and attaching part of it directly to the rectum, or else removing most of the large bowel entirely (colectomy) and hooking up the remaining portions to each other. By 1908 he had performed thirty-nine such operations.[71]

Some of the cases make hair-raising reading: "Case 7. P.S. aged 20, female. Extreme constipation and autointoxication. She was never without a headache. She suffered from severe abdominal pains. She used to be sick every other day. In spite of purges and enemas her bowels would remain confined for ten days. She has been unable to work for two years, being practically an invalid." In

September 1906 Lane performed an initial operation on her, dividing the tip of the small bowel and then connecting part of it directly to the rectum. When this proved unsatisfactory, five months later he removed almost the entire large bowel. Three months after that she was said to be "much stronger, and is fatter. She has no pain in the abdomen, has not been sick since the colectomy was performed. Her bowels are kept regular with some cascara [a purgative], and she is able to do some housework."

Other cases ended less happily. In 1905 he operated on a thirty-nine-year-old woman "completely broken down in health by the results of chronic constipation." She was informed of the risks, yet was said to be "most anxious to be operated on as her misery was great." She went into shock after the operation and died three days later. "E. C.," a woman of twenty-one, was admitted to Guy's in October 1907, "in an extreme degree of exhaustion consequent on chronic constipation. Her condition was so critical that I hesitated to adopt operative measures." Lane was right to be concerned. She died six days after Lane removed her large bowel. In fact of the thirty-nine cases of colectomy for autointoxication that Lane reported in 1908, eight, or 20 percent, died as a result of the procedure. Of these thirty-nine patients, thirty-four were women, most of them under forty. In other words, Lane was performing for such vague indications as "exhaustion" and "constipation" a savage mutilation of young women that was fatal one time out of every five.

Lane's operation did provoke some controversy.[72] But such was his prestige as a surgeon—and indeed from the viewpoint of skill he was probably the ablest surgeon of his generation—that the "Lane operation" went on to become widely adopted. Thus chronic appendicitis and colectomy for autointoxication became the two banners under which battlefield abdomens were carved on thousands of patients, particularly women, in the years before World War II.

In England in the years after 1910, women deformed by meddlesome and unnecessary gynecological and abdominal operations became a familiar sight in the consulting rooms of gastroenterologists. After discussing five such patients, Robert Hutchison concluded:

It will be observed that the road to chronic abdominalism is paved with operations. The usual sequence seems to be this: the patient begins by complaining of pain or discomfort in the right iliac fossa [right lower quadrant], for the relief of which the appendix is removed. For a few months she is better. (It is characteristic of the disease that almost any new treatment, and especially any operation, produces benefit *for a time*.) Soon, however, her symptoms return. This is put down to "adhesions," and another operation is performed to remedy these, with the same result as the first. Warming to his work, the surgeon undertakes bolder and yet bolder proceedings; a complete hysterectomy is probably carried out or some short-circuiting device, or the colon is fixed, or even partially removed, but still the patient is not cured of the pains, whilst the state of the nervous system has steadily worsened.[73]

Such patients were seen in Germany as well. The case of a twenty-nine-year-old patient of Else Neustadt-Steinfeld at the state asylum in Düsseldorf-Grafenberg captures the flavor. Frau "A. B." had come to Grafenberg with an attack of hysterical blindness, from which she recovered in the asylum after a year and a half of psychotherapy. Of interest here is her previous history:

It is extremely difficult to say exactly what was hysterical in the course of her illness. But certainly much was hysterical. The fact alone that the patient had consulted fifteen different physicians inside five years, who on the whole worked without consultation with one another, suggests that the presenting organic symptoms at least have been overvalued. Also, within this period fifteen different operations were performed on her, from an appendectomy, to a sympathectomy [cutting fibers in the sympathetic nervous system], to a trepanation of her skull. It is impossible to miss the patient's hysterical "addiction to operations" [*Operationssucht*]. She speaks proudly of her many operations. Once, when she was reproached with unwillingness to get well, she said that was unfair, that the many operations were not exactly trivial for her either.[74]

The point is that, however ardently she may have desired the operations, she had no trouble finding surgeons willing to perform them.

Doctors' willingness to perform needless surgery, as well as patients' desire for the surgical experience, was probably stronger in the United States than elsewhere—unsurprising given that American medicine remained in the "Wild West" right up to World War II.[75] The trust of American patients in surgery as a panacea was staggering. As Joseph Mathews, a distinguished surgeon in Louisville, Kentucky, said in 1911, "Coming to my office for perhaps every day in the week for many years have been patients who are perfectly willing to go under the knife, and for what? For constipation. They are not suffering from any acute disease so far as we can see; they are not suffering from any marked pathological conditions, but they are willing to submit to anything that you tell them to do."[76] After seventeen years of practice, William Schauffler of Lakewood, New Jersey, concluded, "I know of no more miserable object than the man or woman who has passed into a chronic nervous state. . . . If a woman, she has already been the rounds of the gynecologists with varying degrees of relief and has realized that they can do nothing more for her; and if a man, the chances are that surgery has long since done its utmost by removing a doubtful appendix."[77] Many of these patients had sought salvation under the knife merely once or twice.

But it was lifelong recourse to surgery that, in the twentieth century, would become the lot of many middle-class patients with chronic neuroses. Truly remarkable lifetime histories were compiled. Francis Dercum, a noted Philadelphia neurologist and professor at Jefferson Medical College, described a female patient with "a number of hysterical conversions which were frequently mistaken for somatic diseases. She suffered therefore from many physicians and surgeons. Appendix was removed in 1908, ovary was removed in 1910, a couple of years later the gall-bladder was removed, the kidneys were hitched up a few years later, and again operated on in 1917." His colleagues at this particular meeting of the Philadephia Neurological Society were spurred to tell their own stories. Alfred Gordon recalled a male patient "who, making the rounds of various internists and surgeons, suffered from many diseases and might have had all his organs removed if happily fear had not made him run away from the operating table. This experience seemed to cure him of all his manifold psychogenic pains." Charles Burr added: "Many surgeons seemed to have no conscience at all."[78]

"Polysurgical" patients would constitute an enduring theme in American medical literature for decades to come.[79] In any setting in which chronic nervous patients were encountered, long operative histories came to light. In 1934 internists John Macy and Edgar Allen at the Mayo Clinic discussed the medical histories of 200 of their patients with chronic nervous exhaustion: "This group of 200 patients had undergone a total of 289 separate operations; of these tonsillectomy [done for "focal infection" in the tonsils] accounted for 74. The remaining operations appeared to have been performed in most instances for relief of the [symptoms of chronic nervous exhaustion]." Of the 156 women, 52 percent had undergone pelvic operations. "Removal of the appendix, gallbladder, thyroid gland, hemorrhoids, and [nasal sinus operations] accounted for the remainder." Most of these operations, the authors noted, had not relieved the symptoms.[80]

With these polysurgical patients the whole internal logic of being a bed case was overturned. Whereas the bed case was a passive vessel for the nerve doctor, these patients, however pained and fatigued they might be, became active players in the bedside psychodrama. With the knife now available to them, they grabbed fate into their own hands rather then expressing their symptoms in helpless neurasthenia. Mrs. Carswell, a Georgia housewife who had "reared five children and looked after a large house," was the mirror of the new autonomy. "Her history," as William Houston, an internist at the Medical College of Georgia in Augusta, told it, "was an epic without end. For twenty years or more she had been a great sufferer from headache, backache, obstinate constipation, from severe discomfort after eating. . . . The most dramatic of her symptoms was a formidable eructation of gas. The gas came up with explosive force, like popping a paper bag, and could be heard all over the house." Also, for weeks on end she might vomit everything that she ate and was as a result quite thin. Her family doctor would treat her for malaria and "bad liver," and when the purgatives and quinine involved in this regimen failed, she would seek out a surgeon. "Teeth and tonsils had gone as a sacrifice to the painful knees [doctrine of focal infection]. Her colon was tender throughout and the transverse and descending portions [those across the navel and down the left side of abdomen] very spastic. This condition of affairs had led to an appendectomy, a second operation removing one ovary and breaking up supposed adhesions. A third operation had taken her gall-bladder." Her uterus then followed. "After each of these operations she was better for a while." But then "her zest for activity, or as it appeared to her a proper sense of duty, prompted her to bounce out of bed and start to work at the earliest moment."[81] Mrs. Carswell typified a larger shift in these years from the fainting Victorian heroine to the jitterbugging flapper, from the passive endurance of invalidism to the active quest for radical relief.

Helen Flanders Dunbar, the New York psychoanalyst who did consultation-liaison psychiatry at Columbia University, saw many somatizing patients in the internal medicine service. She was appalled at the surgeons' previous exploitation of the patients' psychosomatic illnesses:

> There are all too many women carrying on their bodies numerous marks of treatment by specialists, who still keep their complaints after being told again and again that anatomically everything was normal. Whole series of operations, curettage, discission of the cervix [incisions on both sides of the cervix], amputation of the portio [tip of cervix], plastic operations, excision of adnexae [ovaries and uterine tubes], appendectomies, nephropexies [fixation of a supposedly fallen kidney], gastroenterostomies [rehooking the intestines to the stomach], and finally extirpation of the uterus—all have been in vain.

Dunbar deplored physicians' refusal to see "the real source of the complaints in the patient's personality" or "in the secrets of her marriage or total life situation. Sometimes, for example, it is the husband that should be treated."[82] It is clear from such testimony that countless women were suffering mutilation and death in this maniacal onslaught of surgery.

Both the bed cases and the polysurgical patients represent extreme forms of culture-bound behavior. The bed cases were at the far end of the spectrum of somatization, patients who let themselves become totally incapacitated by their symptoms. But their incapacity took a passive form: staying in bed in a darkened room and not moving. On the other hand, patients who became addicted to surgery represented the active form of extreme somatization. So unbearable did they find their symptoms that they were willing to contemplate disfigurement and death in order to get rid of them. Both taking to one's bed and seeking out a surgeon represent hyperbolic expressions of the same phenomenon: the chronic perception of illness signals from one's internal organs, and both were at their inception specific to the middle classes.

The occurrence of this transition from passive to active has both a narrow technical and a broad cultural explanation. The rise of modern surgery made it possible technically. Before the 1880s the bed cases had no choice but to remain in bed. Once seeking out the surgeon became an option, the bed cases could resume active lives, minus a few of their parts.

Yet "something in the air" was at work as well. In the 1920s new notions of female roles dissociated women from their hysterical paralyses, causing them to seek out other kinds of symptoms, such as pain and fatigue. As Elisabeth Roudinesco has written of the new woman—actually the new female psychiatric patient—of the 1920s, "[She was] a woman in revolt, a criminal, a paranoid or homosexual, no longer the miserable linen maid of yesteryear, no longer a slave of her symptoms but the heroine of a new modernity."[83] Perhaps the new roles of this new woman also invalidated the bed case, making it unfashionable to lie abed a shut-in for years when one could be out and active in the community, even if as a lesbian or a paranoid.

Thus surgical strategy expanded chronic illness from the wealthy to the broad middle classes, for many people could afford an operation. Given that surgeons were ubiquitous, and that the patient could function normally between operations, it became possible for small businesspeople and even farmwives to take on the lifelong preoccupation with physical symptoms that previously had been an entitlement of the well-to-do.

This chronicle reflects how social class helps to shape illness behavior. These well-off patients had the leisure to occupy themselves neurotically with their bodies, to hive off into private nervous clinics and exclusive spas and to pick up fashionable new diagnoses while the lesser orders were still bemoaning such folkloric ailments as being "all tore up inside." But of course these middle-class sufferers were not aware of having fashionable illnesses. For them their ailments were as real as the suffering of tuberculosis and cancer; it was merely that the doctors could "never find anything wrong" except "chronic exhaustion." We don't know to what extent their ailments were genetically founded because the case histories on which this chapter relies contain so little family history. But the social classes change their composition so rapidly that it is probably unrealistic to expect much that is definitive from "the genetics of class." What we see in the face of middle-class suffering is how powerfully class mandated patients' woes.

Yet men and women did not share equally in these experiences. Women bore the greatest burden. It was the bedridden middle-class women who played out the larger cultural drama of female passivity. The patients with the ploughed abdomens reflected the power that "scientific medicine" had acquired over the female gender in particular. The sage of chronic neurosis is a chilling illustration of the tension between biology and culture in which these women patients danced, for the story ends with direct surgical violation of the body cavities, an intensely somatic result of psychosomatic illness. Why were women so at risk?

CHAPTER

3

Women at Risk

WOMEN SEEM TO HAVE considerably more psychosomatic illness than men. This is not just because they seek help more readily than men, or because doctors tend to diagnose symptoms as psychosomatic in women that they call organic in men—though both sources of distortion do exist. Women are truly more likely than men to define normal bodily sensations as evidence of illness, and to seek medical relief for them. Whether this tendency is genetic, cultural, or a mixture of the two is a big question that cannot fully be answered here. But historically the tentative interpretation seems justified that if, in the past, women have experienced more psychosomatic illness than men, it is because they have suffered a greater burden of unhappiness. We know from research today that women tend to use language differently than men do, and it is likely that both in the past and today women have employed the language of organicity more often than men in order to cope with unhappiness. Psychosomatic symptoms, in other words, may be an extension of other forms of communication that are also distinctively female.

Women's Greater Risk: Not a Myth

A good deal of statistical evidence suggests that the rate of psychosomatic illness among women is higher than among men. In 1967 in the United States, for example, 70 males per one hundred thousand population were under psychiatric care in general hospitals for "psychophysiologic and psychosomatic disorders," 137 females, almost twice the rate. In psychiatric outpatient clinics, 20 males per one hundred thousand were receiving care for such disorders, 27 females.[1] Family doctors, too, report more psychosomatic illness among their female patients than their male. In a survey done in 1961 and 1962 of 147 medical practices in England and Wales, the diagnosis of hysteria was made for 7 percent of all female patients, 4 percent of all male.[2]

Most physicians today have the impression that, when they deal with somatization, they will be dealing mainly though not exclusively with female patients. Psychiatrist Donna Stewart says of patients who present with "such popular nonscientifically documented disorders" as total allergy syndrome, hypersensitivity to yeast infections, and chronic fatigue syndrome: "Such patients are frequently psychologically disturbed, well-educated, single women, aged 30–50, in unhappy life circumstances."[3] How may we evaluate this evidence?

Several issues must be examined before the conclusion may be allowed that women really do somatize more often than men. Has the bias of the investigators, usually males, somehow skewed the results against women? Although such unconscious biases are extremely difficult to control for, if they exist, then it must be said that they are also present among the female scholars who have dealt with these matters. On the subject of psychosomatic afflictions of the pelvis, psychologist Judith Barwick claims that, while men must deal only with impotence and premature ejaculation, "Women experience a range of dysfunctions astonishing in their variability and frequency—every one of the reproductive-system functions in women can develop symptoms."[4] Historian Carroll Smith-Rosenberg takes the surplus for granted, asking, "Why did large numbers of women 'choose' the character traits of hysteria as their particular mode of expressing malaise, discontent, anger or pain?"[5] The whole subject of women and psychiatric illness has proved a prickly thorn for many feminist scholars. As Hilary Allen, a sociologist at Brunel University in England, writes on the subject of surplus female psychiatric morbidity as a whole, "For a polemical feminism . . . whose interest in the matter is political rather than clinical, this apparent female morbidity is a matter of mixed discomfort and concern. To the extent that the figures appear to confirm an unwelcome stereotype of women, they are embarrassing to feminism and there is every reason to deny their validity."[6] Allen herself, however, accepts the apparent surplus as real, a phenomenon crying out for explanation rather than denial.

What about the issue of medical bias? Have doctors diagnosed hysteria and spinal irritation more often in women, while considering similar symptoms in men to be evidence of organic disease? One must indeed be wary of interpreting findings such as this: In 1977 a nationwide, random survey of Americans who visited the doctor showed that in the twenty-five to thirty-four age group, 160 women per one thousand population did so for "neuroses" as against 85 men per thousand. Does this prove that women are more neurotic? Not at all. "Neurosis" is a doctor's category, not a patient's. The same symptoms in men might well have received other diagnoses.[7] It is fatal for historians to limit themselves to studying doctors' diagnoses alone. One must push through the bias of medical diagnosis to underlying descriptions of symptoms and of the course of the illness. Then—on the basis of such evidence as a history of long-standing complaints in multiple organ systems or of response to placebo therapy—one may retroactively assess whether the illness might have been psychosomatic. In this way the bias of the doctors may partially be circumvented.

But even though medical bias may have been real, some psychosomatic symptoms were so striking that it would have been difficult to pass them by. It stretches credulity to think that the doctors would have missed hysterical paralyses or decades-long sofa cases among male patients. A young person immobilized with paralysis at the beginning of adult life who responds three years later to removal of the sexual organs represents either a publishable curiosity or a therapeutic triumph, depending on one's point of view. In either case a doctor would not have ascribed the symptoms to polio, had they occurred in a male patient. Doctors' possible prejudice against women cannot fully explain the reporting of higher rates of psychosomatic illness among women.

Or does the answer lie in some behavioral characteristic of women? Do they seek help earlier and oftener than men, thus giving themselves apparently higher rates? Surveys of people's symptoms done randomly among the population rule out the effect of differences in medical help-seeking. Interviewers knock on people's doors and ask them what symptoms they have. These studies indicate that subjectively, women tend to be more sensitive to bodily sensations than men. Perhaps women also amplify such sensations more often, interpreting them as evidence of disease. In four different community surveys from the 1950s and 1960s, with interviewers going from house to house and inquiring about symptoms, women reported psychosomatic illnesses 60 percent more frequently than did men.[8] A random nationwide survey of the United States in 1989 showed that, for a wide range of "chronic conditions," young women reported more illness than young men. For example, thirty-seven women per one thousand population said they had "arthritis," twenty-five men. Twenty-five women per one thousand claimed "trouble with acne," twenty men. Thirty-three percent more women than men reported "dermatitis." Whereas twenty-four men per one thousand reported migraine headaches, fifty-nine women per one thousand did so. The rate of bladder disorders was thirteen times higher in women than men. And, although men smoked more than women, the rate of "chronic bronchitis" in women was 67 percent higher than in men. For no important chronic condition except asthma and slipped disks was there a male surplus among people younger than forty-five. Again, these are self-reports—not a doctor noting medically the presence of a given condition but a patient telling an interviewer that he or she has it. Clearly, in the United States at the end of the twentieth century, women believed themselves to be sicker than men.[9]

The great paradox is that, even though women are more symptomatic than men, it is not because they have higher rates of organic disease. At every age of life, the death rate of men is higher than that of women. As for life expectancy at birth, in 1990 American men could expect to live only 72.0 years, American women 78.8 years.[10] In terms of organic disease, men are sicker than women, but women more commonly perceive more illness.

Somatic Styles

Some observers think that men and women have different manners of processing and interpreting the signals they receive from their bodies, that they have different somatic styles. These differences have been a continual subject of historical comment. As Pierre Briquet, attempting to explain why hysteria was commoner among women, wrote in 1859, "Women have, at both the psychological and physical levels, a livelier sensitivity than men do." In line with the beliefs of this time he added, "For women everything is a matter of sensation [*Tout chez la femme et une occasion de sensation*]. And all the sensations they feel influence their internal organs." Briquet had actually done an empirical investigation of symptoms, asking all the patients on a women's ward, and all those on a men's, what physical sensations they experienced whenever they felt strong emotions. "The results of these investigations were always the same. In the presence of a strong emotion, the woman loses her breath, sobs, feels a sense of strangulation in her throat, feels compression about her stomach, feels pain and a tremor or restlessness in her limbs, a sort of transitory hysteria. Men become excited, animated, agitated, blush, feel blood rushing to their head, do involuntary movements of a violent, threatening nature. Their hearts race, their breathing accelerates. They feel they are about to have an attack of apoplexy or epilepsy. In summary, in the presence of unpleasant emotions the woman suffers; the man becomes agitated."[11] Briquet's conclusions reflect the values of his day, but the differences he reported doubtless existed at the time.

Doctors as a whole have long been sensitive to differences in the somatic experience of male and female patients. In 1926 Charles Odier, a Genevan physician and early psychoanalyst, said that men's and women's neurotic episodes differed according to time of day. Middle-class men exhibited the "five o'clock sign" (*le signe de cinq heures*), meaning that at the end of the business day they obtained temporary relief from their neurotic symptoms. If the physical problems of a professional man improved around aperitif time, his symptoms were probably neurotic in origin. For neurotic women, on the other hand, symptoms often began around five

o'clock, as the children stormed in from school. Thus Odier believed that men's physical experience of neurosis varied diurnally
from that of women. The male patients, aware of exhibiting the
"five o'clock sign," believed it, too, as did the females with the "in-
verse sign."[12] These are mere anecdotes, not definitive quantitative proof, but they do suggest that in the past for whatever
reason—cultural, social, or genetic—women's somatic styles differed from men's.

Evidence from today also indicates that men's and women's somatic styles diverge. Three researchers from Yale University, won-
dering why chronic neurosis ("Briquet's syndrome") is seen so
much more often in women than men, argued that men were
more reluctant to produce "deviant" symptoms. "Men may be
less likely than women to present symptoms in a histrionic fashion, and are therefore less likely to arouse suspicions that the
symptoms may be of psychogenic origin."[13] Psychologist James
Pennebaker, who in 1982 published a major investigation of gender differences in symptoms, found women "more attentive to internal states." Women perceived these states more often as
evidence of disease and sought medical help more often. For
Pennebaker this heightened internal vigilance reflected the social
precariousness of women, caught up in major life changes and
lacking a sense of control. "The modal high symptom-reporter is
a female from a conflict-ridden home who is anxious and self-con-
scious and has low self-esteem." Pennebaker gave women's somatic hypervigilance a quite specific social address: women of
lower social status, from small towns, obsessed by their weight,
and feeling that life was otherwise beyond their control.[14]

In chronic psychosomatic illness, a certain kind of somatic style
overlaps into pathology, which is to say it disables the person who
has adopted it. For example, sometime in the early 1920s Charles
Symonds of Guy's Hospital saw a young woman of good family
who had been at a "home for incurables," paralyzed with what her
previous physicians believed to be organic disease. Around the age
of twenty-five her parents had lost all their money, and she had
been obliged to accept work as a governess, "work for which she
had the greatest possible distaste." Employed by an officer's family, four years later she went abroad with them to one of the

colonies. There she met a twenty-year-old private soldier who functioned as an officer's servant. The couple was clearly unsuited for each other in the long term, yet, "She was fond of the man and welcomed any opportunity of escaping from the work which she disliked so much." They became engaged. She returned to England to await the wedding, and while back in England contracted some kind of infection that gave her a mild arthritis. Still in bed when her fiancé returned, she was at that moment clearly not well enough to be married.

"Now," said Symonds, "consider her position at that time. So long as she was ill her relatives were prepared to provide for her. She was well looked after and had not to work for her living, and all this without paying the price of a marriage which at the back of her mind she felt would be disastrous." Thus she could rightfully remain abed while in good conscience continuing to put off her fiancé.

Up to this point the case shows a specific somatic style—taking to bed for minor discomforts—that characterized a specific society at a specific time: Edwardian England. But now events got somewhat out of this young woman's control. Her chosen somatic style became toxic. Her fiancé broke off the engagement, and her physician, compounding her woes with a misdiagnosis, broke the news to her that she was suffering from an incurable disease. Her relatives finally placed her in a home for incurables, where Symonds first saw her. By this time the patient had converted herself from an active young woman into a chronic invalid and was reluctant to accept the opinion of the physicians at Guy's Hospital that her problem was similar to "cases of functional disorder observed amongst soldiers during the war." Symonds and his resident physician restored her briefly with a combination of Dubois's rational persuasion and the Freud-Breuer "cathartic therapy." She relapsed. A definitive cure eventuated largely because of her embarrassment at the whispers of the other patients at the "home" that she was malingering.[15] The point of this is that women at that time did have a somatic style that tended to lead them to weakliness. It was seen as socially correct for her to seek a time-out in bed. Yet the styles themselves may leap out of control. The unconscious mind cannot be fine-tuned, and the path of invalidism once trod upon may plunge the bearer of the style into misery.

The Role of Economic and Physical Misery

Before the middle of the nineteenth century, women generally had harder lives than men.[16] Not only were farm women or women laboring alongside their husbands in craft shops expected to pull their own weight, the burdens of childbearing, breast-feeding, and looking after small infants also fell on them. Before the great fertility decline of the late nineteenth century, the average woman would give birth to around six children. This means that for every woman who had only four children, there would be another who had eight. Women paid the cost of this tremendous load of work and care with their health, and experienced real organic disease more commonly than men. For example, among the population aged thirty to forty in rural Denmark in the 1840s, 81 men died for every one hundred women. In urban Denmark the relationship was reversed: 113 men in that age group died for every one hundred women. It is almost certain that one of the reasons for the surplus of female deaths in the countryside was the hard lives of Danish rural women.[17] Many other such statistics could be accumulated.

What toll in psychosomatic illness did this harshness of life exact? Intuitively it makes sense to think that a careworn existence would produce some kind of psychophysical reaction, some formation of symptoms in an effort to escape unrelenting drudgery. The astrologically oriented English divine Richard Napier, rector of Great Linford in Buckinghamshire, functioned as a physician, for his parishioners came to him for the cure of body and spirit as well as of soul. Afflicted with what historian Michael Macdonald has called an "extra burden of disease," women in particular sought out Napier for the relief of mental distress. Napier called four of his female clients "heartsick," an old-fashioned word for being despondent and in pain. Twelve males and fifteen females made "nervous gestures," and fifty-five women (versus thirty-four males) had "no appetite." The largest single category by far among Napier's two-thousand-odd cases was "can't sleep" (250 females, 58 males).[18] It is not inconceivable that much of this anorexia, insomnia, and nervosity were a response to the harsh economic conditions of seventeenth-century English village life.

Reports of women's misery are legion. To contemporary physicians it seemed obvious that the "hysteria" they observed in their female patients was caused by "the stinking, suffocating rooms they inhabit," as Georg Consbruch, a physician in Ravensberg in Germany, said in 1793 of the impoverished linen weavers in that district.[19] Étienne-Jean Georget, a psychiatrist at the Salpêtrière, wrote in 1821:

> Women are generally more patient and better capable of enduring disaster than men. Very quickly they learn to get along following sad emotions, without experiencing effects as disastrous [as those of men]. But nonetheless their health is affected. In such circumstances women almost always have various symptoms whose true cause physicians fail to recognize. . . . I am referring to their headaches, insomnia, and stomach aches. . . . These symptoms are so common, above all in Paris, that some combination of them is to be encountered in more than a half of all female patients. . . . In general, their cause is domestic sorrows [*chagrins*], vexations and anxieties, which announce themselves in the form of headaches and insomnia.[20]

Could Madame Lambert, a thirty-two-year-old patient of Raoul d'Étiolles at the Hôtel-Dieu Hospital in mid-nineteenth-century Paris, have been an example of such domestic "chagrins"? She had experienced her first fit at age twenty-six, caused by "an episode of great sadness [*une forte émotion morale triste*] following the misbehavior of her husband" (The "misbehavior" was unspecified.) Separated from him at twenty-eight, she returned to him after seven unhappy months alone, now having numerous fits, announced by a ball climbing into her throat and by vomiting. At thirty she moved to Paris to escape her husband. "She worried greatly about the future, obliged as she was to make a living for her children." This apparently difficult period in Paris reached a wretched provisional end when in 1853, at age thirty-one, she was unjustly accused of theft and taken to the prefecture of police. "In jail a guard, under the pretext of bringing her to the judge as she had requested, took her to a remote room and raped her." She responded by developing a number of nervous symptoms, whereupon she was confined in another locale, whose nature became clear to her only as she was placed in a straitjacket bearing the inscription "St.-Lazare Prison." She now developed "an unbearable feeling of ants crawling over the skin [*fourmillement*] of her whole body, simultaneously a generalized nervous tremor, her pupils even moving about convulsively." Her saga continued for months, as symptom heaped itself on new symptom. One might infer that the root cause of her hysterical symptoms was the powerlessness and abuse she had endured in her adult life at the hands of brutal men.[21]

Why do we see so much "functional neurosis among women of the lower and lowest classes?" asked Leipzig gynecologist Franz Windscheid in 1896:

> You can certainly say that women around here are the better half in marriage. Earning the daily bread falls mainly on their shoulders. In addition to the work that naturally comes to them from their gender, they must also worry about supporting the family, because very often the men are unable or unwilling to perform this duty, which should by right be theirs. Then, to these purely physical facts are added mental ones—above all that women have to endure mistreatment from the men. Thus their nervous system, labile under the best of circumstances, is further weakened and the ground prepared for hysteria and serious neurasthenia.[22]

Many urban physicians associated hysteria in women with such conditions.

The hardness of women's lives expressed itself also in unrelenting labor from dawn to dusk. Cornelius Suckling, physician to the Queen's Hospital in Birmingham, thought the consequences of grinding toil so distinctive as to constitute a separate variety of paralysis: "exhaustion paralysis." One of his patients was a woman of fifty-one who was admitted to hospital with a paralyzed right leg:

> She had followed the occupation of cook in a large factory, and had been accustomed to standing for many hours a day, the usual hours being from 6 A.M. to 9 P.M. She would perhaps sit down for a few minutes to her meals, but certainly for not more than half an hour in the day. Besides being constantly on her

legs, going up and down stairs, she had to lift and carry heavy weights. She had worked at the factory for some months, and had always left her work completely tired out.

Her paralysis, said Suckling, was not hysterical in nature, "the patient being a hard-working and very matter-of-fact individual, not at all of the neurotic type, and extremely anxious to get out of the infirmary to go to work again." She was cured in ten days by their standard therapies.[23]

If we had only such selected anecdotes to go no, we would easily conclude that physical misery caused psychosomatic illness, and that if women had higher rates than men, it was because they were more miserable. Unfortunately, an equally impressive body of evidence can be assembled to demonstrate the exact opposite: namely that a life of luxury and idleness caused hysteria. It is difficult to see how the doctors of the day could simultaneously have maintained both propositions, so starkly do they contradict each other. Yet the tradition in medicine of assigning nervous illness and hysteria to the soft life of the urban middle classes goes back a long way. In 1772, for example, Hughes Maret, a physician in Dijon, observed: "Members of the female sex, placed by fortune in a class where inactivity is a virtual duty, are frequently attacked by the hysteric passion, a malady that is almost unknown among women whom necessity has condemned to work."[24] Montpellier's Edme-Pierre Beauchêne pointed out in 1781 that "attacks of vapors" in men and women were anything but an affair of poverty: "One must not believe that only women are subject to the vapors, for in the cities where we live in such congestion, men who give themselves over to idleness and the pleasures of luxury [oisiveté et aux plaisirs du luxe] are tormented as well." But the male temperament was naturally hardier than that of women, said Beauchêne, making them less subject to "maladies nerveuses" than women.[25]

In France the authors of the "medical topographies," books on local public health, usually associated hysteria with wealth rather than poverty. In 1786 a doctor Méglin, from the small Alsatian town of Guebwiller, found that, "Women here are very subject to nervous troubles and hysteric affections. These maladies propagate themselves from mother to daughter. One sees entire families in which the daughters, in the very flower of their youth, are ravaged by it. The abuse of coffee, and the inactive life-style of the women—sometimes coquetry as well and maybe even wine—are the causes." For Doctor Méglin "hysterical affections," whatever he understood by the term, were manifestly not a disorder of the poor.[26] François-Emmanuel Foderé, a well-known professor of medicine in Strasbourg, was surprised in 1821 to find hysteria so widespread among the women in the cold valleys of the Alpes-Maritimes Department, "for these women lead very active lives and are very sober [*fort sobre*] at the same time. I have also noted this in Provence, which convinces me that it is not always the luxury of the cities and the reading of novels that gives rise to hysteric affections."[27] And in 1860 a local physician in the Finistère Department, a backward area of Brittany, thanked God that the healthy rural life had spared local peasant women all the "spasms, the migraines, the gastralgias, the hysteria, the chlorosis, the anemia, the severe disturbances of menstruation . . . these ever more frequent affections that damage the health of urban ladies [*les dames des villes*], who, condemned to a sedentary life by the double demands of their physical constitution and their social obligations, experience an extreme nervous lability and an overdeveloped sensibility."[28] In sum, to go by testimony such as this, one would never dream that in France psychosomatic illness in women was connected with the hardness of life as peasant and working-class women encountered it.

Nor was this invocation of comfort some aberrant notion of French physicians. Many Central European doctors, too, believed "hysteria" to be the result of luxury and idleness among middle-class women. In 1813 the local physician in Sankt Pölten, a small town near Vienna, volunteered that "nervous diseases . . . represent a considerable part of the distress and the complaints of the distinguished classes above all. Nervous weakness, spasms, agonizing abdominal pain and torment are the daily lot of the prettier sex."[29] And in 1868 Munich gynecologist Joseph Amann could not have been more scathing about the nervous weakness of his middle-class female clientele, contrasting the emotional lability of these pampered creatures with the stoicism of lower-class women:

"The women of the countryside and the urban working-class have little time to concern themselves with trivial complaints, unwell feelings, apprehensions of weakness, and headache and toothache. These women do not attend anxiously to every little gas bubble and every abdominal woe. They make fun of the apprehensive city creatures, who daily must have the family doctor certify their well-being."[30]

The theme of "women spoiled by tenderness" also resonated elsewhere among German physicians. In 1925 Felix Preissner, director of the psychiatric and neurological service in a public hospital in Breslau, commented on the number of fortyish female patients with "serious hysteria [who] have been treated at home with all too much tenderness and leniency. One such housewife had not taken a step in months and felt quite well as a result. She let herself be brought by her good-humored husband and a second companion to the author, at whom she smiled with pleasure. She thereupon took leave of her concerned husband with a few short tears, and then, cheerful and eager for sensation, began to drink in her new milieu."[31] From such German evidence who would ever dream that hysteria arose from stress and misery?

The same notes were heard in England. In 1843 Evans Riadore, a fashionable London physician, attributed "nervous constitution" to "the present system of education adopted for young ladies amongst the more wealthy classes of society." In his view women of this class expended too much "nervous energy" in education, too little in exercise. As surgeon to the Middlesex Infirmary, Riadore also knew the lower orders, yet he was silent on the subject of faulty nervous energy among them and clearly considered "nerves" to be a middle-class problem.[32] Hysteria "attaches itself particularly to the noble and opulent," wrote Walter Johnson, a tutor at Guy's Hospital, in 1849. "It is well known among the bourgeoisie."[33]

A long line of nineteenth-century English physicians spoke in this vein, and Stephen Taylor's analysis of "the suburban neurosis" in 1938 represents a kind of provisional capstone to this interpretive tradition. Who had this suburban neurosis? "Mrs Everyman is 28 or 30. She and her dress are clean, but there is a slovenly look about her. She has given up the permanent wave she was so proud of when she was engaged." Her clothes, in fact, now looked a bit shabby, and when Mrs. Everyman sat down in front of Doctor Taylor, "I notice that her hands are shaking." She listed her symptoms, declaring, "It can't be nerves, doctor."

Among Mrs. Everyman's symptoms were: "Lump in my throat that goes up and down, or round and round. . . . Trembling all over, and I jump at the slightest noises. . . . Continuous gnawing, nagging headache. . . . Stabbing pains over my heart. . . . Pain in my back which runs up and down."

Mrs. Everyman was clearly a somatizer. Taylor located her socially in the lower middle classes, "Her parents were respectable, and kept themselves to themselves. After school, she went to a shorthand college, and from there to a business house in Brixton." Having met Mr. Everyman, also a clerk at the business house, she marries. The couple acquires "a small semi-detached hire-purchase villa on the wonderful new Everysuburb estate," constructed by "Mr Jerrybuilder" of "the cheapest unseasoned timber, the lightest of breeze brick, and the smartest of bathroom fittings." Bored at home, Mrs. Everyman starts to become somatically preoccupied, acquires the fear that she has cancer, and ends up highly symptomatic in Dr. Taylor's office.[34] One cannot reproach Taylor, who later became Baron Taylor for his contributions to the Labour party, with ignorance of the situation of the poor. Although his account steams with loathing of the lower middle classes, he situated hysteria far from the nineteenth-century Birmingham cook with her poor aching legs.

The above examples trace two alternative realities in the genesis of psychosomatic illness in women. Through selective quotation hysteria was first established as an affliction of hardship and deprivation, then as a result of the idleness of the pampered classes. Both notions—that hysteria was caused by misery and that it was caused by wealth—cannot simultaneously be "true." What seems correct is that psychosomatic illness affected women of all social strata, although only upper-class women allowed themselves a complete debility. In looking for quantitative class differences in hysteria, some authors have missed qualitative differences in the presentation of psychosomatic illness. It is not the rate of illness that is different from class to class, but the form.[35] The middle classes tended to present the picture of valetudinarianism, the lower classes the twitches and spasms of motor hysteria.[36]

What helps us to understand women's special experience of psychosomatic illness is not social class but their experience of shock, violence, separation, and loss.

Trauma

Emotional shock runs like a red thread through psychiatric experience. The first attack of schizophrenia is often produced by a traumatic event. Giving birth elicits occasionally a pyschotic response in women. Shocking the brain by withdrawing sugar from it, battering water against it, or sending electricity through it seems to produce a temporary remission from psychosis. It is therefore not intrinsically implausible to see the onset of psychosomatic illness as one of the mind's mechanisms for coping with unexpected and unendurable information.

This relationship of trauma to hysteria was not unfamiliar to the Scottish "man-midwife" William Smellie. In 1724 Smellie was called to assist a female midwife at Wiston, near Lanark. The midwife had experienced difficulty delivering the child, which had been born feet first, its head still trapped in the birth canal. The midwife, not knowing that Smellie at that moment was hurrying to the scene,

> fell to work immediately and pulled at the child with great force and violence. Finding, as she imagined, the child coming along, she called out that "now she had got the better of him"! The neck at that instant separating, the body was pulled from the head, and she fell down on the floor. As she attempted to, rise, one of the assistants told her that it wanted the head, a circumstance that shocked her so much (being a woman of a violent disposition) that she was immediately seized with faintings and convulsions, and obliged to be put to bed in another room.[37]

If in the annals of hysteria one circumstance stands out above all others, it is emotional trauma as the cause of adopting symptoms. The reaction to stress is a constant theme in psychosomatic illness, but the form of the reaction varies from period to period and from men to women. Relevant here is that women react in a more somatic way than men.

What kinds of trauma did women find unendurable? Loss, physical violence, and sexual assault provide the commonest themes. The sudden death of a child, for example, often provoked the kinds of psychophysical reactions called hysteria. These afflicted responses were certainly common in the nineteenth century, the grand century of maternal love, and possibly before as well. At some point in the 1820s or 1830s the Frenchwoman Mme. X. saw one of her two children suddenly perish within forty-eight hours of getting croup. Mme. X. was twenty-one at the time. "That evening a hysterical crisis eventuated, preceded by no premonition." Sighing and struggling for breath, her heart pounding and belly painful, Mme. X. felt a ball rise from her abdomen to her throat. She then went into fits that lasted for five hours, attacks that recurred for the next two weeks. By the end of the month, the fits having become irregular, Mme. X. removed to the countryside, where she remained sad and somewhat symptomatic for the next four months. Her "hysteria" then terminated in an awful moment, when—believing her surviving child dead of a fall—she fainted. On awakening she burst into paroxysms of joy to discover the little girl alive. Mme. X. was well thereafter.[38]

On the last day of February 1866, Karl von Wertheimstein, a Viennese sculptor of eighteen and son of the great Wertheimstein banking dynasty, came down with scarlet fever. Twenty-four hours later he was dead. This event so affected his mother, Josefine, that she became unable to speak or move. The lad's father, Leopold, was scarcely able to hold himself upright. In the hopes that at least a change of scene would aid the mother's recovery, she was transported from the family's estate in Döbling, outside Vienna, to the Hotel Oesterreicher in the middle of town. "Unfortunately this did not suffice," said Josefine's brother, looking back in 1903 over these sad events. "Her condition worsened from day to day and soon there could be no more doubt that her mind was affected.

Doctors were called from far and near." Only tender nursing care from other family members brought about Josefine's recovery over the years. She was never able again to speak the name of her beloved son. A veil of silence descended over the exact nature of the mother's symptoms during this period, but presumably they represented a continuation of the physical symptoms—aphonia and paralysis—that she had shown at the beginning.[39] During the nineteenth century, many episodes of motor hysteria were touched off by such terrible emotional traumas—a scenario so chilling that physicians referred to it in shorthand as "the telegram."

Then came the physical violence of men against women. Of 289 "slow-onset" hysteria patients of Pierre Briquet at the Charité Hospital in Paris in the 1840s and 1850s, 12 had acquired their symptoms after "prolonged domestic violence [*après les mauvais traitements prolongés*]."[40] It was quite common to find women becoming "hysterical" after being beaten up. The following story represents a typical scenario. On April 5, 1879, Dr. Munk of Verebély in Hungary was called to the bed of a landowner's wife in an outlying village. "As I arrived I had trouble pressing through the gathered crowd. A large number of curious spectators were compelled to leave upon my command. The patient lay recumbent in bed with closed eyes, as though asleep, a feather bolster pulled up to her chest. As I removed the bolster, I saw that her upper limbs were rigidly extended." So were the lower limbs. Everything else seemed normal. Dr. Munk lifted her arm, but it immediately fell back down to the bedside, ruling out "catalepsy" as far as he was concerned. "I dripped hot wax on her lower limb, which did not move, nor did her facial expression reveal pain." Neither did she respond to his repeated questions. He put a spoonful of water in her mouth, which trickled out. Now weighing a diagnosis of "lethargy," Dr. Munk asked what had happened. "Yesterday the patient's husband beat her, and from that moment on she fell into this lethargical condition."

Dr. Munk was uncertain what to do. Only later, on the ride home, did it occur to him that he might have tried the "magnetizer" Carl Hansen's formula: "Wake up!" (*Wach!*) But the patient was Hungarian and might not have understood German, he said.

What happened to her later? The next day she was discovered out of bed trying to cut a slice of bread. She then fled from home for several weeks, finally returning, after which her husband resumed beating her.[41]

One Chicago woman's encounter with invalidism began in the 1890s when, working as a domestic, she quarreled with her employer. "During this altercation she received a blow over the right eye, which caused a contusion and almost instantaneous blindness in the same eye." Although the blindness soon went away, several months later she developed a paralysis of her left arm. "This, too, suddenly disappeared, but the right arm in its turn became paralyzed and recovery ensued in the same manner. For the past three years both lower extremities have been paretic [almost paralyzed], so that she is unable to walk without the aid of crutches." While she was at Cook County Hospital, young doctor Julius Grinker hypnotized her, effecting a temporary recovery, but she immediately relapsed as soon as Grinker left the hospital.[42]

The symptoms that women experience following violence seem to have shifted over the years from paralysis to sensory disturbances, in the manner of psychosomatic symptoms generally. Around 1930 "Lena," a thirty-three-year-old woman of Italian background in New York, sought help at the gastroenterology clinic of the Cornell Medical College because of "abdominal discomfort—accumulation of food, a pinched feeling, headaches, and anorexia at times." She gave a vague history of having fallen on her side. George Stevenson, called in to do a pyschiatric interview, found "that she had not actually fallen but rather that her husband, according to a custom of his, had punched her. In view of her illness, his punching had ceased."[43] Lena's unconscious mind, in other words, had devised a symptom that would protect her. This is a distinctive theme that divides the history of psychosomatic illness in women from that of men: taking on hysterical symptoms for the secondary gain of relief from violence. This element of self-protection is present in all three of the above-mentioned cases, and many similar instances could be adduced from the literature.

An extreme form of violence against women is rape. Because rape has been in the past—as it remains today—one of the most traumatic experiences a woman can undergo, one would expect some connection between this kind of sexual violence and the formation of psychosomatic symptoms. In fact, a number of women who fell sick with such symptoms had episodes of sexual violence in their background. Yet, historically, psychosomatic illness from rape has been little studied. Of such an essential matter in the lives of women we know almost nothing. Here one might merely note that the symptoms women developed following rape and incest seem to match generally the pattern of somatization that prevails in any given epoch. This means that in the nineteenth century we see motor symptoms: in the twentieth, sensory.

In the late 1830s Marie D., a French servant of eighteen, "was attacked in the middle of a field by a number of men who wanted to assault her sexually [*attenter à sa pudeur*]. She was so frightened and indignant at such a brutal act that she had an attack of nerves on the spot. These attacks then repeated themselves over the following days, three or four times a week. They lasted for about three-quarters of an hour." Eight years passed, and by the time Marie D. was seen in Pierre-Adolphe Piorry's service at the Pitié Hospital in Paris, her hysteria had come to incorporate most of the standard symptoms of the day. The attacks were preceded by a bout of sensory symptoms, such as ringing in her ears and a feeling that an iron bar was crushing against her kidneys. Then, after a sensation of a globe mounting from her abdomen to stick in her throat, convulsions would begin with foaming at the mouth. "After the attack she feels exhausted, broken, drained of energy. For about ten minutes her mind is shadowed. She laughs, sings, seems to be preparing to leave [*fait son paquet*], fails to respond to questions, and then she comes back to herself." Moreover, for the last three years, she had developed a total-body anesthesia, so that "a pin stuck into her skin produced no sign of pain."[44] In this case an episode of sexual violence had steered a young woman into a decade of invalidism involving the convulsions, catalepsy and anesthesias typical of the time.

On April 20, 1842, Mlle. X., a thirty-year-old factory worker in Angers, said to be of good health and timid character, was attacked at dusk by a drunken soldier. "In running after her, this man tripped on a pile of stones and fell down clumsily. Mlle. X.'s fright was extreme, and her period was instantly suppressed." Now her belly became distended and painful. She could walk only with difficulty yet did not have to stay in bed. Over the next five months she experienced four major fits in which she fell down and lost consciousness. Her physician attributed the fits to menstrual events.[45] Although these anecdotes are just selections, I have no doubt that they are representative of the larger body of cases in the medical literature. Whatever the nature of the trauma, women who experienced it took on the symptoms of the day.

Similarly, little has been written about psychosomatic symptoms in women who are victims of sexual violence today. Yet, at a psychosomatic clinic in a large city, it is not uncommon to hear of a history of violence or abuse in a young female patient. One notes how the symptom pattern today has changed. For example, a young woman of twenty-two who lived with her parents was admitted to the clinic. She complained of feeling dizzy when she got up from a chair, also of total-body weakness, a burning sensation in her head, numbness in both hands, episodes of fainting, and an unsteady gait. Examined carefully by a neurologist, she seemed to have nothing organically wrong. Over the days ahead her story came out. She had been afraid as a child of her "uncaring and critical father," her mother being "emotionally unavailable." Yet from the age of five until she was thirteen, she had lived quite happily with her grandparents. When at thirteen she moved in with her father and mother, her father, who also beat her, began an incestuous relationship with her. Since then she had been "depressed." Now at twenty-two, feeling herself "unworthy of friends," she was said to have no social life outside the family, a family in which , according to the norms of the ethnic group of which she was a member, she was completely enmeshed. Her horizons were limited to school and study. She had never had a boyfriend. The home atmosphere was unpleasant, with the relatives arguing all evening. A psychologist, who tried to get her to fantasize about images with a Rorschach test, reported her to be "very regressed, morbid and confabulated." Her images of "victims in torment" were thought to reflect her father's abuse. As an inpatient in the clinic she seemed very angry at everybody, and after discharge continued to be symptomatic. Her unsteady, or ataxic, gait harked back to the old motor paralyses of the nineteenth century (her ethnic group being somewhat "traditionally" oriented), while her other symptoms more resembled the garden-variety complaints of late-twentieth-century life. This particular case is not meant as a definitive confirmation of the "symptom shift" but as a reminder that anyone who attempts to deal with the traumatic circumstances under which hysteria once arose in women's lives must confront the subject of rape.

Disappointment and Enmeshment

Only a minority of women with psychosomatic symptoms experienced the kind of trauma described above. But in the nineteenth century another kind of shock lay in store for women: the new intimacy of family life. In entering the sentimental family of the late eighteenth and nineteenth centuries, in which ties of fondness rather than those of property, held people together, women were, in a sense, climbing into a cauldron and pulling the lid shut atop them.[46] As the emotional intensity of the modern family was historically unprecedented, much that was new in the area of illness behavior and perceptions of one's body might have derived from the altered circumstances of sentimental life. How often were the superheated expectations of young women before marriage disappointed by what they actually encountered, the reality traducing the dreams encouraged by the novels!

In accounting for psychosomatic symptoms in women, one might therefore envision a kind of "disappointment-enmeshment" scenario specific for the nineteenth century: Young women in courtship anticipated a delicious mutuality and romantic fulfillment. Indeed, on entering this new style of family life they found an intensity in relationships with husband and children that their grandmother's generation had not known. But relationships can be intensely good and intensely bad. For, unlike the traditional family, based on custom and tradition, the dynamics of love and passion in the modern family could produce crushing surprises. Pierre Briquet warned of this in 1859: "The most powerful of all the causes [of relapses in hysteria] is marriage. Because of the grief and the upset [*des ennuis et des chagrins*] that it causes, marriage was responsible for rekindling in twelve patients symptoms which previously had been dissipated for some time. And two patients resumed their attacks of convulsions as a result of sexual excitement arising from intercourse."[47]

So there was shock at the very intensity of the new-style family life. This shock might come as the surprise of disappointing events, events of which one as a young woman could scarcely even dream. Or it might simply represent shock at enmeshment, at the compelling, all-involving nature of sudden intimacy with a man who had previously been a stranger. One remembers that in bourgeois families it was customary for young women to remain chaste before marriage and to see suitors only when chaperoned.

On the subject of unpleasant surprises, one of Briquet's patients, a woman of middle-class origin, told a typical story:

I was born of normal parents. My relatives had never had a nervous illness. I had a good constitution. My character was gay and carefree. I was well brought up. My period had always been regular, and my health was perfect up to the time of my marriage. From this event onward I suffered, in my own person and that of my children and in my property, all that one can suffer. For fifteen years my life was just one long martyrdom. After six months of housekeeping I had stomach pains, after ten months I could not get my breath and felt I was choking. After a year, following a violent scene, I had my first attack of convulsions. These attacks then became more and more frequent, and might happen two or three times a week. They stopped only with my husband's death, after fifteen years of domestic life. From this moment on I had no further ones, and my usual symptoms [*mes souffrances habituelles*] gradually began to diminish.[48]

This patient experienced no particular trauma, just the total and unaccustomed shock of married life.

A female patient, thirty-three, of the psychologically oriented Paris physician Pierre Janet, suffered from having been "virtually abandoned by her husband and very isolated. She is obliged to conceal the unhappiness she feels about this." Her psychosomatic problems began one night at a concert as she was moved by the performance of a blind violinist. The next morning, with no further explanation, she asked her husband to take her to the oculist. The oculist examined her eyes and found nothing out of order. "The next day she visited a second oculist, and when asked about the reason for her anxiety, ended up confessing that she believed herself to be blind." This notion seemed quite bewildering to her entourage because she could function normally in her daily life, yet she was convinced she was blind. Now she began refusing to eat and sleep, and would spend the days agonizing. Highly agitated, she threatened suicide "in order not to remain blind."[49] One concludes that the husband's neglect of a woman who had had in marriage every expectation of not being neglected gave her the idea that she was blind. Perhaps she had adopted this symptom as a means of arousing his concern and initiating nonverbally a dialogue that seemed verbally excluded. In the disappointment-enmeshment scenario, the reality of marriage had proved disappointing. This woman, like many others, was too emotionally involved to extricate herself. While the choice of divorce was theoretically available to such women, their enmeshment excluded it in practice.

In this context it was not so important whether the patients were overtly miserable. The impact of intimacy was the important factor, for women held tight by intimacy often plastered over their dilemmas with a happy face while becoming hysterical. (The women in these families bear a striking resemblance to anorexic young females, who also on the face of it were "happy" in equally "happy" families.) Thus in hysteria we also encounter women whom marriage seemed to smother with its bliss. In the 1870s Alfred Beni-Barde, the prominent Paris hydrotherapist who functioned as society nerve doctor in the suburb of Auteuil, treated a happily married woman of thirty-two with three children. She stemmed from an old industrial family in the provinces. Her chief complaint was "the inability to hear her husband's voice without feeling a nervous agitation that provoked in her major melancholy and anxiety." She would have to go off by herself whenever he started to speak. "She told me that his voice, in speaking or singing, had once been for her a source of sweet sensations but now aroused in her entire being only extremely painful feelings. As soon as the first sounds reach her ears, she starts to hear an incessant racket that soon gives way to a kind of irregular tremor disseminated in every part of her body." Her eyes filled with tears as she told Janet her story, and her agitation was manifest in her face and manner of speaking. Sometimes the feared voice caused her "involuntary movements which she was easily able to control, other times sharp pains of ephemeral duration that migrated about her body." The patient was also quite emotive about other kinds of sounds, unable to play Chopin "without feeling an extremely painful impression," or anxiety at hearing Schumann.

The main point is that she was, in her own mind at least, not overtly miserable. Her physician husband had swept her off her feet, demonstrating to her during their courtship how beautifully he sang. Then after "twelve years of joy and happiness," one day he returned from duck hunting with a bit of laryngitis. Quite unable to sing, he could emit merely a few hoarse croaks. Now the very sound of his voice began to provoke symptoms in her, a few muscular twitches and involuntary contractions. She began to have crying spells as she saw "happiness passing away." Black depressions commenced. Although the husband soon recovered his singing voice, she did not recover her equilibrium and was brought in a state of nervous exhaustion to Beni-Barde's clinic. The contrast between her marital fantasies and her rejection of her husband at the somatic level is an exquisite depiction of the rejection of intimacy. The whole story illustrates a woman suffering the shock of marital alienation. Beni-Barde cured her by isolating her for months from her husband.[50]

We are dealing with psychological and not economic misery. The loss of ideals, the separation from fantasy if not from loved ones in practice, may have found expression in somatic form rather than in flight or protest. In fact, the disappointment-enmeshment scenario is a historically specific illustration of the general impact of loss and misery on the mind-body relationship. It suggests how the specific cultural milieu of a given time and place can shape enduring and universal aspects of the mind-body relationship.

The Matriarch

A second culture-specific scenario involved the figure of the matriarch. Family life has always known powerful women, and the
nineteenth-century family offered nothing distinctive in this re-
gard. What was new in the nineteenth-century was the strategy of
sentimental blackmail. In the peasant family, where relationships
tended to be instrumental rather than for the sake of happiness, it
was quite difficult to blackmail other family members with one's
suffering. The news that "madame was suffering" would have
been received by male peasants with a yawn, and indeed traditional men might swap proverbs along the lines of:

"If the cow kicks off, mighty cross.
If the wife kicks off, no big loss."
[*Kühverrecke, grosser Schrecke,
Weibersterbe, kein Verderbe*][51]

The sentimental rules of the modern family, by contrast, com-
manded husbands to pay attention to their wives' symptoms and
parents to attend to the symptoms of their children. This atten-
tiveness opened the possibility that these symptoms could be used
manipulatively. The example of anorexia nervosa is instructive.
The self-starving patient could derive few advantages until the ad-
vent of the modern family, beginning late in the eighteenth century. In the traditional family not eating and threatening to starve
oneself to death would have been received with indifference, or
else seen as evidence of insanity. Only when passionately felt emotion clenched family members together around the table did the
threat of not eating evoke an alarmed response.

Taking to one's bed was similar. In the traditional family the figure of the bedridden matriarch aroused little compassion because
other family members were quite complacent at the prospect of female suffering. In the nineteenth-century family, however, the
prospect of another's suffering became intolerable. Other family
members must provide succor and sympathy. Thus was born the
bedridden matriarch who had the ability to command the household on the basis of her claims of chronic illness.

The matriarch became a stock figure in nineteenth-century

medical literature, pounding on the floor with her cane to call the servants, dominating the household on the basis of her requests for quiet and special diets, and summoning the doctor for daily visits. Unfortunately our access to the matriarch is somewhat obstructed by the physicians' loathing of her. Doctors hated being these patients' errand boys. "There are many kinds of fool," said Weir Mitchell in 1887, "from the mindless fool to the fiend-fool, but for the most entire capacity to make a household wretched there is no more complete human receipt than a silly woman who is to a high degree nervous and feeble, and who craves pity and likes power."[52] French psychiatrist Julian de Ajuriaguerra described in 1951 "castrating" mothers who produced hysterical, tyrannical, and frigid daughters.[53] These captivating images of matriarchs doubtlessly owe more to perfervid male imagination— laced in the latter case with a dose of Freudian psychobabble— than to an objective assessment of mother-daughter relations. Yet the figure of the housebound, bedbound middle-class martinet, tyrannizing servants and berating a silent, weary husband, has come down to us in so many forms—literary, medical, and artistic[54]—that we must be nudging against some historically distinctive form of women's experience.

In the twentieth century, with the downward diffusion of the female matriarch to all levels of society, she became an increasingly familiar object of medical irritation. Anthony Clarke, a family physician in Sheffield, described in 1967 "the dominant matriarch syndrome," writing, "The grandmother is the dominant figure" over three generations. "She married a steady, quiet, reliable wage-earner, who soon discovered that any self-assertion on his part resulted in either fierce opposition or hysterical symptoms on the part of his spouse." The ailments—as well as the note of female authority—were passed on from generation to generation. Clarke determined in the case of thirteen three-generational Sheffield families that, "[The granddaughter] suffers the same ailments as her mother, but often to an exaggerated degree. . . . She is a regular patient, and is frequently accompanied to the surgery by both mother and grandmother. In any visit by the doctor to the child's home, grandmother does the talking, mother agrees, and the men (if not out at work) never say a word." The mother and her husband do not move away but go just across the road from the grandmother, "and when either the mother or the girl-child becomes ill both these females move back to the grandmother or she moves in with them." Clarke found these families to be in stark contrast to the normally patriarchal working-class family in Sheffield.[55] Whatever the prejudices of these physicians, they were struggling to describe a core phenomenon of women who were powerful in family life and also chronically ill.

It is difficult to penetrate the veil of medical distaste for these strong yet symptomatic women in order to establish what is really going on in their lives. When a doctor evokes a "tyrannical" or a "castrating" matriarch, what is he actually describing? The core reality of the matriarch's experience was that she was both feared and loved. It was from the affectionate bonds forged by courtship and early motherhood that these matriarchs derived their authority to command, for they had relatively little power in the sense of disposing of resources or means of coercion.

The matriarch's power thus lay in her ability to "concentrate love," in the words of Paul Schilder, a Viennese psychiatrist who later emigrated to New York. In 1939 Schilder assigned to hysteria the function in family life of focusing everyone's love for one another. In family life organic disease "concentrates the love of the parent upon the child. It makes the individual still more dependent upon the parent." So did pseudo-organic disease, or hysteria, for the parent could not know if the symptoms were organic or not. "Hysteria thus becomes the expression of suffering as disease in its human and social aspects," Schilder continued. "It stresses the helplessness and dependence of the child on the love of the parents."[56]

In reality the apparently dominant matriarchal figure may well have been a woman who feared for the continuation of love from husband and children and whose chronic ailments represented an assertion of the need for that love. Why must she be a "dominating matriarch" to achieve this objective? It was probably an accident of the distribution of personality styles, for women by nature less assertive would have been classified as "fragile labile hysterics" by the physicians. Women on the more assertive end of this particular spectrum became known as "dominating hysterics."

Were There Only Female Invalids?

Were there no male invalids? Did the condition strike only women? It is inconceivable that chronic disability in the absence of medical disease affected only one gender. In fact males did have a kind of subterranean existence as invalids, although historically they come less to notice. Information on male invalidism—men who are not bedridden, seem to have little wrong with them, and yet cannot work—is extremely difficult to come by but important because it universalizes what would otherwise seem an exclusively female experience. In past times it was expected that middle-class women would not work. Having little else to do, they had few qualms about taking to their beds. But idleness among males was not socially sanctioned, and the invalid males have covered their traces better. One physician with extensive experience among male invalids in the American South wrote, "It is my impression, poorly documented, that male invalids do not seek out medical attention. The diagnoses they carry are too fragile and subject to refutation."[57]

Clifton Meador, an elderly physician with memories of practicing in the 1930s and 1940s in little towns in southern Alabama, gathered information about at least one male subculture of invalidism. We are dealing here with psychogenic problems, not chronic organic illnesses such as arthritis and heart failure. "Locked bowels" and "fell into a well and remained there overnight" qualified one for a lifetime of disability. Often the men were described as having "almost died." Men with such vague but traumatic-sounding experiences behind them would become permanently unemployed and depend on their wives financially. Unlike the female invalids, the males did not remain housebound, although their energies scarcely sufficed to drive the family car to the parking lot to pick up their wives at the end of the day, and certainly did not suffice for the drive home. Nor, unlike the female invalids, did they remain unmarried. "A man could not be an invalid and remain unmarried. It would virtually rule out the diagnosis," said Meador.[58]

There must have been many other male subcultures of invalidism in the past, though they are less well described. Was there one in southern France? In September 1886 Monsieur A. of Marseilles, thirty-six, was taking a seafront walk. In trying to clamber onto a rock, his foot slipped and he fell into the sea. He was fished out immediately thereafter, unconscious. So in France, too, we are in "almost died" country. Shortly after this episode he developed symptoms such as total skin anesthesia, which would stay with him for the next six years as he haunted the hospitals of Marseilles and Paris. Monsieur A. claimed himself unable to feel anything anywhere on his body. "We can touch, pinch, prick and burn all these mucous membranes and the skin without the patient being able to feel the slightest sensation. When his bladder and rectum are distended by urine and feces, he feels some fulness in his lower abdomen. . . . The last time he had sex was a year ago. He achieved orgasm but felt no voluptuous sensation at all." Taste and smell were abolished, hearing diminished, and in accordance with the doctrines then in vogue at the Salpêtrière (which emphasized the hysterial "stigmata" of Jean-Martin Charcot), he was found to have a constriction of his visual fields. "In summary, Monsieur A. is in touch with the outside world only via the intermediaries of vision and hearing," and even these senses were impaired. Gilbert Ballet, who presented the patient at rounds at the Saint-Antoine Hospital in Paris, considered him a simultaneous example of neurasthenia, hysteria, and hyperthyroid disease.[59] In fact Monsieur A. was just a chronic somatizer who had been suggested into the symptoms of Charcot-style "hysteria." Much of the literature on mesmeric trances and other physiological special states comes from the south of France, often involving males.[60] Perhaps a male subculture of illness existed along the quais of the Vieux Port—the dock area of Marseilles—that validated such behavior in men, similar to the subculture of the chaise longue among the female middle classes in Paris. Perhaps chronic invalidism in France was not as exclusively female as it was believed— or appeared—to be.

The exclusively male upper-class London clubs constituted perhaps another such subculture of male invalidism. "It is a marked peculiarity of hypochondriasis," wrote Francis Anstie, a London consultant, in 1871, "that it is far more common in men than in women." He called it "pre-eminently a disease of adult middle life," continuing, "the patient who today complains of the most severe gastralgia, or liver-pain, will tomorrow place all his sufferings in the cardiac region, or in the rectum, or will complain of a deep fixed pain within his head." Situating the condition especially among "the rich and idle classes," Anstie described one of his patients from the group of "rich and gloomy old bachelors who haunt some of our London clubs." The man had "been a repeated visitor at the Westminster Hospital during many years. He has had pseudoneuralgic pains nearly everywhere at different times." After giving an account of the man's groin pain and similar afflictions, Anstie concluded, "He will never be really cured, and I suspect that the secret of his maladies is an inveterate habit of masturbation."[61]

Hugo Gugl, chief physician of the private Maria-Grün clinic near Graz, Austria, had acquired extensive experience with the wealthy and chronically ill males who drifted from clinic to clinic and from spa to spa. Treating these cases of "cerebral asthenia ranks among the most thankless tasks, especially when the patients have consulted every possible specialist—and naturally have not always heard the same diagnosis, when they have visited a whole series of spas and read all the relevant medical literature. . . . I am thinking here mainly of males, for female patients accept authority much more easily."[62] Writers such as Anstie and Gugl were describing the kind of "international hypochondriac elite" with which Frederick Parkes Weber—a turn-of-the-century Harley Street physician with a well-to-do clientele—Weir Mitchell, and the other society physicians were not unfamiliar.

The men among this elite might be incapacitated in every way imaginable, except that they were not in bed. Paul Dubois gives a picture of Monsieur Y., a lawyer aged forty-six, who came in 1897 to Dubois's clinic in Berne. "For twelve years he had found it impossible to walk for more than a few minutes. He could stand up for a moment only, and that by putting the right knee on a chair and holding on to its back."

Monsieur Y.'s problems went back to "a violent emotion caused by a fire" in 1884. His condition worsened as he almost lost his position two years later, his brother dying a year after that. Monsieur Y. had done the international circuit for hypochondria.

"I have been to Néris and to Lamalou [French spas]. I have taken treatments of hydrotherapy, electricity, massage, and magnetism. I have been cared for by homeopaths, allopaths, and empiricists. . . . I am obliged not to wash myself except with alcohol, for I have such a fear of water."

"To sum up," he wrote Dubois, "All my organs [have become] weaker. In a few moments and even in a few seconds I would exhaust the strength which others could draw on for several hours." Intestinal problems led to great dietary restrictions. "I became greatly emaciated, either as a consequence of my intestinal troubles or in consequence of too strong magnetic treatment." Monsieur Y. had twice been to Lourdes.

After Monsieur Y. checked into the clinic, he gave Dubois a record of his symptoms. "It was an excellent piece of calligraphic work, which showed with what attention the patient noticed the slightest variations in weight. He noted his symptoms year by year, remarked that his parents were cousins, noted his diseases and his emotions which seemed to him to have played an etiological role." He had statistics on precisely how long he was able to stand upright. "Sometimes," he said, "when I went out of my office into the room where my clerks were I could stand up very well, and walk if the door opened easily. But my limbs would immediately sink from under me if the lock stuck or turned with difficulty."[63] This is not a picture of someone with an organic disease of the nervous system. On a statistical basis, men such as Monsieur Y. were probably found less often than female invalids. Yet the Monsieur Y.'s of this world assure us that the cross of invalidism did not fall entirely on one gender alone.

Constant Themes

The lives of women have changed greatly since 1900. Yet psychosomatic illness has not diminished at all. It has merely changed its form. The medical community has been scrambling to find labels suitable for the forms of today. For example, in 1980 two physicians at Harvard Medical School described the "Oklahoma complex," a reference to "Ado-Annie's" song in the musical

Oklahoma: "I Cain't Say No." The authors described a population of symptomatic young women who, "overextended by peer pressure, social demands, and their own aspirations," acquired somatoform symptoms as "an excuse for their recent failure to live up to their growing responsibilities." One typical patient was a twenty-seven-year-old woman who "had married early in life, worked, and attended night school. After becoming involved in the feminist movement, she left her husband and took prelaw courses in college. She worked at night in order to support her family." Under these pressures the woman lost strength on the left side of her body. Then she successfully obtained a scholarship, was able to stop working, and her symptoms disappeared. The authors said of their patients with the Oklahoma complex that all were "friendly and accommodating, experienced difficulty turning down invitations or responsibilities, and registered feelings of 'miles to go' before they rested. Clearly, all had bitten off more than they could chew."[64]

Although the sobriquet "Oklahoma complex" did not catch on, the authors nonetheless had uncovered a portion of a larger reality: that the lives of women at the end of the twentieth century, with "two careers" of job and family strapped to their backs, retain the potential for misery as much as ever. The range of missteps one might make today is, indeed, broader than before. Choices once limited to intimate decisions about husbands and lovers have now extended themselves to embrace the kind of career, the place of work, whether to undertake a commuter marriage, and what alternative arrangements to make if the baby-sitter is sick or the nanny quits. Under these circumstances it would be astonishing if the levels of what was once called "hysteria" were reduced.

There is a common theme of psychological misery and sociological unhappiness in women's experiences of psychosomatic illness that is transhistorical and transcultural. The tendency to convert unhappiness into physical symptoms is probably universal in the human species. But why is it so much more common in women than in men? Is it genetic, stress related, culture related, or a combination of all three? If this quality were genetic, all women would potentially possess it. Yet only a minority of women become symptomatic, so clearly psychosomatic illness in women is not driven by biology alone. If somatization were culturally determined—a "sex role" mandated for women—it would be specific to certain cultures and not found in others. (Anorexia nervosa, for example, *is* culturally specific, found almost exclusively in Western society.) Yet "hysteria," psychosomatic illness, and the like are universal, found everywhere and clearly embedded in the human condition. We saw in volume 1 how specific historic periods selected specific templates of illness from the symptom pool. Obviously culture does play a role. Yet women have higher rates of "hysteria" than men in *every* culture[65] so culture itself does not explain the female surplus. As for stress, meaning the conditions of social life to which women are subject, women in Victorian society doubtlessly perceived their more restricted social roles as "stressful," reacting perhaps with psychosomatic symptoms. Yet although the social position of women today has vastly changed, women still somatize more often than men. Merely the kind of symptom is different: Patterns of "oppression" alone do not provide the answer.

In accounting for the female surplus of psychosomatic illness, one basic circumstance about the differences between men and women is striking. Both historically and today, women have always borne the greater burden of unhappiness. Robert Peirce (also written Pierce), the spa physician at Bath in the late seventeenth century, had some insight into this, for his well-to-do patients, suffering from psychosomatic symptoms, were often miserable with their lives. Departing from his usual custom, Peirce refused to publish the names of these patients in writing up their cases, on the grounds that, "since God and Nature hath given them [women] the heavier end of the staff, in bearing the burdens of this life, we ought (in good manners as well as in justice) to make it as easy to them as we can."[66]

Perhaps Peirce's gallantry now seems dated. Yet his underlying insight is probably as valid for the twentieth century as for the seventeenth: Women seem to be more affected by the shock of loss and separation than are men, and across the ages they have suffered more than men from the deaths of their children and their relatives. We know from much research on "women's speech" that in conversation women expose themselves more to hurt than men do.[67] They make themselves more vulnerable and suffer more when wounded by an interlocutor. Universal in the female gender seems to be a coping style, a certain expressiveness that—some researchers believe—accompanies the basic nature of femininity itself.[68] The possibility should at least be explored that, if women have more psychosomatic illness than men, it is because they have suffered more than men, and the development of such symptoms is one way of coping with this suffering.

4

———

Ethnic Components

EVERY ETHNIC GROUP HAS its own interpretation of bodily symptoms. Cultures with a low tolerance of mental illness interpret sadness and loss of energy as signs of tired nerves rather than depression. Ethnic groups that prize male virility interpret the physical sensations of anxiety as a sign that the penis is shrinking back inside the body. Ethnic groups that value family togetherness tend to be hypervigilant about bodily sensations as an expression of caring. Ethnicity, in other words, gives cultural meaning to one's perceptions of one's body. As Arthur Kleinman has written, "Illness is like a sponge that soaks up the peculiar meanings that differentiate each of our personal lives and interpersonal situations."[1]

Because some ethnic groups have genetic characteristics in common, the biology of the group may lend its own stamp to bodily behavior. This is a subject about which virtually nothing is known. By contrast, a great deal is known about how the culture of an ethnic group helps to shape the presentation of illness. If we ask how culture matters in psychosomatic illness, it matters a great deal in the realm of ethnicity.

Some anthropologists believe that as cultures become more sophisticated, their capacity to express unhappy emotions (dysphoria) shifts from a somatic vocabulary to a psychological one. It is said, for example, that the Xhosa people of South Africa use such phrases as "His heart is very sore" because they lack a sophisticated psychological vocabulary for talking about anxiety and depression.[2] Yet this theory dismisses as primitive many Third World cultures that have attained a high degree of psychological sophistication, such as the Buddhists of India, but who use language different from our own. And it assumes our own culture's sophistication, when the fact is that most chronic somatizers in Western society have very little psychological insight, rejecting psychological analyses of their difficulties and expressing their dysphoria in the most blatantly somatic terms.[3] The notion of psychological sophistication explains little of the difference in the symbolic use of symptoms from culture to culture. It is cultural differences, not psychological sophistication, that determine difference in the meaning of somatic symptoms for individuals.

As an example of the cultural interpretation of bodily symptoms, middle-aged Malay women, who tend to be dependent on men, are prone to *latah,* a somatic reaction after a sudden fright. The patient, or victim, falls into a trancelike state, exhibits automatic obedience that puts her "completely at the mercy of those who surround her, doing almost anything they command her to do, imitating all their actions." She may also repeat exactly everything that is said to her (echolalia) and, rather spasmodically in an involuntary manner, imitate the movements of another person (echopraxia).[4] Here a culture of female enthrallment tells women that the physiological sensations of anxiety turn those who experience them into will-less automatons. In a society in which women are so beholden to men as Malaysia, *latah* has a certain internal logic.

In parts of Latin America—Mexico, for example,—men and women have a quite different reaction to fright. Suddenly alarmed, they might experience nausea, stomach cramps, and difficulty in breathing. Called *susto,* or fright, these extreme psychophysiological reactions are said to lead even to death. For Mexicans the symptoms make sense as an expression of the breakdown of one's internal strength, or *consistencia.* If one's *consistencia* has crumbled, naturally one will be vulnerable.[5]

The world is filled with such cultural diversity in the expression of internal states. Because mental illness is highly stigmatized in China, Chinese people often deny being "depressed," although they may exhibit the classic symptoms of depression such as insomnia, loss of appetite, and feelings of guilt. Instead they tell themselves they have "neurasthenia," a diagnosis of supposed organic nervous disease imported from Western society in the last century. Some Chinese may interpret their psychological dysphoria as a "big internal fire" or as a pressing on the heart—thus rendering a psychological experience a somatic one—and seek relief in herbal remedies.[6] The drugstores of the Chinatowns in North American cities contain on their shelves yard after yard of herbal preparations, the pharmacological benefit of which is little more than a placebo effect.

Within Western society as well, differences exist from one ethnic group to another in how the body's internal signals are conceptualized. A study in the 1960s of illness behavior among the Italian and Irish communities of Boston showed that the Irish emphasized difficulties of the eye, ear, nose, and throat and tended to deny pain as an aspect of the illness. The symptoms of the Boston Italians, by contrast, tended to be spread more diffusely over the body, to be greater in number, and to entail "more types of bodily dysfunction." Some observers attribute these differences to a greater "expressiveness" of Italian culture, and to a kind of plodding stoicism of Irish culture.[7] As for Jews of East European origin, they have a distinctive kind of psychosomatic illness that illustrates nicely the interaction between culture and biology.

The Psychosomatic Symptoms of Jews

At several levels, Jews of East European origin experience an interaction between genetic influences and culturally determined coping styles. East European Jews are subject to certain distinctive hereditary diseases more often than non-Jews, such as Tay-Sachs disease, a fatal neurological disorder that develops about six months after birth and is one hundred times commoner among East European Jews than in other populations.[8] More speculative is the argument that Jews of East European origin may possess a certain cognitive style, or way of knowing and acting, and that this style may have a genetic component.[9] Is it true that Jews are more sensitive to psychosomatic illness than non-Jews? If so, what proportion of this psychosomatic sensitivity is genetically determined and what proportion culturally?

The whole issue of Jews and psychosomatic symptoms is inseparable from the history of the Jews of Eastern Europe, which arguably has been more traumatic than the history of most other European ethnic groups. This is because of the collective experience of the "two great stresses." Members of most ethnic groups have a historic memory of but a single great stress, the migration from peasant life to the big city, be that city in the Old World or the New. East European Jews historically have had two great stresses. The first epochal change in Jewish history began late in the eighteenth century. After a thousand years of living in small towns and villages flung across Europe from western Czechoslovakia to the eastern Ukraine, a first great upheaval began. Young men and women began to look to the culture of urban Western Europe and to question the validity of traditional Jewish culture and religion. Throughout the nineteenth century young Jews from Eastern Europe migrated in enormous numbers to the great cities of the West such as Vienna, Berlin, and Frankfurt. There they established for themselves middle-class existences that had very little in common with the lives of their parents in the shtetl, or small town. This migration from village to city, the first great stress, was quite similar to migrations undertaken at the time by non-Jewish groups. Perhaps the only difference was that the Jews on the average bounded higher up the social ladder once they arrived in the cities, a large number finding their way into the middle class in cities such as Vienna.[10]

This first migration was dislocating enough. One can see what enormous psychic cost it must have demanded from a man like Hermann Nunberg, a Viennese psychiatrist who was one of Freud's collaborators in the 1920s. Nunberg was born in 1884 (as Hirsz, not Hermann), in the small town of Bedzin (then known as Bendenor or Bendzin) in Russian Poland. Of his original given name he in later life mentioned not a word, either to his wife Margarethe or children (and his daughter was quite astonished to learn of it when I told her).[11] Nor did he divulge much about what his own father did for a living or the family's circumstances. After Hermann Nunberg arrived in Vienna from Cracow in 1914 it was as though he was a "new man," born from nothing. In the 1920s in Vienna, Nunberg embodied the upwardly mobile young physician, marrying the daughter of wealthy pediatrician Oskar Rie and becoming something of a connoisseur of art. Up to this point, little separated Nunberg from the many non-Jewish physicians and other professional people in the big city who had started out from lowly Polish origins.

Then came the second of the great historic stresses: the rise of racially based anti-Semitism and the Holocaust. Secure for decades in a comfortable urban middle-class life, the Jews of Central Europe now found themselves—literally from one day to the next—with their property confiscated and fired from their jobs, subject to public humiliation such as washing paving stones on their hands and knees, and forced either to flee or be brutally murdered.

This story is too well known to require further telling here, but—modern Jewish history in microcosm—Hermann Nunberg moved from Vienna to Philadelphia in 1932, and thence to New York. He dropped the second *n* in his name. He never discussed life in the Old World with his two children, who, embarrassed because he and his wife spoke German together, would always walk well in front of the couple on the sidewalk. Never, ever did the children hear a word of Yiddish pass Nunberg's lips or notice a manner of speaking German that recalled the singsong accent of the East European Jews. One can only imagine what psychic penalties these two migrations must have exacted from Nunberg, what an act of repression must have been necessary to put not one but two pasts behind him. Nunberg was typical of the hundreds of thousands of Jews of East European origin who were fortunate enough to find refuge somewhere beyond Europe. In the memory of family members, he "regarded himself very much as an invalid," and, in addition to the very real organic problems he developed as an older man, he also complained of chronic bowel difficulties. If the Jews of Eastern Europe displayed psychosomatic symptoms, one does not necessarily have to look far for the causes. The collective experience of persecution that surrounded the Jewish community made individual Jews more likely to exhibit psychosomatic symptoms of their pain.

Jewish and Non-Jewish Perspectives

Jews of East European origin seem in fact to have been more subject to psychosomatic illness, and various sources allow this to be demonstrated. But first one must come to grips with the question of anti-Semitism in the sources. Here is an example of the kind of evidence with which one has to contend: Parkes Weber apparently believed his Jewish patients were more subject to neurosis than his non-Jewish patients. When treating Jews he often would inscribe in his notes such words as "hypochondriacism," even in the presence of demonstrated organic disease. For example, when Mrs. X., a twenty-eight-year-old "Russian Polish Jewess," came to see him in June 1915, she had been "ailing three weeks with digestive troubles and a 'globus' [*globus hystericus,* or lump in the throat]." "No appetite," he said. "Palpitation. Pains in epigastrium. Rumbling in abdomen." Parkes Weber could find nothing wrong. Mrs. X. seemed to have an irritable bowel. Over the next few weeks she was troubled by "windy spasm" and "all kinds of 'feelings,' especially an inclination to be sick when her bowels act." Mrs. X. was also quite anxious. August 31: "Patient fears she has a tumor in the abdomen." In November 1915 Parkes Weber finally sent her to the German Hospital in London, where he had admitting privileges, for an X ray. "To my astonishment," Parkes Weber said in his notes, "Dr. James Metcalfe reported that the Röntgen photograph of the thorax showed a good deal of thickening at the hilus [the part of the lung where the windpipe enters] on each side—also many small consolidations in both lungs—he thought that there was probably early tuberculosis of the lungs."

Yet, due to the patient's high level of psychic distress, Parkes Weber did not really believe the consultant's report. Both doctor and patient continued to fix upon her varying "feelings," which included "globus hystericus, crawling feelings in the limbs (formication) etc. . . . and all kinds of imaginary fears for herself and her life." Parkes Weber had to reassure her repeatedly that she did not have appendicitis.

In the spring of 1917 Mrs. X. became pregnant and acquired some kind of bloodclot that drifted up to the artery that supplied her left eye, obstructing most of the field of vision in that eye. Yet Parkes Weber, now totally uninterested in the possibility of tuberculosis, was also indifferent to her plugged retinal artery. When he saw her on June 12, 1918, he maneuvered the interview back to her "neurotic troubles" and found it interesting that the act of giving birth had suspended her "sensations" for a while.

Parkes Weber had news of Mrs. X. for the last time in 1921, when he met her husband in Charlotte Street, near where the family had opened a shop. In his summary note of the case Parkes Weber wrote, "Nervous dyspeptic, neurasthenic. Hypochondriacism, approaching an acute melancholic type of insanity."[12] One imagines that had Mrs. X., the Russian Jewess, been Countess Y. or Baronness Z., Parkes Weber might have focused on organic features of the case. Yet she *was*, without a doubt, somewhat hypochondriacal.

Let us say that Mrs. X. was a somatizer. Was she typical of East European Jews generally? Quantitative data on rates of psychosomatic illness by race or ethnic group are very difficult to come by. Qualitative observations, by contrast, abound. It is possible of course that these physicians were merely being anti-Semitic in their labeling of Jewish complaints. Yet Jewish physicians tended to believe the same thing.

These observations by both Jewish and non-Jewish physicians must be set in the context of history. From the 1870s onward a great tide of East European Jews came flooding westward, partly in search of newly opened economic possibilities, partly in flight from the pogroms, or violent acts of persecution, that had started to oppress Jews in the Russian empire. These newcomers arrived in the midst of established, middle-class Jewish communities in the West. Small colonies of Jews had dwelt in the large cities of Western Europe and Britain since the late eighteenth century and even before. By the late nineteenth century they had achieved acceptability, intermarrying widely with Christians and even joining the nobility. Many Jewish physicians were drawn from the ranks of these comfortably well-off and long-established Jews, as the names of such medical dynasties in Vienna as Federn and Obersteiner testify. By the 1870s, therefore, the Jews who were most likely professionally to observe the behavior of the newcomers had nestled into a kind of clubby social status in which the rites of Orthodox Judaism appeared as bizarre as the caftans and sidelocks of the shtetl Jews.[13] As for non-Jewish observers, though they were anything other than philo-Semitic, their prejudices against Jews were most often the commonplace reproaches of "Christ killers" and "moneygrubbers." Until the 1870s few maintained that Jews constituted another race; nor was there any expectation that Jews would bear the biological stigmata of nervous disease that might characterize "degeneration" in a people.

Onto this scene of harmonious assimilation and integration burst the Eastern Jews, or *Ostjuden,* whose arrival was a shock for Jews and non-Jews alike. The newcomers were just emerging from desperate poverty, intent on closing the book on centuries of separateness. They spoke the languages of the West with funny accents and were often peculiar in dress and appearance. Popular opinion labeled them "dirty" and "unhygienic," although back in Russia and Poland their children had had a lower mortality than the children of non-Jews (at a time when infant mortality was a good indicator of the filth in which a family lived.)[14] The patronizing reactions of non-Jewish and established Jewish physicians alike to the *Ostjuden* reflect a willingness to believe the worst of the newcomers.

Among non-Jews the belief that Jews were especially vulnerable to nervous illness went back to the early nineteenth century or even to the mid-eighteenth, when nervous disease was first described.[15] Was this belief the result of bias or did it correspond to the facts? In 1824 Anton Müller, head of the psychiatric service of the Julius-Hospital in Würzburg, noted that it was harder to heal Jewish patients than others: "Of seven, only one recovered completely."[16] If Jews were, in Müller's opinion, more difficult to treat, it could only be because their nervous illnesses were more deeply ingrained.

Spa-going was a classic health-seeking activity of the day, and Jews were known as devotees of the "powerful" mineral waters at spas. Puzzled at the refusal of Jewish patients at the spa of Schwalbach in Hessen to seek out milder springs, Francis Head, an English visitor, said in 1834, "As the cunning Jews all go to the Stahl brunnen [the iron-rich spring], I strongly suspect that they have some good reason for this departure from the fashion."[17] Although Head did not specifically mention nervous complaints, the link between spas and nerves was indissoluble, and many of the famous spas of Europe, such as Bad Vöslau near Vienna, Bad Ischl in western Austria, Territet-Montreux in Switzerland, and the German island of Norderney in the North Sea, later became associated with a Jewish clientele.

If late-nineteenth-century German physicians commented widely about Jewish nervousnesss, it was partly because the doctors had nerves on their mind. They were adhering to the new central-nervous paradigm.[18] But they also saw in their daily practices many apparently nervous East European Jews. Ludwig Hirt, a Breslau neurology professor who treated many *Ostjuden* at his university clinic, said in 1890, "As to race, the Slavonic (Poles, Russians), the Latin races (Frenchmen, Italians), and above all, the Semitic, are more liable to hysteria than the Teutonic. The severest forms of hysteria are seen in French women and in Polish Jewesses."[19] Valentin von Holst, head of neurology at the Riga City Hospital and director of a private nervous clinic, argued in 1903 that Jews had a "national burden" (*nationale Belastung*) toward hysteria.[20] And Harald Siebert, who like Holst had extensive experience in dealing with the large Latvian Jewish community, said at the time of World War I that, "Nervous disorders appear most frequently by far among the Jews." Writing of the city of Lepaya (now Liepāja), Siebert claimed that, among the working classes such disorders concerned mainly Jewish men, among the middle classes mainly Jewish women. "Their labile constitutions constantly alternate between manifest psychoneurotic disorders and apparent health. To the practiced eye, their pathology presents as paralyses, mood disorders, localized or total-body convulsions, shaking, and, within the internal viscera, as autonomic insufficiency [*Sekretionsanomalien*], perverse disorders of respiration and swallowing, irritation and other disorder in the gastrointestinal tract, such as belching, vomiting, and constipation."[21] All this was deemed specifically Jewish. Indeed, German doctors held forth about Jewish nervousness in a voluminous and inexhaustible literature.[22]

In France non-Jewish doctors considered Jews and nervousness to be but two sides of the same coin. Especially at the time of

Charcot, who saw as "stigmata of hysteria" every nervous complaint imaginable, the Jews became known as a nervous race. When discussing in 1888 a twenty-year-old Jewish woman with hysterical dyspnea (shortness of breath), Charcot said, "Nervous illness of every kind . . . occurs incomparably more often in Jews than non-Jews."[23] In 1891, in an editorial on "Jewish Pathology," the medical weekly *Progrès médical,* house organ of Charcot's school, said: "The Israelite is nervous *(L'Israélite est nerveux)*. . . . Monsieur Charcot has continually pointed this out. This pool of neuropathy can manifest itself in the most varied expressions: neurasthenia among the men, hysteria among the women. We should not be surprised at the frequency of neurosis in Jews, for intermarriage among the co-religionists and even consanguinous marriage have ineluctably developed in them a predisposition."[24] Charcot delighted in singling out as instances of a pathological subtype the poor East European Jewish males who had made their way to Paris for a consultation. He referred to them collectively as "the wandering Jew" *(le juif errant)*. When, for example, a Herr Klein from Budapest staggered into the hospital after an exhausting journey, Charcot said, "He may have been predisposed to hysterical neurosis from early on. One notes that he is an Israelite, and the very fact of his bizarre peregrinations shows that he is mentally subject to driven behavior."[25] Charcot was not inhibited by Freud's own Jewishness from expressing sentiments about Jewish degeneration to him. In an 1892 letter, Charcot told Freud that, to find examples of "inherited arthritic diseases," one might search in Jewish families. They would display the condition alongside inherited neurosyphilis and epilepsy.[26]

Among Charcot's students, most of whom become influential neurologists, the master's doctrines about Jews turned into great verities. As Henry Meige expounded in 1894 on the "wandering Jew": "Above all, their preoccupation with health obsesses them and they impulsively abandon one experimental treatment after the other. It is with inexhaustible volubility, with tears, sobs and frantic gestures that they hound every physician with their complaints. One would never see an end of their lamentations, if one did not brusquely interrupt the interview."[27]

The most famous of Charcot's students was Pierre Janet. In

presenting Mlle. D., a young Jewish woman with "abulia" (lack of will), to the medical students around 1903, Janet said, "It suffices to point out that she comes from an Israelite family, and to remind you of the clear predisposition of the Israelite race to mental disorders. It is probable that the predisposition was accentuated in this family."[28] Thus the notion of a special "Jewish predisposition" infiltrated the French neurological school root and branch.

Because their personal incomes depended on the continued custom of wealthy Jewish families, these French and German physicians had to bridle their tongues in overly ascribing degeneracy to Jews. In the Anglo-Saxon world, however, spirits were less constrained by pecuniary prudence. The Jewish communities of London and New York were historically more recent than those of Paris and Vienna, and the Jewish middle classes less numerous. Accordingly Anglo-Saxon nerve doctors permitted themselves in public the most malignant remarks about "Jewish hypochondria" and the like. Harley Street physician Alfred Taylor Schofield, who referred to his Jewish patients on Warrington Crescent in London as "the New Jerusalem," struck the consultant's disdainful tone: "Their houses were all alike; the moment the hall door was opened a spacious odour of fried fish . . . assailed the nostrils. You were shown into the dining-room where the furniture was all mahogany, never oak; and on the sideboard there was invariably a decanter of wine" (though he noted that his Jewish patients were never drunkards). Did Dr. Schofield's patients have many psychosomatic illnesses? "I soon found to my dismay [after qualifying in medicine in 1883] that private patients did not as a rule have Hospital diseases. They had curious, indefinite mixed complaints of their own, which were very difficult to classify."[29] Schofield clearly believed his middle-class Jewish patients more subject to psychosomatic illness than his non-Jewish ones. He may have held this belief out of anti-Semitism or because it corresponded to the reality of the day.

For Cecil Beadles, on staff in 1900 at the London asylum of Colney Hatch, "the insane Jew" was almost an object of loathing:

For those who come in contact with the race in hospital and private practice, the men are looked upon as neurotic, the women as hysterical. Neurasthenia . . . would seem a common complaint amongst those seeking medical aid. Hereditary insanity probably figures high in the race. . . . The mental strain resulting from excessive zeal in acquiring riches, and the worry and annoyance which must invariably accompany this greed for worldly goods, doubtless play no small part in the mental breakdown of these people.[30]

Beadles went on to quote the opinions of another London psychiatrist, Ernest White, who was unable to attend the session at which Beadles spoke: "The Jewish patients supply many of the noisy and troublesome patients in an asylum; they are all very indolent, frequently faulty in habits, morally degraded, and are destructive of clothing." Beadles added, "This excellent summary corresponds in all respects with the estimate one arrives at from a study of the Jewish insane in Colney Hatch Asylum."[31]

In the comments of American physicians, who knew few middle-class Jews, Jewish immigrants were made particularly to sound like alien beings. Smith Ely Jelliffe, reviewing the results for 1905 of New York's Vanderbilt Clinic, said, "As in former years, foreigners preponderated greatly among the neurasthenics, the Russian Jew being greatly in evidence."[32] In 1911 Harvard neurologist Philip Knapp wrote of the nervous clinic at Boston City Hospital, "In the last twenty-five years the great influx of Russian and Polish Jews into the city has occurred, and has been very noticeable in the clinic. It is an admitted fact that these new immigrants are a peculiarly neurotic race."[33]

Walter Alvarez often emerged as a sympathetic figure, fighting against unnecessary colectomies and ovariotomies. But there is no doubt that his bias against Jews was characteristic of much of the medicine of his day. Alvarez found Jews irremediably hypochondriacal: "Many a time, especially when dealing with a much-frightened Jewish patient, I have tried for a half-hour to reassure, only to learn later from the wife that the man was still hopeless and sure that he had cancer." Alvarez considered them doctor-shoppers: "The Jewish patient with an anxiety neurosis is particularly likely to keep traveling from one clinic to another, hoping that some day he will get a run of three opinions all alike!" "In my experience," Alvarez mocked, "intra-abdominal quivering is always a sign of nervousness; and epigastric 'burning,' especially in the Jew, points almost as certainly to a neurosis." A patient who reported sieges of belly pain was, naturally, "an excitable Jew." "Every so often I see a patient, usually a woman, and usually a highly nervous Jewess, who complains that for some time after moving her bowels she suffers from pelvic or abdominal distress [and] a sense of faintness and exhaustion." Jews were people who fainted after their bowel movements.[34]

At issue here is not whether these physicians were anti-Semitic but whether their assessment of psychosomatic illness in Jews exhibited a bias. Clearly Alvarez and his American and European colleagues deemed Jews hereditarily predisposed to psychosomatic symptoms. We must assess the reality content of this judgment. Were these doctors merely blinded by their anti-Semitic prejudice, or were they reporting—albeit through distorted lenses—a behavioral reality?

In evaluating the testimony of non-Jews, it is useful to know that most Jewish physicians as well believed that their Jewish patients had a special disposition to hysteria and neurasthenia. As early as 1777, Elcan Isaac Wolf, a Jewish physician in Mannheim, spoke of "the extraordinary sensitivity of the nervous structure" of Jews, of whom there were many in the small towns of the Palatinate. For Wolf this sensitivity was an understandable consequence of the

> ceaselessly gnawing worry, the constant rumination about one's daily bread, the terrifying thought of what might happen in the future as the energy of the aged declines, the loss of wealth as one's capital vanishes, the endless taxes and imposts which are almost impossible to bring up—these are the plagues which befall our race in particular and which are unimaginably injurious to the nerves. It is no surprise if people see us as having so many nervous hypochondriacs, who over the years might well become deeply depressed.[35]

This is among the first statements by a Jewish physician on the existence of a special tendency to nervous illness among Jews. Of course it does not mean that Wolf was correct, for unbeknownst to him, just as many non-Jews might have complained of the same ailments as his Jewish patients.

Just as the medical profession generally broke into a chorus of concern about nervous illness late in the nineteenth century, Jewish physicians chimed in on the subject of Jews. In 1894 the Munich psychiatrist Leopold Löwenfeld said, "As for a supposed predisposition of the semitic race [to hysteria], it is clear that a dis-proportionately large contingent of neurasthenics and hysterics is to be found among the semitic race. But whether this condition is attributable to a special predisposition of the race as such is ques-tionable." Instead Löwenfeld ascribed Jewish nervous illness to "the physical misery in Eastern Europe, in addition to the enor-mous psychological pressure [of the pogroms], the custom of mar-rying early and the large number of children. In the West the problem is the selection by Israelites of predominantly white-col-lar occupations."[36] Environment plus heredity were at fault, said Heinrich Singer—a Jewish family doctor in Elberfeld with the ex-perience of seven years of practice—in 1904. "The general Jewish predisposition to nervosity" was explained in his view by the over-lapping of biology and society. "The diseases of the nervous sys-tem have reached such an extraordinary expansion among Jews, that the norm seems almost to have become the exception and we have difficulty re-establishing the customary boundaries between normal and pathological." He called "nervosity . . . a characteris-tic racial quality of the Jews. . . . The hereditary dimension has be-come steadily greater over the years, and is further increased by familial inbreeding."[37]

These Westernized middle-class Jewish physicians directed many comments specifically against the Eastern Jews. In 1923, for example, Max Sichel, on staff in psychiatry at the university hos-pital in Frankfurt, called Warsaw "an inexhaustible reservoir of [Jewish nervous illness] that now is flooding the entire Continent with male hysteria."[38]

One might question if assimilationist Jewish physicians had just absorbed the anti-Semitic values of the surrounding culture.[39] Yet Jewish physicians themselves born in the East did not believe any

less in a special Jewish propensity to nervousness. Martin
Engländer, a Viennese family doctor born in a small town in
Hungary who graduated in medicine in 1900 from Vienna, said in
1902 that, "the Jewish brain has been fighting a heavy battle for
centuries. Right up until Emancipation it had to struggle for a mea-
ger, naked existence." This two-thousand-year struggle, he believed, had left its mark upon the nerves. Nervosity among Jews was
one of the forms of "degeneration." These forms had a "common
origin in the inferior organization of the central nervous system."
Therefore Jews had inherited more nervousness. Jews also had acquired more nervousness from the stresses of life, and now all were
pressing into the cities, prime breeding grounds for nervousness.
Many of Engländer's Jewish patients had bowel problems.
"Neurasthenia of the gastrointestinal tract, with its numberless
complaints of ill digestion and disrupted colon activity is a typical
lament of urbanites, with their racing mental processes and lack of
physical exercise."[40] Likewise Arthur Stern, a psychiatrist born in
Zary in German Poland, expressed the opinion that "the Russian-
Jewish population," a population then streaming into the cities of
the West, had a psychopathology of its own with "hypochondriacal,
anxious-depressive coloration."[41]

Jewish physicians believed that the nervousness of the *Ostjuden*
was more determined by culture than by poverty. For this same
nervousness was encountered in private clinics for the wealthy. In
1912, Salomon Behrendt and Salomon Rosenthal, chief physicians of a private nervous clinic especially for religious Jews in
Sayn near Coblenz, said that hysteria, often in combination with
mood disorders, was notable among their Jewish patients.[42]
According to Rafael Becker, who had a background in private
Swiss clinics but in 1919 was at a public asylum in Switzerland,
not only were the major mental illnesses more frequent among
Jews, the "functional nervous disorders" were so as well, even
though such patients were less often admitted to asylum. "The
Jew . . . sees what a disaster his national renaissance has become
and begins to believe what the anti-Semites tell him, that his God
is a bad God." "In short," said Becker, "the Jew begins to believe
himself inferior" and acquires as a result the kind of "organ inferi-
ority" that Alfred Adler had described.[43]

It is hard to find a Central European medical writer of Jewish origin who did not believe that psychosomatic illness was commoner among Jews than non-Jews, although there was considerable discussion of the reason for this. But Jewish physicians wrote more sympathetically of their Jewish patients than did non-Jewish physicians, whose accounts usually succeeded in making the Jews sound ludicrous or bizarre. Jewish doctors customarily sought exculpations. If, for example, Hermann Oppenheim's patients in Berlin cried out "Gewalt! Gewalt!" (Heaven help me!) as he pricked them with a pin during the neurological examination, it showed, said Oppenheim, how accustomed they had become to persecution.[44] Oppenheim said that neurasthenia even had a positive side for the Jews: It extended their life span. As one pupil recalled Oppenheim's words, "The neurasthenic anxiety of Jews causes them to see the doctor more frequently and leads to the early detection of many diseases."[45] These doctors picked up a theme already sounded a century earlier by Wolf: Jewish physicians almost never sought out hereditary causes alone in considering the high nervosity of the Jews, but invoked instead the difficult conditions of material life or family patterns.

Although Central Europe contained the amplest number of Jewish physicians writing on Jews, the theme of elevated psychosomatic illness was truly international. Georges Wulfing, a young Parisian Jewish physician who before World War I had spent several years on Pierre Marie's service at the Villejuif Hospital, had been struck by Charcot's remark that a study of "la médecine nerveuse des Juifs" was needed. Wulfing therefore focused on neurasthenia:

"Jews are particularly predisposed to this disorder of our times," because of persecution rather than a love of luxury. "Jewish people become a people whose nervous system takes precedence over the muscular system. Jews are, as one says in common parlance, 'all nerves.' "[46] Wulfing did not reach these views all on his own— indeed he cites extensively the contemporary literature—and his dissertation represents a distillation of what both Jews and non-Jews believed. The French psychiatrist Henri Stern made precisely the same comments about Jewish hypochondriasis when he encountered it after just after World War II, not in French Jews but in the East European Jews who had survived the Belsen concentration camp in Germany. Stern was employed by an American relief organization as a consultant at the camp, which was in the British sector, for six months between the winter of 1947 and the spring of 1948: "The general inclination of the Jew towards hypochondria is another thing which must be allowed for," wrote Stern apropos the physical health of camp inmates. "It is another manifestation of the insecurity which tortures the Jewish spirit, and I found it expressed most often in the anxious preoccupation shown in the case of illness."[47]

Within the American Jewish medical community, too, East European hypochondriasis was judged to be a familiar phenomenon. Maurice Fishberg, a young physician born in Russia who had an office on West 115th Street in Manhattan, said in 1901: "Neurasthenia and hysteria are mostly found among the Jews." Moreover: "Mental diseases occur more frequently among the Jews."[48] "Step into any clinic for nervous diseases in any large city in Europe or America," said Boston psychiatrist Abraham Myerson in 1920, "and the Jew is unduly represented among the patients." Myerson argued that, as a result of "social heredity, . . . the Jew has an innate character, different from that of other races, which perhaps predisposes him to psychoneuroses and other mental disease."[49] These impressionistic quotations do not in and of themselves prove that hysteria and mental illness were commoner among Jews than non-Jews. But they do establish that this opinion was not just an anti-Semitic slander.

The problem with most of these abstract accounts, emphasizing diagnostic labels and generalizing across millions, is that we cannot reach the reality of individuals' experience with illness. One study—carried out in 1907 by Hyman Morrison, a fourth-year medical student at Harvard who spoke Yiddish and was evidently of Russian Jewish background—did break this barrier: "The term 'Hebraic debility,' " he said, "has been used for some time at the Massachusetts General Hospital to designate the condition of many of the Jewish patients coming to the clinics. These patients complain of 'burning' and 'sticking' pain, generally in the chest and epigastrium, but often all over the body. 'Es brennt mich,' 'es stecht mich,' and 'schmerzen überall' are familiar expressions in their stories." (I have a burning feeling, I have a piercing feeling, pain everywhere)

Morrison studied fifty-one cases of "Hebraic debility" by going to their homes. Almost all were recent immigrants. Eighty-six percent of them came from Russia, and all were poor and uneducated. Seventy-five percent were women. When he visited them virtually all were well. As he spoke to them in Yiddish, "pain" often turned out to mean distress. By "heart" they meant upper body. In 73 percent of the fifty-one patients, the chief complaint was constipation, which Morrison attributed to sedentary occupations and to irregular habits in the New World. But the patients themselves were highly fearful of cancer, turberculosis, and heart disease. One woman, for example, had "been to see one of the most prominent physicians in the city about her heart; she had already been to about all the clinics in Boston, and everywhere was assured that her heart was all right, but she thought that the doctors would always talk differently among themselves about her."

Morrison concluded, "The Jews, always a highly imaginative people, have been for centuries cradled in fear, so that it has become one of their keenest emotions, provoked by trifles." But it was not just a folkloric memory of age-old fear that had provoked the symptoms of these recent immigrants, especially the women. In Boston they led much harder lives than they had in Russia. Almost all worked in the New World, while back at home many had not. "Many a home in the North and West Ends is to be found in the rear of stores. One woman living under these conditions told me that she was up from seven in the morning till one at night, running back and forth from the kitchen to the store,—it was a little lunch room." Another had been out collecting bills all afternoon, "though she was pregnant and quite miserable," while her husband minded the shop. Morrison concluded that "Hebraic debility" did not exist, and that psychosomatic illness among these recent Jewish immigrants was related to exhaustion.

But then Morrison added one final circumstance. Their problems had, perhaps, as much to do with culture as with material conditions. In these families there was a tradition "from time immemorial [that] women have been sick. It is a sort of privilege tolerated with them; it is even expected of them. 'A woman keeps on dying all the week, but recovers on the Sabbath,' " was one saying Morrison heard. Also people said, "A woman has ninety-nine souls." The women themselves gradually began to believe this, and their self-diagnosis was aided by the proximity of hospitals and clinics in the Jewish districts of Boston. "In Russia the Jewish woman can hardly afford to consult a doctor for the least thing that ails her, and hospitals and dispensaries are very rare." But in Boston they were nearby. "These help the Jewish woman to keep her attention on herself; she goes to the hospital or to her lodge-doctor for things which in her old home she had to overlook and forget." Morrison sketched out, in other words, a milieu in which somatic hypervigilance was a cultural norm, not just a response to stress.[50]

Morrison's account reminds us how misleading the abstraction of symptoms into medical diagnoses can be. Constipation and heartburn became in the hands of Harvard's clinicians a hereditary "Hebraic debility." Abdominal discomfort among other young women at other times became "ovarian reflex hysteria" or "autointoxication," justifying life-threatening surgery on ovaries and colon. It is only a step further to suppose that such abstract disease conditions characterize not just individuals but entire peoples, such as Jews. Tay-Sachs disease does affect East European Jews disproportionately, but we must be extremely cautious in generalizing this kind of organicity to illness caused by the action of the mind.

On balance what distinguished the East European Jews was not so much a pattern of illness as a pattern of help-seeking. Jews were thought to be distinctive not because they suffered more but because they sought out the doctor more.

East European Jews as Hypochondriacal Patients

Toby Cohn, a prominent Berlin nerve doctor of the 1920s, had a hypochondriac as a patient. He was a German Jew "who dictated daily to his secretary page-long reports for her to type about his temperature—which moreover he believed to be elevated already at 36.5 C. [normal; only temperatures over 37.8°C, or 100°F, are considered "feverish"]—also about his various bodily sensations and health experiences. He then presented these extremely monotonous and as one would expect boring disquisitions to his physician on a daily basis."[51] This was garden-variety hypochondriasis.

Such hypochondriasis could strike Jew or non-Jew alike. It is of interest in a larger work on the history of psychosomatic illness only when it appears to befall an entire culture. Distinctive of East European Jews was not that they were ill more often than other people, but that they combined exaggerated concern about symptoms with a reverence for medical authority. There are cultures, such as the parishioners of Richard Napier in seventeenth-century England, that are concerned about symptoms without necessarily revering medical authority. And there are cultures, such as the American middle classes of the 1930s and 1940s, that revere medical authority without being especially attuned to bodily symptoms.[52] The Jews of Eastern Europe combined these two qualities: hyperalertness to bodily states together with a belief in the physician as a man of science. The Berlin neurologist Hermann Oppenheim summed these up as *"furor consultativus."*[53]

The small-town Jews of Eastern Europe rushed first to the prestigious university clinics of nearby cities like Königsberg (now Kaliningrad) and Breslau (Wroctlaw) and then, depending on income, to great international centers such as Berlin and Vienna. Paul Rosenstein, the first Jew to be accepted in Prussia in a program for gynecological surgery, recalled the East European Jews as they sat in the waiting rooms of the university clinics where he trained, "because they had insufficient confidence in the medicine of Poland and Galicia." They were drawn, for example, by the reputation of the great surgeon Johann von Mikulicz, the chief of Rosenstein's clinic, who had migrated in 1887 from Cracow to Königsberg, and then in 1890 to Breslau:

In Germany we had been conditioned to treat these [Eastern] Jews with some contempt. They were a totally different kind of person, and we did not understand their language, Yiddish. I was therefore astonished at how easily all of the Christian professors and assistants got on with these people. Thus the deputy-chief physician [*Oberarzt*] of the surgical clinic spoke perfect Yiddish. And I, the son of a rabbi, felt somewhat ridiculous at my own inability and must confess to my shame that at the beginning I often laughed at some of the peculiar expressions. But under the direction of [the non-Jewish Dr. Johannes] Storp, I soon learned Yiddish and was in my later medical career especially thankful that I had trained at Königsberg.[54]

Emil Kraepelin, head of psychiatry at Tartu (Dorpat) University in Estonia from 1886 to 1890, opened an outpatient clinic to which "few patients came, for the most part Polish Jews with every non-specific nervous complaint one could imagine, only very exceptionally a real organic neurological problem."[55] The psychiatrist Johannes Schultz, who later invented "biofeedback therapy," remembered the hordes of Eastern Jews "from farmhand to wholesale merchant," who pressed into the outpatient clinics of Breslau "in order to consult in the spring and fall about spa-visits and spa-cures and to have themselves examined." (Schultz, a non-Jew who had married a Jewish woman, commented favorably upon "the meticulous body hygiene and the cleanliness, the intelligence and vivacity of these people." This is in contrast to the customarily uncharitable observations about "the dirtiness" of the *Ostjuden.*)[56]

Letting oneself be examined does seem to have struck a particular note. The Berlin psychiatrist Emanuel Mendel, himself Jewish, told the following story from his outpatient clinic:

A Polish Jew comes in.
"What's the problem?"
"Nothing."
"Well, then, what are you doing here?"
"I heard you examine people for nothing. Take a look at me. Who knows? Maybe you'll find something."[57]

Of course the story demonstrates the kind of contempt for the *Ostjuden* that Rosenstein mentioned above. But it shows that these patients sought examination because they were anxious about falling ill rather than for the relief of physical complaints.

But Orthodox Jewish respect for medical authority could be mediated in strange ways. Many patients often relied on their rabbis for major decisions, in life generally and about medical care in particular. Friedrich Torberg, a journalist who left a treasurehouse of anecdotes from the coffeehouses in the 1920s of Prague and Vienna, told the story of a businessman from one of Austria's eastern provinces who had some kind of nervous disorder. "He appeared one day in [Otto] Pötzl's private office." Pötzl, a Viennese psychiatrist, was before 1922 Julius Wagner-Jauregg's deputy chief physician. Although Wagner-Jauregg was by that time world famous, Pötzl also had the honorary title "Professor."

Torberg continued:

Most people—but not Pötzl—would have thought this kind of illness was rather in Wagner-Jauregg's competency. So when Pötzl, pleased to have the business, asked the patient why he had not consulted Wagner-Jauregg instead, the patient burst forth with a surprising confession. Before leaving his hometown, he had sought the advice, not just of the local physicians but also—as the Jews in that area had the custom of doing—of the local rabbis. And because in this case money was no object, the man had asked two of the most notable rabbis of the region, the rabbi of Belz [in Galicia] and the rabbi of Sadagora [in Bukowina].

The latter had recommended Professor Wagner-Jauregg but the former had sent the patient "to you, Herr Professor."

"Well?" asked Pötzl, highly curious as to why he had been chosen.

The patient looked at Pötzl trustingly. "Herr Professor," he said, "I know that Wagner-Jauregg is greater than you. But *I* believe in the rabbi of Belz."[58]

For some hypochondriacal patients of Orthodox belief, the path to the revered Western doctor thus led through the rabbi.

Knowing that their patients had excessive anxieties about illness, the Western doctors would jolly the Eastern Jews along a bit.

Unlike the Western Jews, many of the Eastern customarily negotiated over the price of medical services. An elderly Jew wanted
Mikulicz to operate on his wife but found his six-hundred-mark
fee too high. The man asked if Mikulicz would operate for three
hundred marks.

"Oh, I probably can," Mikulicz said, "but then I'll use the knife
with the dull blade."

On another occasion—according to Adolf Strümpell, who
recorded these stories in his memoirs—Mikulicz responded to a
similar request, "Oh, all right, but then my hand will shake during
the operation."[59]

The only reason the Polish Jews would forsake the excellent surgeons in Cracow and Lemberg for the great names of the German
university clinics was their respect for medical authority. If the
Eastern Jews converted many family issues and bodily sensations
into medical problems, it was on the basis of belief in the miracles
of science. Neurologist Strümpell witnessed this in his university
clinic in Breslau: "These people always attempted, even in the
most hopeless cases and under the most difficult conditions, to
find truly the best and most able physician. Their unconditional
belief in the authority and knowledge of a university professor had
at times something truly touching about it."[60]

An exaggerated respect for the accomplishments of Western
medicine runs throughout accounts of life in Eastern Europe.
Bernard Naunyn, professor of internal medicine at Königsberg in
the early 1870s, whose office was filled in the summer often until
ten at night with Eastern Jews, said in his memoirs much later,
"The Jew decides on the basis of the physician's scientific reputation. This brings him to the office of the professor, at best to
the clinical professor. . . . For a Jew to go to a quack is almost
unheard of."[61] As Austrian novelist Elias Canetti was growing up
in the Jewish community of a small Bulgarian town, he overheard
the family discussing medical problems. "They often talked
about relatives who had gone to Vienna in order to consult famous doctors. The names of the important specialists of the day
enjoyed in our house the greatest possible celebrity. When I myself later went to Vienna, I was astonished to discover that all
these great names—Lorenz, Schlesinger, Schnitzler, Neumann,

Hajek, and Halban—actually existed as people."[62] The internist
Ernst von Leyden remembered from his own years in
Königsberg the masses of Orthodox Jews, the men in black silk
caftans, the women with silk wigs on their shaved heads, who
would flock to the lodging houses of the Jewish quarter. "Despite
their poverty, they would not content themselves with the many
family doctors who practiced in the city. No, it had to be a professor whom they consulted." They would summon the professors to the lodging house, always three at a time. "The number
three was chosen so that, if differences of opinion arose, there
could be a vote, and the diagnosis of the majority selected."
Leyden would usually go with two surgeons, and the three professors would progress from room to room, accumulating the
modest fees. "The custom was that the honorarium was always
paid in silver thalers carefully wrapped in paper, and thus we
would return home our pockets filled with clinking coins."[63]

Naunyn recalled of these conferences, arranged in the "second-
class Jewish inns in the outskirts [of Königsberg]": "Three, even
four of us university professors would have to attend such a 'council.' Even at that time there were people in Königsberg who made
their living by arranging these affairs." So the professors would go
from inn to inn for two or three hours, each receiving six marks per
consultation. (Finally it was the professors, and not the Jewish patients, who negotiated a change in fees: from six marks to ten.)[64]
Only because the consultation of medical authorities had been elevated to the status of one of life's highest prizes did the East
European Jews devote so much time and collective energy to it.
Preoccupation with bodily symptoms became a focus of public life.

Such collective consultation survived even—or perhaps was accentuated by—the ghastliness of the concentration camps. In his
report on Belsen, Stern said that the commonest manifestation of
hypochondriasis was

> the employment of a multiplicity of doctors all at the same time,
> and more particularly of a 'professor.' There were families who
> for one patient would mobilize a whole battery of doctors of all
> kinds, carefully seeing that the different doctors remained un-
> acquainted with the treatments prescribed by the others. Hence

distrust and hypochondria competed to the detriment of the patient, and it was difficult to persuade such innocents of the absurdity of their stratagems.[65]

To contact these stellar professors people would undertake arduous voyages and then be prepared to spend hours in waiting rooms. In Breslau one might see in the waiting rooms at midday the same Jewish figures who had been there since early morning, demonstrating, as Strümpell saw it, their "truly astonishing patience." Strümpell's own neurology-psychiatry waiting room was also full:

> One evening around seven, as I was just about to go out with my wife, an old Polish Jewess came up to me with her daughter to ask for a consultation. I saw that the daughter was not in apparent distress and therefore told the mother that I could not with the best will imaginable see her that evening and said that she should come to my office hour the next morning. We went out and thought no further of the patient. As we returned fairly late that evening and unlocked the door to the building, we heard in the darkness a strange noise and saw just as soon as we had lit the candle two female forms sitting on the steps. We looked at them somewhat astonished, and recognized the elderly Jewess and her daughter. With a friendly smile she said that she had permitted herself to wait for me here, and asked me if I could not now prescribe something for her daughter. Half angry, half amused, I finally granted her request.[66]

If this woman was at all overeager in grasping for the healing prescriptions of the great "Herr Professors," it was just by a bit. The larger point is that this overeagerness to consult demonstrates a deep anxiety about bodily symptoms—the true meaning of hypochondria. The Western professors told these tales with such relish precisely because most of the Eastern patients had nothing wrong with them.

The epicenter of the Eastern Jews' *"furor consultativus"* was not the provincial eastern universities but Berlin. Rivaled at that time for world medical leadership perhaps only by Vienna, Berlin represented the greatest pool of "professors" then in existence. In the *pas de deux* of the Berlin consultation, there were two actors—the largely Jewish psychiatrists, neurologists, and other specialists and the Jewish patients.

The "professors" themselves were divided between the chair-holders in the Faculty of Medicine and the specialty physicians settled in the community, who had teaching privileges and honorary professorships but not the prestige of a chair. All counted as academic medicine. In Berlin the tradition of Jews in academic medicine reached back to Ludwig Traube, who joined the teaching faculty of the Friedrich Wilhelm University in the 1850s. Rudolf Virchow, a non-Jew who was the most famous basic scientist in Germany at that time, had in the late 1860s and 1870s brought in a number of young Jewish physicians as residents *(Assistenten)* at the Charité Hospital. This opened the door for many Jews to lesser university posts if not to professorships.[67] By the end of the nineteenth century, 5 percent of Berlin's population as a whole was Jewish, as were a third of the physicians.[68] By 1933 50 percent of the physicians were Jews, and a third of the medical faculty as well.[69] Kept from the best professorships, Jewish specialists created an academic world of their own, based on private clinics and funded by fees of wealthy patients seeking consultations. As public health specialist Alfred Grotjahn said in the early 1930s:

Circling about the fixed stars of the faculty chair-holders were the planets of scarcely less brilliance, the senior lecturers *[Privatdozenten]* and honorary professors *[Extraordinarien]* who in clinical medicine scarcely took a backseat to the professors. Indeed they even surpassed the professors in significance for us medical students or as consultants for the prosperous domestic population, and even more for the crowd of foreigners who every year would flood in from abroad. As Jews, these men had not been selected for chairs at other universities, and so they created for themselves in Berlin their own clinics and circles of students. Among them were to be numbered [Emanuel] Mendel the neurologist, the dermatologist [Oskar] Lassar, the pediatrician [Adolf] Baginsky, the surgeon [James] Israel, the gynecologist [Leopold] Landau and the syphilologist [Georg] Lewin.[70]

So Jewish did the great Berlin consultants appear that elsewhere anti-Semitic slurs arose against the "Jewish Berlin spirit."[71] Several non-Jewish physicians in Berlin who flattered themselves as scientists scorned the Jews as moneygrubbers.[72]

The Berlin academic nerve doctors in particular formed a very special kind of scene. Virtually all were Jews.[73] Settled in the pleasant suburbs to the west and south of Wilmersdorf, Charlottenburg, and Schlachtensee, these men constituted a magnet for an international clientele of somatizers, often arriving, as Karl Bonhoeffer, the professor of psychiatry, put it "with bundles of prescriptions from Parisian, Viennese and English physicians." Bonhoeffer referred to these international patients as "psychopathic neurotics who add to the burdens of the nerve-doctor and his office hours. I attempted to keep this category away, present in the years before the war in such numbers in the West End of Berlin, because it was not in my interest to take over the treatment of such a time-consuming clientele."[74] However, the nonchaired consultants, whose salaries (unlike Bonhoeffer's) were not paid by the state, were indeed prepared to take on this population of hypochondriacs.

Many of these "international hypochondriacs" were Jewish. Hermann Oppenheim, who directed a large and profitable outpatient clinic for nervous diseases, spoke in 1908 of the "enormous confidence" the East European Jews placed in "German scientific medicine. It reaches the point that they lose entirely from view that many diseases are incurable. Or they acquire the idea that the illness will be healed and must be healed in Berlin. This dominates them completely, so that they repress every other consideration or thought."[75] As the internist Johannes Alfred Goldscheider described his East European patients in 1926: "They are terribly anxious about their health, in both an egocentric and an altruistic sense (parents about the children, children about the parents), and have a high predisposition to suggestion in the subjective aspect of the experience of illness. . . . This, it seems to me, represents a large part of the Jewish pathology."[76] (Goldscheider himself was Jewish.)

Because so few of the records of the physicians and of the private clinics have survived the Holocaust and World War II, the trail grows cold here. We know little more about the social composition, origin, or religion of the patients seeking consultations in Berlin. The Berlin physicians quoted above emphasized the Jewish component either because it was in reality quite large or because these Westernized specialists wanted to distance themselves psychologically from the Jews of Eastern Europe, whom they knew to be figures of fun in the eyes of their non-Jewish colleagues. But the Jewish nerve doctors of Berlin did think there was something peculiar in the presentation of their patients from Eastern Europe. They located this distinctive trait in anxiety about illness and in confidence in Western medicine. Both qualities came across to Western eyes as somewhat bizarre and parochial, and so the Westernized physicians spoke of a characteristic East European "hypochondria." This hypochondria probably did exist at one time, and may even have been passed culturally from generation to generation right into the New World.[77]

The evidence certainly does not demonstrate the existence of a genetic component in psychosomatic illness among Jews of East European origin. Yet other kinds of psychiatric disorders having a genetic basis, such as manic-depressive illness, did tend to occur more often in East European Jews than in the population as a whole.[78] It is not inconceivable that further research will establish that somatization as well has the same kind of genetic source. For the moment, however, cultural arguments suffice to identify the Jews of Eastern Europe as distinctive in a history of psychosomatic illness.

Ethnicity and illness constitute a tangled pathway. On the basis of our present knowledge, it is virtually impossible to separate the operating rules of a culture from biologically based components. Until now the entire subject has been more or less taboo. Virtually none of the extensive literature on cross-cultural psychiatry even contemplates the possibility that culture-specific illness behavior might possess biological as well as social roots. Given the explosion of genetic knowledge in psychiatry, it is a subject whose turn to come out of the closet has now arrived.

CHAPTER

5

The Cultural Face of Melancholy

MELANCHOLIA, THE DEEPLY SAD FORM of depression, is an excellent illustration of how social class and values on the one hand and genetics and biology on the other can shape the way people interpret their bodily symptoms. Depression, involving feelings of sadness, loss of self-worth, and numberless somatic complaints, usually has its origin in the biology of the brain, in disruptions of neurotransmitters. Yet the disruptions in the brain cells must be socially and psychologically interpreted in the patient's mind. Why am I in so much pain today? Why have I no energy? Why am I so sad? How the surrounding culture valorizes, or devalorizes, these varying perceptions of the body will influence how sufferers interpret them. If people believe that their deep sadness will be interpreted by others as a sign of craziness, they may downplay the depression of mood. If they believe their chronic feelings of fatigue will be accepted as evidence of a supposedly organic disease called chronic fatigue syndrome, they may dwell on how tired they feel.

Depression thus stands at the crossroads of two pathways. There is the biological pathway to illness, or events taking place deep in the brain. Then there is the social pathway to illness, or how the culture helps us interpret our bodily sensations. Depression has a clear biological side. It tends to run in families, to respond to antidepressant medication, and to be found in its essential elements in all times and places. But depression has a cultural side as well.

Other of its symptoms vary from era to era and are shaped by notions of what is legitimate or acceptable in disease at particular times. All these factors are highly germane to psychosomatic illness because depressed people tend to be plagued with physical symptoms. Indeed, the aches and fatigue of depression may be its sole outward form and are often chiefly what the doctor sees.

In a centuries-long tradition of medical terminology, *melancholia*, an old-fashioned term for the sadness of depression, has always been something akin to madness. Severely sad people may often hallucinate or become delusional, evidence of psychotic illness. Melancholia resonates with the ring of profound disturbance, of loss of contact with reality. What has shaped the evolution of the term *melancholia* has been an enduring fear of madness among the middle classes. As a condition that qualified one for admission to an asylum, melancholia was a diagnosis that no one wanted to have. It was the fear of hereditary madness and degeneration that would provoke the transformation of melancholia, with its connotation of disorder of mood, into the more acceptable form of depression having to do with somatic symptoms. The psychosomatic aspects of depressive illness thus represent a complex interaction between patients' hopes of organicity and fears of madness, and between physicians' ever-changing theories of psychiatry and their desire to be accommodating to the well-paying middle classes. The longing for social acceptability, and fear of social exclusion, helped shape the physical symptoms of severely depressed middle-class people.

Physical Symptoms and Depression

Herbert C.'s problems illustrate the psychosomatic side of depression. A thirty-nine-year-old single man who had been "assisting his father in the carpet business" in London, Herbert C. was admitted in March 1890 to the Holloway Sanatorium, a private nervous clinic in Virginia Water, Surrey. Herbert C. had a history of depression, the first attack occurring several years previously, when his eldest sister died, the second when a brother who had been living in America—and to whose visit Herbert had been eagerly looking forward—died. During this second attack Herbert was sent to Colney Hatch, an asylum in London. "While there he had two fits, the result of excessive fear. He had hallucinations of sight when there, says he saw men in white robes with fire coming from their mouths, and at other times saw a funeral passing in front of him. He was put into the strong room and this made him very timid."

After being discharged from Colney Hatch in 1885, Herbert was well for three years, then lapsed into depression again in 1888 when his mother died. Now, in 1890, Herbert had voluntarily requested admission to the Holloway, a sanatorium founded in 1885 "for the lower middle classes." Frederick McKettrick, a young Scots medical student then working as an assistant at the sanatorium, found Herbert to be "depressed and moody. . . . He weeps easily, there being loss of emotional control. He has slight impairment of memory both for recent and remote events." Herbert's mental functioning was also slowed, and he could not subtract 53 from 92. "He believes he has committed a serious crime, and thinks he is a criminal lunatic, hence his great intimidation." He often "sighs greatly and says music affects him very much, recalling to his mind past events and making him weep." Once in the sanatorium, Herbert shunned the company of other patients and avoided work as well, "complaining of it being too great for him. The real reason being"—in the opinion of this rather puritanical young Scotsman—"that he prefers to lounge about lazily, or sit indoors if he could do so." So Herbert C. was clearly depressed, but he was also physically symptomatic. "He is hypochondriacal and often talks a great deal about his bowels, muscular action very slow. . . . He says he has a feeling in his head as if the upper half of his scalp were being lifted off."[1]

Herbert was a mirror of both the biological and the cultural shaping of depression. He had all the aspects of classic depression through the ages, such as feelings of sadness, inability to remember, loss of appetite, insomnia, and feelings of fatigue.[2] But Herbert's experience with melancholy was also shaped by his cultural context. Guilt is universal in depression. But its more particular forms, such as the false belief of having committed a great crime, are more culture-specific. Similarly, psychosomatic symptoms are universal in depression, but Herbert's particular variety were shaped by the culture of his day. At Colney Hatch he had the fits typical of typical nineteenth-century hysteria, symptoms on the motor side of the nervous system involving dysfunctions of the muscles. At Holloway Herbert manifested "hypochondriacal" bodily concerns in general (his bowels, and so on) and also reported feeling that his scalp was being lifted off. He was discharged apparently well half a year after his admission.

Herbert's experience reminds us how some things have changed while others have stayed the same. Psychosomatic illness arising from depression is common because depression today is very common. A few statistics establish this reality. The average person today has around a one-in-eight, or 12 percent, chance of becoming depressed over the course of his or her life.[3] (The lifetime risk of manic depression is about one-half of 1 percent.) Rates of depressive symptoms in women tend to be about 60 percent higher than in men.[4] Many door-to-door surveys have been done to determine what percent of the population is depressed at any given moment. The results of these surveys differ somewhat because the populations themselves differ and also because the investigators often have different criteria of what constitutes "depression," notably whether to include chronic pain, tiredness, and the like, even if the individual denies feeling sad. But the figures tend to converge.

One may distinguish between having some of the *symptoms* of depression and having a clinical depressive *illness*. The symptoms of depression are extremely common and occur at a minimum in one person out of ten, as in a survey done in rural Tennessee.[5] At a maximum they strike one out of five. Twenty percent of the population of Kansas City, Missouri, in the early 1970s reported symptoms of depression.[6] Let us say the truth lies in between Tennessee and Kansas. That still means that one American in seven has some of the symptoms of depression at any given point in time.

Other studies attempt to move beyond the cataloging of individual symptoms to establish the frequency of clinical depression as a distinctive disease. The disease statistics are somewhat lower than the frequency of the individual symptoms, yet one study of Iceland in 1957 found 4 percent of the population at any one time to be frankly depressed (2.7 percent of the men, 4.9 percent of the women).[7] Iceland is in the midrange of such studies. At the top a survey in 1976 of Canberra, Australia, found 11 percent of the population clinically depressed.[8] If this particular investigation were generalizable, one out of every ten people at any given moment would have the major physical symptoms—sadness, insomnia, loss of appetite, tiredness, and so forth—as part of the package of depression. Yet even if the surveys converging at about 4 percent are more representative, one person in every twenty-five at any given moment is depressed, suffering the consequences of loss of joy in life, loss of purpose or goal, and potential risk of suicide.

The point is that perhaps a third of depressed individuals are also major somatizers. At any given time, therefore, the total amount of psychosomatic illness caused by depression is enormous. These individuals often have masked depression and turn up at the doctor's office complaining of pain, fatigue, and bowel problems instead of depressed mood and anxiety. Indeed, of the various psychiatric problems that present themselves in family medicine, such masked depressions are the most frequent.[9]

Physicians have a long history of failing to diagnose such masked depressions, treating the physical symptoms instead as a result of supposedly organic disease. In 1844 Edward Bulwer-Lytton, a thirty-one-year-old upper-class English writer, dragged himself to the spa at Malvern. He had a depressive illness of many years' standing, which his physicians had somehow overlooked. "Formerly, it was my favourite and querulous question to those who saw much of me, 'Did you ever know me twelve hours without pain or illness?' " Consulting his doctors before embarking on the journey to Malvern, he was counseled to take further stomach medication. "What had I not yet tried? A course of prussic acid [hydrocyanic acid]! Nothing was better for gastrite irritation, which was no doubt the main cause of my suffering!"

Bulwer-Lytton bore the obvious signs of a somatic depression. He explained that his nerves were "thoroughly shattered. . . . The least attempt at exercise exhausted me." He arose from bed in the morning "more weary than I laid down to rest." And the *joie de vivre* had vanished from his life. Morning walks, to which he had once responded vigorously, had been replaced by, "Headache, languor, a sense of weariness over the eyes, a sinking of the whole system towards noon, were all that I obtained by the morning breeze and the languid stroll by the sea-shore." He had stopped reading, only to be afflicted, in addition to the "profound dejection of the spirits," by "intolerable ennui." Clearly depressed by modern standards of assessing illness, Bulwer-Lytton localized his symptoms in his stomach.[10]

It is clear that psychosomatic and depressive illnesses overlap considerably. Whether the patient presents him- or herself to the physician with a downcast mood, easily diagnosable as depression, or whether he comes complaining of chest and back pain, will depend on whether the larger culture accepts or stigmatizes mood changes. In some Asian cultures, where mood changes are taboo, patients complain primarily of physical symptoms.[11] Historically as well, Western civilization was more tolerant of mood changes before 1800 than afterward.[12] Only in the nineteenth century did melancholy receive the hideous stamp of degeneration, driving black despair underground in favor of back pain.

Melancholia

Severe depression has a biological component that has probably not changed much historically, visible in the form of melancholia, or deep sadness. As far back in time as we care to look, we find melancholia and suicide transmitting themselves within the same family across the generations. The Schmid family in eighteenth-century Zurich, for example, began its spin into pathology with the suicide in 1728 of Jakob, a judge. Of Jakob's six children, two sons committed suicide. All the children of those two sons had melancholia. Of the known descendants of Jakob's other four children, all were either melancholic or committed suicide.[13] Clearly in the Schmid family depression had a genetic basis, transmitted over the generations.

The Schmid family's melancholy was part and parcel of the larger disease of depression. Even though this larger disease may be biologically driven, the actual occurrence of melancholy, meaning the willingness of patients with an underlying biological depression to present this great sadness, does seem to be variable. And it varies both from society to society and from historical period to period.[14] With roots in genetics and in the biology of the brain, melancholia is never entirely absent. Yet the degree to which it is present in the overall illness called depression seems to be culturally determined.

Melancholia has been described by doctors from the earliest days of medicine onward. It is mentioned in the Hippocratic writings as early as the fifth century before Christ.[15] But little sense of the frequency of the disorder may be gained from the ancient and medieval literature. Only with the writings in 1621 of Robert Burton, a reclusive English cleric who was the vicar of the parish of Saint Thomas in Oxford and himself melancholic, does the "modern" history of melancholia begin. In that year Burton, then forty-four, published his great treatise, *The Anatomy of Melancholy.* Although Burton had no medical experience, he must have had wide knowledge of his parishioners, as well as awareness of his own symptoms. Burton gave a clear description of the three important components of depressive illness—mood, cognition, and physical symptoms—suggesting that all three were well represented in the melancholia of his time. Of the depressed mood itself Burton wrote:

> Sorrow is that other character and inseparable companion [in addition to anxiety]. . . . [The melancholic are] without any evident cause, grieving still, but why they cannot tell. Never laughing, sad, thoughtful. . . . And though they laugh many times and seem to be extraordinary merry (as they will by fits) yet extreme lumpish again in an instant, dull and heavy, simultaneously merry and sad, but most part sad: pleasant thoughts depart soon, sorrow sticks by them still continually, gnawing as the vulture did Titus's bowels, and they cannot avoid it. No sooner are their eyes open but, after terrible and troublesome dreams, their heavy hearts begin to sigh. They are still fretting, chafing, sighing, grieving, complaining, finding faults, repining, grudging, weeping.

Burton struck the note of indecisiveness that has echoed in the literature on melancholia across the ages: "Inconstant they are in all their actions, vertiginous, restless, unapt to resolve of any business, they will and will not, persuaded to and fro upon every small occasion."

In psychotic depression the blackness of mood is such that patients often accuse themselves of unbelievable crimes or believe themselves damned without redemption in the eyes of God. This Burton describes too: "Some are afraid that heaven will fall on their heads, some afraid they are damned, or shall be. They are troubled with scruples of conscience, distrusting God's mercies, think they shall go certainly to Hell, the Devil will have them, and make great lamentation."

Burton also details the disorders of cognition frequently present in depression, the inability to concentrate and to remember. "As a man that's bitten with fleas or that cannot sleep turns to and fro in his bed, their restless minds are tossed and vary. They have no patience to read out a book, to play out a game or two, walk a mile, sit an hour [and are] erected and dejected in an instant."

Finally Burton described somatization in depression, the physical complaints. He himself had experienced these, for when he visited his own physician, Simon Forman of London in July 1597, Forman noted of the case, "much pain [in] head and much wind and melancholy." A month later: "Much stopping in the stomach and wind in the belly." In October 1597: "A burning in his hands and knees and a wind in the belly."[16] Burton later wrote in the *Anatomy of Melancholy,* "Hypochondriacal or flatuous melancholy . . . is, in my judgement, the most grievous and frequent." After citing a long series of ancient authorities on turmoil in the innards, Burton told his readers, "Now go and brag of thy present happiness, whosoever thou art, brag of thy temperature, of thy good parts, insult, triumph and boast. Thou seest in what a brittle state thou are, how soon thou mayest be dejected . . . how many sudden accidents may procure thy ruin, what a small tenure of happiness thou hast in this life."[17] No truer words were ever spoken.

References to melancholia slip so easily into the medical writing of the late seventeenth and eighteenth centuries that the condition could not have been uncommon. The famous English physician Thomas Sydenham, in his "Letter to Dr. Cole," written in 1682, casually alluded, for example, to the sobbing gentleman. Although the patient had been feverish several days previously, when Sydenham arrived he was "out of bed, with his clothes on, and talking reasonably. Upon asking why I was sent for, I was told by one of his friends that *I should soon see* [Sydenham's emphasis]. So I sat down and began to converse with him. In a short time, I observed that he pouted his lower lip . . . and finally burst out in such a flood of tears, accompanied with sobs and groans almost convulsive, as I had never seen before." Sydenham was more accustomed to this kind of behavior in women than men.[18] On June 10, 1736, James Clegg, physician-pastor in Chapel en le Frith in Derbyshire, wrote in his diary, "At home till afternoon. Mr. Oldham and his daughter came to my house. She is under a melancholy disorder. I had much conversation with her, prayed with her."[19] Such examples come easily to hand in the casual medical writing of the late seventeenth and eighteenth centuries.[20]

Eighteenth-century textbooks make clear that the average physician could have every expectation of encountering melancholia. As the young London physician John Purcell said in 1702 of "vapours" that typified the condition: "Those who have laboured long under this distemper are oppressed with a dreadful anguish of mind and a deep melancholy, always reflecting on what can perplex, terrify and disorder them most, so that at last they think their recovery impossible and are very angry with those who pretend there is any hopes of it." This is a succinct description of the bleakness of affect in melancholia. He continued, "Melancholia in hysterical people is easily cured in the beginning, but when it has taken deep root, and the patients avoid and shun company, then it is hard to be cured; nay it is to be feared they will endeavour to make themselves away."[21] Richard Blackmore, another elite London physician, described in 1725 the familiar bon vivant, or "hypochondriacal man," one minute "entertaining the company with a great eruption of wit and facetious conversation," the next "his spirits exhausted and sunk, and suddenly relapsing into his dull and lifeless melancholy. . . . Thus are his days varied and checquered with black and white, calm and stormy, fair and cloudy seasons, nor ever does his glass of life stand at a settled point." Physicians many generations later would put such technical terms as *cyclothymia* or *soft bipolar spectrum* to this bon vivant, yet the point is that in London society of the early Georgian period, he was a familiar figure.[22]

By the end of the eighteenth century, doctors were regularly describing the principal components of major depression—the affective, cognitive, and somatic symptoms. James Sims, who had a London society practice, said in 1799 of melancholia: "In the first approaches of melancholy the persons become silent and absorbed in thought, dislike being spoken to or roused, and seem always occupied in some grave contemplation. Jests, laughter, and every species of hilarity seem irksome to them." This downbeat mood might then accelerate into formal psychosis: "They think all their friends are become enemies." Or: "They complain of some action that they have done against some friend or relative, or some crime that they have committed, which can never be forgiven by God or man. This action is often totally imaginary."

Sims also mentioned disturbances of cognition, although at this time medical writers were little sensitive to psychological styles. "Their memory, which is the most diseased part, constantly makes them worse than what they are, and sometimes suggests to them their having undergone the most whimsical, ridiculous, or degrading bodily changes."

Finally Sims dwelt on somatic changes in melancholia, changes relating to the interior of the body, such as loss of energy, not eating, and disordered sleep. "They enjoy but little sleep, and that anxious, waking often in a fright," he said. "They become emaciated, although their appetite may be far from bad. At other times they refuse nourishment, fasting for days, nay, often weeks." And their bodies seemed generally slowed as well (what would later be called "psychomotor retardation"): "When obliged to move, their motion is slow, measured, solemn, or torpid, with folded arms. Their speech is slow."[23]

By the beginning of the nineteenth century all the aspects of what we understand by depression were thoroughly familiar in medical writing, although physicians used different terms for them. Nonetheless, the emphasis in these accounts was on mood—melancholia—not on pain, tiredness, insomnia, or any of the other nonmood elements of the disease.

Although melancholia is always indentifiable from the medical literature of any period, whether it is frankly exposed or concealed depends on the depressed patients themselves—on their own sense of what the legitimate expression of illness is and of what constitutes "madness." In the past the deep sadness of melancholia counted as madness. Not wanting to be thought insane, nineteenth-century patients would be at considerable pains to interpret their problems as nervous rather than psychiatric, somatic rather than mental, for nervous illness was thought to be due to a physical affection of the nerves, was not deemed evidence of degeneration, and would be seen by a nerve doctor rather than by an alienist.[24] For example, the private clinics that flourished toward the end of the nineteenth century for the middle classes all trumpeted themselves as dealing with nervous illness. "Mental illness" was excluded, they insisted in their advertisements.[25]

It is interesting that although the lower classes shared in this longing for nervosity as opposed to melancholy, lacking the finely tuned feelings of their betters for what was acceptable, they might get the signals wrong. Elise G., a thirty-six-year-old farm woman from a village in Lower Austria, became tired and upset in December 1902 after giving birth. The child, unlike her previous children, had survived. The local doctor recommended that she leave the infant behind and go to live with her parents for a while to recover. "That was her disaster," said one of her doctors later. "She was always lamenting about the infant and feared something might happen to her only child. . . . She cried constantly, and screamed that either the baby be brought to her or she would go home." Her mother, sizing up the situation, told her "that she would be brought to Vienna to a professor who cures people who cry a lot," meaning a nerve doctor. Elise ended up in an asylum anyway because she had chosen a symptom that would be taken as evidence of melancholy rather than of nerves.[26] As peasants, she and her family, perhaps did not realize that the strategy of the middle classes for not being considered mad was to dwell on physical symptoms.

Nonmelancholic Depression in Past Times

To sidestep the stigma of melancholic insanity, a series of diagnoses came into fashion during the nineteenth century that represented supposedly separate nervous diseases but in fact centered
on different aspects of depression. By World War I most of these
new terms had been subsumed under the term *depression,* and the
term *melancholia* had gone out off style. These new diagnostic labels incorporated bodily symptoms and stressed the nonpsychotic
side of sadness. They had the effect of downplaying deep mood
changes that could be taken as evidence of insanity, and shifting
the whole phenomenon of depression from the psychiatrist to the
neurologist, from the asylum to the oak-paneled consulting rooms
of Harley Street and Park Avenue.

The first of these depressive-equivalent diagnoses was
"hypochondria." Before the mid-nineteenth century the term was
mainly a synonym for psychoneurosis in men, the equivalent of
"hysteria" in women. (Later it came to mean semidelusional preoccupation with illness.)[27] But many of these patients clearly had
a non-psychotic depression, as for example the "hypochondria"
patients of James Rymer, a family doctor in late-eighteenth-cen-
tury Surrey. After describing the usual pains and bowel upsets of
hypochondria, Rymer continued, "In consequence of these sufferings of the body, the temper and mind are often wonderfully affected. The patient becomes peevish and touchy at mere trifles;
dejected, timid, distrustful, bereft of hope as to his cure and all future events, with aversion to society." "All the great powers and
generous passions of the mind," said Rymer, were "subdued by
the depressing influence of melancholy and the conception of a
variety of evils, fantastical, and groundless." With hypochondria
Rymer and his patients may have been trying to sidestep the stig-
matizing aspects of melancholia, concentrating on the physical. Or
perhaps in the patients' experience of illness the physical aspects
were simply more enhanced. What for Rymer was hypochondria
would a century and a half later become depression.[28]

When the young Paris physician Jean-Baptiste Louyer-Villermay
wrote of hypochondria in 1802, he was essentially depicting an

anxious depression that might end in suicide. After gastrointestinal symptoms at the onset of illness, patients would become anxious and develop chest pain. Other pains would dart about the body. Finally a sense of nameless terror would seize them. They avoided society, became sleepless after horrifying dreams, and finally ended up praying for sleep that never seemed to come. As their illness advanced, symptoms now hailed down on Louyer-Villermay's poor "hypochondriacs": hot and cold flashes, headaches, vertigo, tinnitus (ringing in the ears), hypersensitivity of hearing, taste, and so forth, "profound sadness," a feeling of heaviness in the limbs, even an unsteady gait, "extreme irascibility, added to natural morosity, and worsened by their physical condition." The "hypochondriacs" might end up longing for death and commit suicide.[29] Again a century and a half later Louyer-Villermay's hypochondria would be redefined as depression.

To give a final example: Evans Riadore noted in 1835 that "hypochondriac complaints" were often accompanied by "low spirits" and tiredness. "There is something in active duty, or hard labour of every kind, that tends to avert them," he noted censoriously. "Low spirits and hypochondriac complaints are more commonly met with in person under thirty years old, and more common in females than in males."[30] This sounds like a description of depression. None of the above-cited authorities used the term *melancholia* for what they were describing.

Among the first to recognize hypochondria as a subform of depression was the Viennese psychiatry professor Max Leidesdorf. Leidesdorf owned an expensive private nervous clinic in the suburb of Döbling and had ample opportunity to watch his patients over a period of time. In his textbook, published in 1860, he ranked hypochondria among "the conditions of psychic depression." The difference between hypochondria and melancholia was merely that, while the hypochondriac was busily seeking medical consultation, the melancholic, to the extent that he did anything at all, was planning his suicide.[31] After Leidesdorf hypochondria came increasingly to mean either preoccupation with psychosomatic symptoms or a kind of delusional disorder centering about bodily states.

Other depressive equivalents boiled up. Between the 1860s and

World War I, somatic preoccupations in people who felt blue became assigned to "dysthymia" and "neurasthenia." Both diagnoses were heavily associated with middle-class life, particularly
with the cosseted world of the private nervous clinic. The popularity of both represented, without a doubt, an effort on the part
of the middle classes to avoid stigmatization, not just that of
melancholia or of insanity but of "degeneration." The last third of
the nineteenth century was the heyday of the doctrine of degeneration, which insisted that mental illness was almost invariably inheritable, and that it worsened successively when passed from
generation to generation.[32] When melancholia meant degeneration, it was something nobody wanted to have. Organic-sounding
neurological diagnoses were far preferable.

Karl Kahlbaum, owner of a private nervous clinic in Görlitz in
eastern Prussia, brought dysthymia into the world in 1863.[33] As a
tidy classification for recurrent, nonpsychotic melancholia, it enjoyed a vogue among staff physicians at the kinds of private nervous clinics that did not have locked wards and barred windows.
Theodor Tiling, for example, chief physician at a private clinic in
Saint Petersburg, recommended that Kahlbaum's *dysthymia* be
used as the diagnostic term on open wards, where the patients
came and went. "The patients who suffer from dysthymia are not
unapproachable and reticent, but give their opinions quite openly
and without reservation to the physician. They complain of a feeling of pressure and heaviness in the skull, along the forehead, and
about the stomach, which they take for anxiety or pangs of conscience." Tiling said the patients themselves identified their problems as psychic, not physical (except for insomnia), and could
usually point out some "moral" or catastrophic cause of their distress. Filled with guilt and despair, they feared the onset of madness. He observed that, while dysthymia usually recurred, rarely
did it deteriorate into graver insanity. Although patients with dysthymia were quite at risk of self-harm—three of his having committed suicide—only seldom did they end up in asylums.[34] The
term *dysthymia,* it is true, emphasized more a disorder of mood
than somatic symptoms. Yet it implied that mildly depressed
mood was not tantamount to insanity, and that middle-class patients could be treated outside asylums in chic private clinics. It

therefore caught on among the kinds of people able to pay for these clinics, and among the physicians avid to staff them.[35]

Neurasthenia, on the other hand, was torn directly from the fabric of nervous illness and was not supposed to connotate madness of any kind. The term had been revived by George Beard in 1869 and reached the height of its popularity around 1900. Neurasthenia incorporated two core entities: chronic fatigue and nonmelancholic depression. Both conditions do in fact overlap, for the chronically fatigued are frequently though not invariably depressed, and vice-versa.

So why did physicians in the 1880s and 1890s prefer the term *neurasthenia* to *depression?* Because depression did not sound sufficiently neurological, in an era when psychiatric patients craved neurological rather than psychiatric diagnoses. Neurasthenia meant an organic disease of the nervous system, and was tailor-made for patients who seemed disgruntled, dyspeptic, or anxious, and who manifested psychosomatic symptoms. As Ludwig Hirt said in 1890 of neurasthenia, "First, the patient is down-hearted and worried and sees everything in blackest colors, and, above all, despairs of recovery. He becomes irritable and impatient, unsociable with his friends, and feared by his family." He is slow and unable to concentrate at work, suffers insomnia, as well as "a disagreeable pressure in his head," dizziness, and bowel upset.[36]

Neurasthenia, with its emphasis on physical symptoms, became a favored diagnosis among the psychically distressed middle classes. The patients of Paris psychiatrist Maurice de Fleury at the turn of the century would come in the door and say, "Docteur, je suis neurasthénique." They might take from their pockets "sheets covered with notes . . . a phenomenon that Charcot called 'the man with the little notes' [*l'homme aux petits papiers*]. The patient is sure to add that his memory is very imprecise. He asks permission to read his history, which he had taken care to write out."

What are his complaints? "At first, there was a profound and lasting tiredness, more marked in the morning after arising from bed." He wants constantly to lie down. Then he has a dull, preoccupying ache in his neck, or perhaps in the lumbar region.

"The nights are awful. Either he goes to sleep only very late, after having turned in bed for a long time. Or after having fallen heavily asleep just after dinner, he awakens around midnight or one in the morning, completely wide awake, and tries in vain until dawn to fall to sleep again." There were digestive complaints too: The patient arose disgusted from the table, bloated and unable to work. On and on the list of physical woes went. Then Fleury's patients would describe their state of mind: weakened memory, inability to remember numbers or proper names, panicky about forgetting so much. "Work becomes a bother, painful and impossible. To carry on a conversation or write a letter to a supplier, he has to marshal all his forces to accomplish an act that previously was the easiest thing in the world." And the sense of "emptiness in the head"! Finally, said Fleury, the patient becomes frankly sad and has had enough of life, "la fatigue de vivre." He becomes hypochondriac, stops eating, and contemplates suicide. This, for Fleury, was "neurasthenia."[37]

Other accounts of neurasthenia included such symptoms as obsessive-compulsive traits or personality derangements that normally would not be reckoned to depression. Yet at the core of reports of neurasthenia was either a chronically tired individual, downcast because of fatigue, or someone who was depressed, having the core physical symptoms of insomnia, loss of appetite, and a blizzard of physical ailments, plus thoughts of suicide.

Doctors with a middle-class clientele encountered neurasthenia on a daily basis. Heinrich Averbeck, director of a sanatorium in Bad Laubbach on the Rhine, described "acute neurasthenia," the sudden "collapse of nervous energy, the bankruptcy of the nervous system." High officials admitted to his clinic might complain of feeling "all worn out [*das Verbrauchtsein*]"; academics would describe feeling "ossified" or having their minds "go to seed." Army officers, in an officer corps that prided itself on being "colossally dashing," would turn up in Bad Laubbach feeling "deadened."[38] Hugo Gugl treated a population of "extreme neurasthenics" who bordered on melancholia. But unlike true melancholics, Gugl said, these patients had no active plans for suicide and responded to the "consolation of the physician." Such cases were suitable for admission to a voluntary wing such as the one in his clinic because the patients retained some insight—they had voluntarily chosen to be admitted and did not have to be kept under close supervision. Nor did they appear to other patients as "insane" (always bad in a sanatorium for psychoneurotics) or become bothersome to others "as long as appropriate measures [were] taken."[39]

In a university town the true target group of neurasthenia was the fatigued and stomach-plagued students. "For them," said one French physician,

> the most terrible moments are those spent alone, their noses buried in Roman Law or Testut's *Human Anatomy*. Whatever the charm of these studies, they cannot captivate the [student's] imagination. At first he simply returns to his work too soon after eating and falls asleep over his book, victim of a more or less marked hyposthenic gastrointestinal condition. Then after an hour of crushing slumber, broken with nightmares and abrupt wakenings, he emerges from his torpor and while still rubbing his eyes, begins to think of suicide. He resumes reading at the line where he left off, but finds it impossible to fix his attention. Between his eyes and the book a thousand incongruous images are interposed, or he imagines himself in interesting sexual positions with idealized feminine forms. . . . Discouraged and exhausted by the struggle [against sex], he throws his book aside and slumps in an armchair, watching the hours tick away on the clock, dwelling on the nothingness of a miserable life that, for him, forbids the only pleasures that make living worthwhile.

The author believed that involuntary sexual abstinence was a cause of neurasthenia.[40] To this physician neurasthenic students presented themselves as organic cases. If such students were to turn up today at a counseling service on campus, it is difficult to think they would not receive a diagnosis of depression.

In Paul Hartenberg's practice in pre–World War I Paris, the face of middle-class melancholia offered itself as a businessman saying, "Doctor, I've come to consult you because I'm always tired and can't work. In the morning when I get up, I'm tireder than when I went to bed. All day my body feels tired, my arms and legs exhausted. The slightest effort finishes me off. I can no longer take walks or do any physical exercise. Even standing is painful."

But it was not just fatigue. The patient continued:

It's not just my body that's tired but my brain. I constantly feel as though an iron vise were tightening on my cranium. My head feels empty. My mind won't work. My ideas are confused and I can no longer concentrate. My memory is shot. When I read, I can't remember by the bottom of the page what I've read at the top. I forget my appointments, my business affairs. And with all that, I feel sad. I get no joy out of anything. Everything that entertains other people doesn't amuse me at all. . . .

As for my will, my energy, they're gone. I no longer know what I want, what I'm supposed to do. I doubt, I hesitate, I don't dare take a decision. Moreover I've no appetite and I sleep badly. I have no sexual desire.

Hartenbeg's diagnosis was neurasthenia, a highly frequent condition among the Parisian middle classes.[41] A century later the condition is no less so, merely that it is called depression. There is little evidence that the high rates of depression today were not also present among middle-class people in former times. The difference is that the stark mood changes of melancholia were driven into the background while somatic complaints advanced to center stage.

In dismantling melancholia, somatic complaints finally became, in and of themselves, evidence of depression. Among the first psychiatrists to use the term depression was the Leipzig professor Johann Christian Heinroth in 1818.[42] In 1856 Louis Delasiauve, staff psychiatrist at the Bicêtre Hospital in Paris, insisted that "depression" be isolated out of the larger complex of psychoses the French had been calling "lypémanie."[43] Other physicians as well began to question the suitability of melancholia—basically a diagnosis used in insane asylums—for outpatients who were dejected or anxious and who had numerous physical symptoms. In the influential fifth edition of his textbook, published in 1896, Emil Kraepelin described "simple depression," in contrast to the term "depressive insanity" he had employed in earlier editions.[44] That was probably the European turning point.

The American turning point came in 1904, when Adolf Meyer, a Swiss psychiatrist who had come to the United States twelve years before, attended a meeting of the New York Neurological Society. Meyer, at the time director of psychiatric research in the New York State hospital system and later professor of psychiatry at Johns Hopkins University, was probably the most prestigious figure in American psychiatry before World War II. The subject of this 1904 meeting was "the classification of melancholias." When Meyer's turn to speak came, he said he would "rather favor a different classification. On the whole, he was desirous of eliminating the term melancholia. . . . If, instead of melancholia, we applied the term depression to the whole class, it would designate in an unassuming way exactly what was meant."[45] Meyer's views then filtered into the standard Anglo-Saxon textbooks and became dogma for the twentieth century. Thus, by the early twentieth century, melancholia came to be called depression.

By now depressive illness had been unhooked from psychosis and from degeneration. It had been tamed for outpatient practice among the middle class. A final step in rendering depression almost as innocuous as the common cold was the concept of depression without sadness, or depressive-equivalents. Here sadness, anxiety, and agitation became dispensed with altogether. Walter Cimbal, a deputy chief physician *(Oberarzt)* on the psychiatric service of the municipal general hospital in Altona near Hamburg, popularized this view of depression before World War II. (Cimbal later played an inglorious role in the history of psychiatry during the Third Reich.) In 1929 he gave a paper at a psychiatric meeting on "vegetative equivalents of depressive states." "Vegetative" was the technical term for symptoms produced by the autonomic nervous system (once called the vegetative nervous system), and vegetative symptoms meant somewhat vaguely all those not related to mental processes. For Cimbal depression existed when a patient had disquieting feelings plus "the physical sensation of dejection and weakness, or the inability to resist anything or achieve anything."[46]

Cimbal's work was the thin end of the wedge. Psychiatric diagnosis would ultimately get away from his precise views about weakness and achievement to delineate a certain pattern of psychosomatic symptoms as evidence of depression. By the 1980s patients who denied feeling depressed but who were physically symptomatic (as long as the symptoms included pain, anorexia, and insomnia), would be eligible for the diagnosis of a mood disorder. One authority wrote in 1986 that even if the patient denied feeling sad, "one needs to look for supporting evidence of depression and such symptoms as loss of interest and pleasure in activities of daily living, food and sex, insomnia, lack of drive. A history of a constellation of these symptoms justifies a presumptive diagnosis of a depressive or anxiety disorder, or both."[47] Thus depression was to become the commonest diagnosis in psychiatry, beloved among physicians because it suggested that some kinds of physical symptoms had a psychological origin, and acceptable to patients because it had ceased to connote madness.

Although depression strikes people of all classes, the transformation of *melancholia* into *depression* as a term had been driven by the middle classes and by physicians anxious for their custom. Ridding the scene of degeneration and madness would favor the middle classes as they sought to marry off their daughters and sons, whose ailments might otherwise suggest poisoned heredity. Neurasthenia and "neurotic" depression became seen as treatable in expensive private clinics and spas. An alliance of class interests and new medical theories thus converted socially unacceptable forms of depression into acceptable ones.

Changes in the Physical Experience of Depression

The subjective nature of depression—what the patient feels in his or her own body—seems to have changed as well as the objective medical diagnoses. In the physical experience of depression there are variables and constants. By constants are meant the somatic symptoms that have always accompanied depression, permanent biological outriders to the core mood changes. In 1874 Richard von Krafft-Ebing, then professor of psychiatry at Graz, reviewed the major physical accompaniments of melancholy.

Among symptoms attributable to the nervous system, he listed "little energy and quick exhaustibility of the muscles, hesitant movements, soft speech, flaccidity and weakness of the muscles. . . . As a rule sleep is disrupted, unrestorative because of the nightmares. The patients feel exhausted and wrung out as they awaken. Headache, neuralgic sensations in the back and limbs, and palpitations are frequent complaints." He went on to mention "disturbances of appetite, pressure in the pit of the stomach, anorexia, constipation."[48] These symptoms have more or less always accompanied a depressed mood.

In psychotic depression too there have been common physical moments—fantastical ideas about the body or disordered perceptions of what is happening within. No outside observer can gainsay the reality of these perceptions for the patient, but the patients' feelings bear no relationship to any organic process, hence they are hallucinatory. To take an example, in April 1889 Caroline D., the thirty-six-year-old wife of a greengrocer, was admitted to Holloway House, the private nervous clinic in Virginia Water near London. Normally "healthy and good tempered," she had been ill off and on for about the previous eighteen months. She told one of the doctors who signed the certificate required for her involuntary admission that she "carries about pieces of stick which she says she coughed up. Had lumps on her belly which worked to the top of her chest. Has sensation of beads in her head and creeping bugs over her body at night." To the other physician whose signature was needed for her certification she reported herself "full of something moving and has real human hair in her bowels."

On admission to Holloway House she was said to be "a tall, stout, obese woman [with] sad and depressed expression, often crying. Tongue moist and furred, bowels constipated. Appetite bad, says she cannot swallow." Mentally she is suffering from hypochondria, with delusions that she coughs up pieces of stick. She also says she has had several miscarriages one on top of the other, which instead of coming away have been passed upward and fixed themselves around her throat. Sometimes she says she has wires fixed in her throat." She reported these experiences around April 23.

She then started to pull out of what retrospectively seems to have been a psychotic depression. May 25: "Mentally she is slightly improved; she remembered she had told me her miscarriages had passed up to her throat and blocked her oesophagus and she now believes this is nonsense, though she still experiences the sensations."

June 25: "She remains querulous and hypochondriacal, is perpetually complaining of queer sensations in various parts of her body to which she gives various whimsical interpretations."

On July 1 her husband came and took her "on leave to the seaside." "Though experiencing these sensations, she is decidedly improved and does not appear so sad." She was discharged definitively six weeks later as "recovered."[49]

Was there something distinctive about these lower-middle-class, genteel Englishwomen and their hallucinatory perceptions of their bodies? We might contrast them with an entirely different population: the working-class and peasant women admitted around the same time for "melancholia" to the provincial Austrian asylum at Kierling-Gugging, just to the north of Vienna. On April 18, 1901, Barbara L., a fifty-two-year-old single woman who worked in the vineyards in the wine regions near Vienna, was admitted to Kierling-Gugging. Three months previously she had seen her sister's sixteen-year-old son killed while he was cutting down a large poplar tree. About a month and a half after that she started to become symptomatic, loudly complaining to friends about her "sinfulness," filled with self-reproach, and unable to sleep. Once in the asylum at Kierling-Gugging she started to develop somatic hallucinations. "She can't eat anything because she doesn't have any stomach or innards." When the Commissioners on Lunacy came by for a visit, she told them in a monotone that she would be hacked to death. "I've done nothing to anybody. I'm not sick. I'm not sleepless." Four weeks later, on June 30, "she ripped a hook loose from the bed and tried to tear open her abdomen with it."

"I can't stand it any longer for the pain," she said. "Just give me a knife, please."

August 15: "She says she has no head and no hands. Her stomach has been quite full of food for many years. She asks for a knife so that she can cut open her stomach. She also requests that she be hanged so as to save her from death. She doesn't have any breath left and feels quite dizzy." Barbara L., who offers us this garden-variety example of somatization in psychotic depression, had still not fully recovered when she was discharged in November 1901 to the care of friends.[50]

Despite the great cultural dissimilarity of middle-class English women at the Holloway and lower-class Austrian women at Kierling-Gugging, the biological side of depression gave them a good deal in common. Their physical symptoms were actually little different. Of the nineteen Englishwomen admitted in 1889 for melancholia whose charts were analyzed in detail, 26 percent had somatic delusions, of the thirty-five melancholic Austrian women in sample years between 1885 and 1905, 14 percent. (The difference is not statistically significant.[51]) About one in five among seriously depressed patients in starkly contrasting cultures experienced such delusions.

But at another level cultural factors do matter. In a given historical period the physical symptoms seen in depression reflect the general patterns of psychosomatic illness prevalent at that time. For example, the twentieth century has seen an increasing sensitivity to bodily symptoms within the population as a whole. This growing somatic sensitivity seems to have been registered in psychotic depression, in which delusions and hallucinations relating to the body have become more frequent (though this conclusion is based on only a few studies). At the university psychiatric clinic in Basel, only 17 percent of the depressed patients in 1878–1914 expressed "hypochondriac ideas," 24 percent in 1915–30, and 23 percent in 1940–51.[52] At the Royal Edinburgh Asylum the percentage of depressed patients having delusional ideas about disease rose from 7 percent in 1892 to 29 percent in 1942–43. This occurred in the context of a large decline in delusional depression generally, so it is all the more interesting that the hard-core group shifted to concerns about the body (instead of concerns about persecution or whether strangers were taking an interest in them).[53]

Depressed people who are not psychotic and not in an asylum—the great majority in other words—have always tended to take on whatever psychosomatic symptoms were popular at the moment. In the eighteenth century it was fits, so depressives developed hysterical fits in addition to the standard somatic changes. As John Purcell said in 1702, "Melancholy in hysterical people is easily cured in the beginning, but when it has taken deep root, and the patients avoid and shun company, then it is hard to be cured; nay it is to be feared they will endeavour to make themselves away."[54] By "hysteria" Purcell meant fits. "Sometimes the development of hysterical attacks," said Étienne-Jean Georget in 1821, "is preceded by a more or less intense state of melancholy. The patients are sad, morose, susceptible and irritable. They seek out solitude for their crying spells. . . . One often finds them absorbed in daydreams, inattentive to what is being said. They suffer complete or partial insomnia."[55] Georget was probably describing patients whose basic problem was depression but who unconsciously selected fits as a suitable accompaniment to the dejected mood.

In the nineteenth century, the century of paralysis, we also find many depressives unable to stand or move their legs. Alfred Beni-Barde told the story of a young woman from a fine family, raised by her parents "with an affectionate solicitude," who had married an up-and-coming painter. Unfortunately her new husband had been "not impervious to worldly pleasures and had not shunned what one used to call les liaisons dangereuses."

One day, when they were walking along looking in the windows of jewelry stores, another young woman suddenly appeared, "well known to him, who gave him a terrible public tongue-lashing. She accused him of having irresponsibly abandoned her with a young child whose paternity was his. Then she went for his face with her clenched hands, which concealed a bottle of sulphuric acid.

"The young wife, horrified and outraged at this unexpected scene, ran away without saying a word and took refuge at her parents'. The husband, who emerged physically unscathed, hastened to join her, and the couple had a coming to terms." Aghast at the scent of scandal, her mother and father tried to persuade her to move back home, while the son-in-law was supposed to leave under the pretext of an extended voyage, after which a marital separation would ensue.

All this affected the young bride's health, and she, who previously had been perfectly well except for a bit of migraine and some stomach upset, began falling down. She complained simultaneously of "great nervous excitability," of exhaustion, and of muscle twitches, at which point the family doctor, the distinguished internist Pierre Potain, recommended that she see Beni-Barde.

"When I saw her for the first time," said Beni-Barde, "I was struck by her state of collapse. Her face was pale and expressionless; she had a sad and languishing air. Her previously vibrant voice has lost its sonority. She spoke but little and obtained from her mutism at least the satisfaction of not having to order her thoughts." She said that her intellect seemed to have undergone a decline, and for this condition she had already asked a surgeon friend of the family if he could not do something (a possible reference to sexual surgery). She had become forgetful and was unable to fix her attention. To these psychic problems were added some physical ones: Her eyes were quite sensitive to light. She had a ringing in her ears and declared herself hypersensitive to the slightest odor. She feared she was slipping into irreversible neurological illness. Most interesting of all was the great muscle weakness she experienced in rising from bed in the morning, for while many of her symptoms belonged to the more-or-less-eternal somatic companions of depression, falling down and collapsing in the morning after getting up were specific to the motor hysteria of the nineteenth century. Beni-Barde restored her health with a course of hydrotherapy, and she reconciled herself to living with her parents.[56]

Young women who somatized their depression in the form of weakness and paralysis were legion among the Parisian upper crust. Maurice Krishaber, a Paris nerve doctor who had grown up in Hungary and studied in Vienna, had a chic consulting practice. Around the late 1860s a twenty-two-year-old woman of Armenian origin came to see him. She had been married at age sixteen to a man of forty-two, who had taken her to Italy. There she had had a baby. Then she left her husband, abandoned the child, and three months previously had arrived in Paris, where she was now living isolated and semi-impoverished, smoking and drinking tea constantly. She had sought out Krishaber because of insomnia, fainting, and a sudden attack of paraplegia that had come on after vertigo, causing her to fall to the floor (but without losing consciousness). After that she took to her bed, where she found herself hypersensitive to light, sound, and the weight of the covers and also extremely irritable. For the next two years the patient was plagued by insomnia, nightmares, feelings of great anxiety, and in the year following that by a sense of going through life as though in a dream. "The patient tried . . . to walk, but the pain in her heart reawakened after the first steps." She was finally able to walk "only by frequently touching her legs with her hands to make sure they were moving, not being able to see where she was going without becoming vertiginous." Over her long course she developed numerous other symptoms, which failed to improve after Krishaber sent her to Saint Moritz. "It seems to me that I'm just not myself," she would say. She attempted suicide several times. Finally all her symptoms vanished except her sadness, and she returned to Armenia, where she was completely restored.[57] The case is a quintessential example of century-specific complaints: a young woman depressed because of life's stress, who takes to her bed, cannot walk, and begins edging toward a second state (feeling that she is "not herself"), all characteristic of the nineteenth century.

Charcot-style hysteria represented a special cluster in the symptom pool. People with depression often selected Charcot's specific stigmata at the end of the nineteenth century and beginning of the twentieth. In March 1992 "la dame R.," age forty-nine, presented herself at the Montpellier University neurological clinic with all the signs of a somatized depression: "The patient complains of being depressed, has no energy, despairs of recovering, suffers headache, a vague gastralgia accompanied by vomiting that is not related to meals. A melancholic depression has increased for the last two months, and the patient is supposed to have declared, without any particular conviction, a desire to end her life." She had had an unhappy marriage, one moreover that never had been consummated because of a congenital malformation of the vagina.

On physical examination "painful points are found corresponding to various hysterogenic zones as well as a marked hypoesthesia [lowered sensitivity] on the right side of her body." Corneal sensitivity was reported dulled, and she seemed entirely anesthetic in the pharynx. "Her visual fields are constricted." The reader will recall all of these "findings" as corresponding to Charcot's stigmata,[58] so she had clearly learned of them somewhere in order to produce them for physicians who expected them.

The most interesting part of la dame R.'s physical exam, however, was yet to come. The doctors discovered her malformed vagina. She had an acute inflammation of the vulva. "Thinking that there was a narrow connection between her state of melancholic depression and her vaginal anomaly, we tried to abolish the latter with the progressive use of dilators of different calibers." Success! The vulvitis disappeared. At forty-nine she finally had "a coital act which her husband found completely satisfying [!]. This changed completely Mme. R.'s mental state." Her depression vanished. Indeed, the story had a gratifying outcome, but it showed how closely the presentation of Mme. R.'s depression was influenced by her own ideas of what constituted nervous illness—she had gone to the neurological clinic, after all, believing in Charcot-style hysteria. She had completely internalized the medical doctrines of a reflex link between vagina and brain and agreed with her doctors that successfully treating the one meant curing the pathology of the other.[59]

In his psychological clinic in Paris, Pierre Janet encountered every fashionable symptom imaginable among the young women who came in with depression. For complicated theoretical reasons, Janet did not see their problems as depression but as "abulia," or lack of will. But the basic problems of these patients, who presented with everything they had read about in the newspapers, related to their mood. Some of them believed they were in chronic trances, called "catalepsy" at the time, though Janet does not use the term. Mlle. E., twenty-seven, had been well until her mother died six months ago "last October." (The year is unclear). Then she began blaming herself for the death and for all kinds of imaginary crimes. In January she flipped into a "very exalted" state, to resume self-reproach in April. "Bit by bit she starts refusing to move, to respond." Admitted to the Salpêtrière ten days previously, she was now in a "stupor," awakening from time to time to ask, "Where am I?" She passively let herself be fed liquids. "She clenches her teeth if something solid is given her." This deliberate clamping of the jaw and letting nourishment trickle down the side of one's face occurred commonly in catalepsy.

A month after Mlle E. was presented at rounds she began to get better, first eating and then talking again. Totally recovered three months later, she told her own story, a long history of such highly mannered forms of pathology as "a feeling that everything is strange, an inability to perceive, a kind of veil covering things." All this recalls exactly the kind of chic dissociation—patients spinning in and out of second states and "seeing everything for the first time"—that were witnessed at Paul Sollier's private clinic in the Paris suburb Boulogne-sur-Seine.[60] These phenomena were evidently also encountered among Janet's less-well-to-do patients at the Salpêtrière. Yet Mlle. E. was probably genuinely depressed, and after her recovery discussed the sad feelings and tiredness of life she had experienced following her mother's death.[61]

Has the twentieth century seen distinctive somatic accompaniments to depression? The characteristic features of psychosomatic illness generally in the twentieth century are pain and chronic fatigue. To what extent do these appear today more often in depression than in past times? The question is a very difficult one. Fatigue seems a natural enough companion to a depressed mood, when all bodily and mental functions are slowed. But how about pain? Is the pain of depression somehow distinctive to the late nineteenth and twentieth centuries?

References to physical pain do not leap out of accounts of subjective depression before the late nineteenth century, although pain was often used as a metaphor for psychic distress. To give just a sampling of the evidence, here is a private patient around the early 1860s interested in being admitted to Max Leidesdorf's private clinic in Vienna: "A still young, very well educated, extremely well-bred woman," she was writing to him about her subjective sensations. "No one can imagine what has been going on inside me for the last year. No one could even guess how horribly the pain in my mind [*Seelenpein*] has grown over this time, how I have had to conceal it and bury myself ever deeper in this evil state. A continuous agitation drives me from doctor to doctor. I have found peace nowhere, nowhere a resting place. I tried to busy myself. All, all, in vain." The patient described having anxious, compulsive thoughts as well as contemplating suicide, which she had twice attempted unsuccessfully.

Another example: In 1887 American feminist Charlotte Perkins, in the midst of a psychotic depression and domestic unhappiness, noted in her diary, "I am very sick with nervous prostration, and I think some brain disease as well. No one can ever know what I have suffered in these last five years. Pain pain pain, till my mind has given way." She later clarified what kind of pain she was experiencing: "I went home [from Silas Weir Mitchell's rest cure in Philadelphia], followed those directions rigidly for months, and came perilously near to losing my mind. The mental agony grew so unbearable that I would sit blankly moving my head from side to side—to get out from under the pain. Not physical pain, not the least 'headache' even, just mental torment, and so heavy in its nightmare gloom that it seemed real enough to dodge."[63] These accounts represent typical nineteenth-century presentations of pain in depression: The patients cast it as mental anguish without believing themselves somatically ill.

Later, however, physical pain emerges prominently in subjective accounts of depression. For example, in September 1917 Princess X. was brought by her son and personal physician to a private nervous clinic in Vienna for the treatment of the latest episode of her lifelong manic-depressive illness. She had now been depressed for about a month, demonstrating indecisiveness, delusional notions about impoverishment, self-reproach, insomnia, and "stubborn constipation." In the family's view, she had "overexerted" herself in caring for her sick daughter and grandchild.

At admission she knew where she was and the date, and was well groomed but complained of feeling as though "an iron wheel went about her head. . . . Earlier she had been so happy, so interested in everything, had always a whole bunch of ideas in her head at once. Now she can no longer think, nothing occurs to her, she can't understand anything, her memory is getting worse and worse. In short, she has the feeling that she's becoming demented. . . . God was," in her view, "punishing her for the many sins she has committed." Thus far Princess X. exhibited a typical major depression, of which we have already seen several examples. But on the somatic side she complained of more than just the shopping list of somatic complaints Krafft-Ebing had enumerated. She was tired, so tired that "she was incapable of any activity." And "she is much more sensitive to pain than formerly. Now she always has such a painful feeling at the cervical verterbrae [the neck], it tortures her terribly." Two months later she was discharged well and pain-free.[64] Although it remains to be confirmed by systematic quantitative studies, Princess X. seems to have belonged to the advance guard of twentieth-century depressives, patients whose symptoms focused not so much upon their mood, in the sense of frank melancholia, but on cognitive and physical symptoms. Her paramount symptom was pain. In terms of the fashionability of symptoms, the upper class was leading the way for the rest.

To this upper-class advance guard also belonged Miss Y., a twenty-five-year-old woman from Durham whom Frederick Parkes Weber treated in 1908. Her chief complaint was the continued presence of pain at the site of an appendectomy incision made eight years earlier. She had also been vomiting for the last eight months. "No actual abdominal or thoracic pain [is] connected with the vomiting," noted Parkes Weber in the chart, "but 'feeling of nausea' under the lower part of sternum! Subject to headaches and bursting sensation in head this year. . . . 'Lumbago' [lower back pain] six weeks ago. Formerly right sciatic pain occasionally."

Parkes Weber examined her, describing a "well-built, rather slight, rather pale" woman. There were no organic findings. "The man to whom she was engaged for three years or so has lately broken off his engagement and gone to South Africa—and this, I believe, accounts for some of the gastric disorder et cetera." Prescribing the spas of Baden-Baden, Territet, and Saint Moritz, Parkes Weber noted at the top of the chart, "Nausea of uncertain cause; mental depression."[65] Miss Y. represented a still more enhanced form than Princess X. of somatized depression in the twentieth century: Her mood complaints were minimal and emphasis was entirely on the somatic, especially on pain.

A final somatic pattern that characterizes twentieth-century depression is gluing oneself to a fixed diagnosis, attributing all one's problems not to internal guilt or inadequacy but to some external agency, such as a virus or an immune disorder. Such unshakable self-diagnoses as chronic fatigue syndrome and fibrositis have made great progress since the 1960s.[66] Many though not all patients who have given themselves disease labels of this quasi-delusional fixity are depressed. One study showed, for example, that 67 percent of chronic fatigue patients were currently depressed, and that 50 percent of them had experienced a major depression prior to the onset of their present illness.[67] Of a sample of chronic fatigue patients seen at the Institute for Psychiatric Research in London, Simon Wessely and his colleagues found that a minimum of 47 percent currently had an affective disorder, which usually means depression.[68] While the fashionable diseases of today may not simply be reduced to depression, to some extent they do represent new somatic forms of age-old illnesses of mood.

In the interaction between biology and culture, depression sits astride a fence. On the one hand, major depressive and manic-depressive illnesses have a clear biochemical foundation in disturbances of neurotransmitters within the brain and in a history of affective illness within the family.[69] From recent research it seems that one of the chemical bases of melancholia is a disruption of the metabolism of a class of chemical called amines.[70] But the physical symptoms of depression also mirror, in the way that psychosomatic illness generally does, larger cultural conceptions of what constitutes legitimate and illegitimate disease. In the eighteenth century stricken individuals developed pseudoepilepsy in addition to the standard somatic accompaniments of depressed mood; in the nineteenth century, paralyses, peculiar anesthesias, constrictions of vision, and catalepsy; in the twentieth, chronic pain and fatigue syndromes. These disorders are all culturally, not biologically, determined. They are mandated by the views of the patient's larger social group about the appropriate presentation of distress. It is more this cultural context than individual life circumstances and history that determine the specific somatic symptoms a depressed person will take on. Here again, as with the influence of ethnicity, social class, and other social factors, we see the cultural world the patient inhabits determining the kind of psychosomatic symptoms he or she will adopt.

6

———

Youth and Psychosomatic Illness

AMONG THE SOCIAL CATEGORIES that seem to shape certain symptoms is age. People of a certain age usually share the ideas about illness they all acquired when they were young. Elderly people today, for example, often dwell on "hypoglycemia" as the cause of their woes, for it was a fashionable diagnosis in the 1950s, while young people now ascribe their problems to "chronic fatigue syndrome," an unusual diagnosis in the elderly. But certain kinds of psychosomatic symptoms do cluster by age, regardless of when the individuals grew up. Men over sixty-five have six times as many problems with irritable bowel syndrome as do men under forty-five.[1] In the past, young women were much more prone to develop a psychologically caused paralysis of the muscles than older women, and "hysteria" counted as a young woman's illness.[2]

For both biological and cultural reasons youth are more prone to psychosomatic problems than the elderly. In our society young people are often less sure of themselves and may fend off anxiety about attaining adulthood through a defensive screen of physical symptoms. Chronic psychosomatic problems may have a genetic basis and would afflict the young before the elderly, as genes express themselves early in life. For a variety of social and biological reasons, one's relationship to one's body is different in youth than in maturity.

Doctors have always known this without necessarily being able to explain why. Medical theorizing about differences in symptoms between young and old reaches far back in time. Edinburgh physician John Buchan, author of a best-selling eighteenth-century health care guide, said in 1769 that "proper attention to the patient's age," among other things, would "greatly assist both in the investigation and treatment of diseases.

"In childhood the fibers are lax and soft, the nerves extremely irritable, and the fluids thin; whereas in old age the fibres are rigid, the nerves become almost insensible, and many of the vessels imperviable. These and other peculiarities render the diseases of the young and aged very different."[3] Though couched in physiological terms, such descriptions were used in the eighteenth-century to explain hysteria in the young.

Nineteenth-century writers uniformly associated hysteria with youth. Hysteria, said London society doctor Russell Reynolds in 1872, "usually commences at about the time of puberty, i.e. between twelve and eighteen years of age; but when once developed, the symptoms may remain throughout life."[4] Men were subject to it after thirty-five. "On the basis of my own impressions," said Leopold Löwenfeld, who had an extensive private practice toward the end of the nineteenth century, "the ages fifteen to twenty-five seem to me to offer the most favorable conditions for the development of hysteria."[5] For Löwenfeld and his contemporaries, hysteria was chiefly an illness of the young.

Statistics also point to an early onset. In the 1830s, when Hector Landouzy was an intern in the Paris hospitals, he collected information on 355 female hysteria patients. Forty-three percent of these women had experienced the onset of their symptoms by the age of twenty; in only a handful did symptoms commence past thirty-five. By hysteria Landouzy understood the standard items of the day, such as a lump in the throat (*boule hystérique*) and fits.[6] Pierre Briquet divided his 450 female hysteria patients from the Charité Hospital into those who were predisposed (a family history of hysteria) and nonpredisposed: Among the nonpredisposed, the first attack occurred on average at age twenty-two; among the predisposed the age of the first attack ranged from fourteen to twenty-one.[7] (Even when we get away from the term hysteria and look at young people with other kinds of psychosomatic diagnoses,

the female disproportion remains. During the late 1830s, in the
Paris hospitals, among patients with "neuralgia," which then
meant localized pain without an obvious organic cause, women
outweighed men by four to one up to age thirty.[8]) Of 92 patients
with long-standing psychosomatic illnesses seen at a clinic in the
1980s in Toronto, 26 percent were under the age of twenty when
they first experienced their symptoms.[9]

Early onset of psychosomatic illness is probably a durable characteristic that reappears in most times and places. It may be that
adolescents somehow feel more in need of coping strategies than
do adults, or that their strategies tend to involve the body more.
So little research has been done on these matters that it is difficult
to say. We know only that youth are more at risk of breakdowns in
the mind-body relationship.[10]

Among the psychosomatic disorders to which youth have been
heir, those affecting the appetite have figured prominently. This
has been especially true of young women. In 1936 William
Houston, a Georgia physician and professor of medicine, noted
how enduringly feeble the appetites of his young, middle-class female patients could be. He recalled "Miss Thelma Smallwood,"
who by the age of thirty had become a classic somatizer. "Her ro-
bust and cheerful sister was happily married, but the only attention from men that Miss Smallwood had was from the various
doctors who came, listened, and prescribed. Her life was a martyrdom of headache, backache, menstrual disturbances, insomnia,
and particularly discomforts connected with eating." It was odd,
remarked Houston, that "she had reached the age of thirty without an appendectomy." To all proposals for betterment Thelma
was receptive enough but would add, "I know I can't do it."

Thelma evoked in Houston the same reaction that chronically
neurotic patients provoked in many physicians: "Thelma was the
kind of patient that seems to take strength out of the doctor and
leave him limp. Listening to her gentle toneless wail of symptoms,
he feels disposed to make a quick exit and go where the therapeutic field is more promising."

"I never want to eat," she said. "I try to eat to please Mamma,
but everything I eat makes me feel worse."

Houston prescribed chocolate milkshakes "to be taken at 10 A.M., 4 P.M. and 9:30 P.M. with thickly buttered crackers." "On this regime, Miss Smallwood gained weight until she was almost plump, her smiles became more frequent, her tears rarer. This gain, I regret to report, was not very solid. Each family embarrassment and difficulty bowled her over, and the climb had to be made again."[11] Dr. Houston gave us a very specific cultural address for the Thelma Smallwoods of this world: They were middle class, young, and female. He might have added one more quality: late Victorian. Thelma Smallwood and her fellow sufferers were a creation of the nineteenth century. Her genteel lack of appetite would spill over in a new century-specific illness: anorexia nervosa.

The Symptom of Self-Starvation

Disturbed eating lends itself easily as a symbol of dysphoria. Youth are very sensitive to weight and easily acquire modish ideas about diet and appetite. Eating too much or too little may communicate subliminal messages in a household in which the giving of food is associated, as it is in the modern family, with the giving of care. When food refusal spills over into truly pathological self-starvation, threatening death, it is called anorexia nervosa, a throwback to the time when psychiatric illness was called "nervous" (anorexia means lack of appetite). A variant illness is pathological cramming, often alternating with purging and vomiting, called bulimia nervosa (bulimia literally meaning "the hunger of an ox"). Such food-related symptoms, which are psychosomatic in nature, deranging the relationship between mind and body,[12] affect women ten times as often as men.[13] Self-starvation, which arose in the nineteenth century, offers an important insight into the cultural creation of symptoms among the young. Anorexia nervosa today offers an equally interesting example of how the larger culture and the medical profession perpetuate and legitimate symptoms that in and of themselves are no more independent disease entities than were spinal irritation and ovarian hysteria.

With anorexia nervosa, culture and biology intersect. The disorder pays a heavy tribute to biology, ending fatally in perhaps one case out of ten.[14] It is, along with suicide in depression, one of the few psychiatric illnesses that can have a fatal outcome. It has a genetic component as well. Researchers at Johns Hopkins University and the National Institute of Mental Health studied the first-degree relatives of twenty-four patients with anorexia (and the relatives of forty-three normal individuals as controls), finding affective disorders of all kinds to be far commoner among the families of the anorexics. The transmission of major affective disorders from generation to generation within the same family seems to be genetic, and the authors speculated that anorexia, which clusters alongside such disorders, might also be genetic.[15] An English study found that, among twenty-five female twin pairs from the same egg, in which one twin had anorexia nervosa, the other twin had it too 56 percent of the time. By contrast, when the female twins were from different eggs, the second twin got it only 5 percent of the time. On the basis of these and other data, the authors concluded that "the propensity to develop anorexia nervosa is significantly genetically determined."[16] So the biology of illness is powerfully implicated.

But society is drawn in as well. Anorexia nervosa is highly culture-specific, virtually unknown outside Western Europe and North America.[17] Nor was anorexia nervosa familiar before 1800 in any setting, with the possible exception of the self-denying saints of the Middle Ages and the isolated fasting maidens of early-modern Europe—young females who were said to go "for years" without eating.[18]

The term *anorexia nervosa* is often used as though it were a separate disease, like mumps or polio, a condition that nature itself has defined that will manifest itself in any time or place as long as the conditions are right. But is anorexia nervosa a distinct disease, or is it merely an item in the symptom pool that the unconscious mind may call forth as an expression of distress? If it is merely one among numberless interchangeable psychosomatic symptoms, it would be overblown to speak of the "discovery" of anorexia nervosa, just as one would not speak of the discovery of hysterical aphonia or of reflex paralysis. These phenomena are culturally induced artifacts. Talk of discoveries and diseases also tends to reinforce the behavior of patients who have taken on the symptom of self-starvation, encouraging them to cling to it the more fiercely in the belief that they have a real disease, as opposed to an almost whimsical symptom choice on the part of the unconscious mind. (The argument that many anorexia patients deny illness is unconvincing; to the contrary, they cherish their diagnosis and are loathe to part with symptoms that they readily agree are pathological.[19])

Medical writers today ascribe to anorexia nervosa certain presumably fixed and recurrent characteristics that are supposed to differentiate it from other forms of food refusal. To qualify for the diagnosis, a patient must exhibit several supplementary features, in addition to not eating and losing weight, such as having a distorted body image or an intense fear of fatness.[20] Historians of anorexia as well have engaged in the same game of differentiating true anorexia nervosa from other manifestations of self-starvation. Because of the impossibility of knowing whether patients in past times had a distorted body image, some writers have proposed the added criterion of hyperactivity, in an effort to apply the diagnosis retrospectively.[21]

The problem with insisting on all these extra features in order to identify true anorexia nervosa, is that food refusal is merely one symptom among many and not a distinct disease at all. The search for additional qualifying criteria therefore needlessly limits the scope and creates artificial categories. If the individual's refusal to eat is not the result of some other psychiatric illness such as depression,[22] or of an organic disease such as cancer or tuberculosis, then we are dealing with anorexia nervosa, or voluntary self-starvation.

There is a curious discontinuity in anorexia's history. Self-starvation has been familiar ever since the second half of the nineteenth century, and experienced an increase in frequency some time after World War II. But the explanations that seem to work well for this original nineteenth-century increase are largely inapplicable to today, and vice versa. The majority of young women who refused food in the nineteenth century manifested neither intense fears about overweight, nor hyperactivity, nor distorted body images (or at least if they had them, they were silent about them).[23] Yet the outcome of their behavior was the same as today: emaciation and death.

If they did not exhibit today's extra features of anorexia nervosa, neither did they suffer today's presumed cause: the mania for thinness. The first great increase in the disorder seems linked to distinctive patterns of intimacy in nineteenth-century family life, in which young women sought refuge from all-devouring smother love by fleeing the family dinner table, an elective focus of this new intimacy. Just as hysterical paralysis could serve as a pretext for retiring from the ebb and flow of family life, so could the refusal of food.[24] Today, however, the modern family of the nineteenth century—with its common mealtimes, its omnipresent stay-at-home mother, and its patriarchal father—has largely disappeared. Postmodern family life has become so fragmented that escape from it seems hardly an issue—so little remains to escape from. Yet young women today refuse food more often than ever before, giving rise to a flock of other explanations stressing societal demands for slimness and an idealized beauty. These explanations are largely inapplicable to the nineteenth century, when young women felt little social pressure to be slim. Indeed many women believed that men preferred corpulence in feminine beauty. Therefore in the history of anorexia nervosa the form of the illness remains the same—self-starvation and subsequent wasting away—but the explanations that seem to work for the nineteenth and twentieth centuries are entirely discontinuous.

How Symptoms Are Created

When one wants to achieve emaciation there are basically three ways to do it. One can refuse food on the grounds that one's stomach hurts or on the grounds that one is not hungry, or one can vomit up one's meals. All three forms of food refusal became common in the nineteenth century, well before the appearance in 1873 of the formal diagnosis of anorexia nervosa. It is these three forms that are historically new—the widespread use of refusing food in order to attain emaciation—and not the specific disease of anorexia nervosa. These are the culture-specific symptoms called forth by the nineteenth century.

Of the three, refusing to eat on the grounds that one's bodily organs simply cannot accept the food—that eating makes one's stomach hurt—is probably the most archaic, in that it dates back longer in time and dissolves earlier as a justification for modern anorexia. This kind of justification once flourished because it corresponded to the medical diagnostics of the day, and because it was then impossible to "disprove." For example, patients in the nineteenth century often refused food on the grounds that it "would not go down" or "got stuck in the throat," a kind of early self-diagnosis that would later disappear as X rays made it possible to show when getting stuck possessed an organic basis and when it did not. In 1823, Salomon Stiebel, a physician in Frankfurt, reported the case of a sixteen-year-old girl who had fallen in love. She was the only daughter of wealthy parents who had "spoiled her greatly." Unfortunately, the parents disapproved of the romance and

> it became clear to the girl that she must terminate relations with her friend. . . . The moment that this was told her, she felt a heavy pressure on the lower region of the esophagus [*die Cardia*], became pale and breathless, was unable to speak, and had to sit down. . . . From this day on, the unpleasant, anxious, pressing feeling in the esophagus returned daily; it came at the same time, midday, as on the first occasion, and lasted with variable intensity until nine in the evening. Neither during this interval, nor at any other time, was she able to eat solid food. The food remained sticking in the esophagus, and only after some time, as a result of its natural weight, did it reach the stomach. The patient felt that even tube-fed liquids remained sticking.

She began to shudder every time food was offered, able to ingest only tea. Other symptoms developed: pain at the slightest pressure on her sternum, an anesthesia of one hand, a dry cough. After a month had passed, she was able to drink a glass of milk every night at nine but at no other time. Now the skin of her face and brow could tolerate no touching; her facial muscles began to twitch. She started to become emaciated. Signs of catalepsy began to appear, "in which she heard everything but did not answer and was unable to move. For a long time to come she was able to eat only in the evening, and whenever she became emotional, she was thrust again into this somnambulic state with a feeling in the esophagus as though a wheel were turning in there."[25]

The case indicates that patients who selected the symptom of self-starvation were merely grasping one among many items in the symptom pool. This young woman responded to her parents' abrupt decision by not eating. Having no recognized diagnosis of anorexia nervosa on which to pattern her behavior, she selected for her protest other symptoms as well, such as paralysis, anesthesia, and catalepsy.[26] These symptoms made sense to the medicine of the day. (Stiebel, her doctor, had been a strong believer in animal magnetism, in which such symptoms flourished.) Later, however, catalepsy, paralysis, and the like would become illegitimate, and patients who selected self-starvation would cease choosing them as well.

Numerous patients in the years before the official discovery of anorexia nervosa justified their inability to eat on the basis of pain and misfunctioning body parts. In the late 1860s Guendalina X., a seventeen-year-old daughter of one of the fine old families of Bologna, suddenly began eating less and less. As the anxious family observed her day after day at the dinner table, she claimed, "It simply won't go down," or that she was able to swallow only after great effort. Giovanni Brugnoli, the head of medicine at the university hospital in Bologna, examined her with a long tube, or sound, and was unable to discover any defect in the esophagus. Her menses disappeared. Even though emaciated, she still was able to undertake long walks. The desperate family granted her wish to enter a nunnery in Rome, where she continued to refuse to eat, dying three months later in July 1869. A second young female patient of Professor Brugnoli's also complained that the food would "not go down" and also died of starvation.[27]

Other patients wanted to bring their behavior into close conformity with medical diagnoses, and would give up refusing food when they failed to convince. Some time in the 1860s, Frederic

Skey, a London society doctor and consultant to Saint Bartholomew's Hospital, admitted a young woman whose troubles in swallowing dated back two months. "She was a very respectable person in character and position, and had been for several years a much esteemed servant in a good family, and was a young woman of some education." A number of other consultants had already examined her esophagus with sounds ("probangs"), finding nothing. "As the obstruction increased, nothing but semi-liquid food passed into her stomach, and this was only effected with a difficult and painful effort. She became emaciated by reason of defective nutrition, and by the time of her admission into the Hospital was weak and somewhat attenuated in form." Skey immediately discarded the diagnosis of cancer of the esophagus, refused to examine her throat any further, and began treating her with medicines and nutrient enemas. Within three weeks she was eating steak. "She was in high spirits at her recovery, and the only vexation she suffered arose from my refusal to pass a probang down her throat before she left the hospital."[28] Her idea of a satisfactory justification for refusing food had been a "stricture" in her esophagus and she felt obliged to abandon the symptom once she realized that Skey entirely disbelieved in it.

Here, for example, is "inability to chew" as a patient's idea of a medical diagnosis justifying food refusal. In 1881 Silas Weir Mitchell described a female patient in his private clinic (when she was admitted is unclear) who suffered from "an apparent inability to chew. Food rests in the mouth until helplessly removed by a nurse or is half passively let fall out by the patient." Mitchell advised her to move her jaw with her hands, "which she did for a while until the power or the belief in the power to chew came back."[29] After anorexia nervosa became widely known as an official diagnosis, such behavior would be abandoned, as patients realized how they had to behave in order to be taken seriously with the diagnosis of this new "disease."

Internal medicine in these years created a number of alternative diagnostic labels for patients whose basic problem was self-starvation, labels that surfaced before the term *anorexia nervosa* was invented and that flourished alongside it for decades.[30] As early as 1840 the Berlin neurologist Moritz Romberg described "gastric neuralgia" as a separate disease entity.[31] In the 1850s and perhaps earlier patients began turning up with self-diagnoses of neuralgic stomach conditions as the justification for their unwillingness to eat. Louis-Victor Marcé, director of a private asylum in Paris, described in 1860 a strange form of "dyspepsia" that struck young women at the time of puberty. To be sure, some of the patients complained only of a complete distaste for food. Others, however, were hungry enough, but implicated "painful digestion, accompanied by the production of gas, of tiredness and malaise." This was the new stomach-pain complaint. Both varieties of dyspepsia, Marcé claimed, were "very common." In both "the patients arrive at the delusional idea that they must not and cannot eat. In a word, the gastric neurosis transforms itself into a cerebral neurosis." After describing how little these patients ate, Marcé pointed out that "their emaciation reaches the outer limits. Any trace of adipose tissue has disappeared, and the patients are reduced to a skeletal state."[32] Romberg, Marcé, and other midcentury writers on stomach disorders had legitimated the refusing of food on the grounds that a neurotic stomach was incapable of receiving it.

In the last quarter of the nineteenth century, food refusal on the pretext of gastric neurosis flourished in Central Europe. The distinguished internists and neurologists of Berlin and Vienna described ever-newer forms. In 1882 Ernst von Leyden, the professor of medicine in Berlin, attributed the refusal of his young female patients to eat to "nervous dyspepsia. . . . The sensitivity of the stomach can reach such an extent in these cases that the most intense pain arises after each meal, or else there is an unpleasant sensation of anxiety and oppression, so that the patients eat less and less and find themselves in an extreme degree of emaciation and marasmus. I have seen such cases last from six months to three years."[33] In 1897 the Berlin internist Ottomar Rosenbach used the term "emotional dyspepsia" to describe female patients who, troubled by digestive complaints, simply stopped eating, becoming "almost cachectic."[34]

In Vienna it was quite common for professors of the university faculty and for owners of private clinics to see young women wasting away on the pretext that their stomachs felt unreceptive to food. In 1880 Moritz Rosenthal, professor of electrotherapy and owner of a select private clinic, treated a twenty-year-old woman who had stopped eating everything except milk and raw eggs because of "intense stomach pain," and had grown "very thin and weak." Diagnosing "gastric neurasthenia," Rosenthal gave her the usual clinic therapies, so that by the fall of that year she could again "enjoy roasts [Braten] and beer." "In two other similar cases of extreme anemia with gastric complaints, which also affected young women, I was struck by the extreme emaciation."[35]

It is clear that long before anorexia nervosa became a familiar medical concept, refusing food because the anatomical parts did not appear to work was common among middle-class young women. Medical theories of the day, which emphasized reflex neurosis and gastric neurosis, abetted this belief in jaws that would not chew and stomachs that failed to digest. These theories would be discredited by the invention of the gastroscope (1889) and the X ray (1895), which showed if an ulcer was really the cause of the stomach pain or a stricture the reason for the esophagus's failure to swallow. Once this medical technology began to disallow patients' theories about body parts that would not work, food refusal shifted to justifications that science would find it more difficult to disprove.

The two justifications for not eating that have prevailed from the late nineteenth century until today were vomiting and lack of appetite. Both were impossible to disprove medically, for the doctor could not explain to the patient that science had made the symptom impossible, as it had belief in a supposed esophageal stricture. The mechanisms of appetite and vomiting even today are too dimly understood for science to rule them out as illegal symptoms. Accordingly these new symptoms suited perfectly the needs of young patients who, for reasons of their own, wished not to eat. Patients who were "just not hungry" or "just felt like vomiting" could not be contradicted.

If a symptom as ubiquitous as vomiting can be said to have a modern history, the role of vomiting in self-starvation became established sometime in the last quarter of the nineteenth century. Vomiting without an organic cause, known as "chlorosis" or "hyperemesis hysterica," is probably as old as time.[36] But not until late in the nineteenth century was it purposely used to achieve significant weight loss.

Before these developments women who vomited systematically do not seem to have lost weight, which means they were not vomiting very resolutely and probably not intent on self-starvation. The York physician Thomas Laycock said in 1840 of "hysteric vomiting," that often the stomach was "so irritable that it rejects every kind of food and drink for many weeks in succession . . . without inducing much emaciation, but often rather increased embonpoint."[37]

In January 1854 Louise Lesage, age twenty-two and an assistant teacher in a girls' school, was admitted to the Charité Hospital in Paris for exhaustion and limb weakness of apparently psychological origin. Her problems had started at age seventeen with a year-long attack of depression, in the midst of which she "acquired a distaste for all foods and was taken by vomiting which lasted for eighteen months. During the first ten months she was given nutrient enemas." She was finally cured by a "folkloric remedy" involving placing hot bricks dipped in brandy between her thighs. What is of interest is that during this year-and-a-half-long seige of vomiting she did not become emaciated. Self-starvation was clearly not on her agenda.[38] Nor was emaciation evidently the goal of Sarah G., a delicate twenty-year-old woman admitted to Saint George's Hospital in London in October 1869 with a yearlong history of abdominal pain and vomiting. Although she vomited continually on the ward and could not be moved from bed, "no positive emaciation [was] produced." After some conflict with hospital staff and a change in wards, she evidently attained whatever goal the vomiting had served: "She entirely ceased to complain of pain and to vomit; and gradually she ate ordinary food."[39]

These anecdotes capture the setting. But quantitative observations as well suggest that psychogenic vomiting, though common throughout the nineteenth century, did not produce the kind of emaciation required by anorexia nervosa until the century's last quarter. Among the 312 female patients with hysteria seen by Joseph Amann at the Munich university outpatient clinic and in his private practice between 1861 and 1868, 12 percent experienced regular vomiting. Amann observed that such vomiting was seldom accompanied by dramatic weight reduction.[40] In 1869 Samuel Wilks said of hysterical vomiting: "Sickness is one of the most troublesome and obstinate of all hysteric disorders, because the organ having got into the bad habit of discharging its contents upwards can with difficulty be broken of it. It is remarkable that in these cases of daily vomiting, [that which is] characteristic of the hysteric condition, the plumpness or absence of emaciation, still persists."[41]

Writing in 1881 of his long practice, Weir Mitchell said of such vomiting: "I can now recall five cases of hysteria lasting from fifteen to twenty-five years. All are bed-ridden; and while four have [stomach] contractions, three are in the habit of vomiting every meal, and have done this for years. One has actually grown stout under this. . . . The others are at least not wasted, and you ask yourself in vain how they live upon the small amount they seem to retain."[42] It is highly likely that in these years psychogenic vomiting was not used for the purpose of weight reduction.

The big change seems to have begun in the 1870s, a possible result, though unacknowledged by patients, of the forging in 1873 of the formal diagnosis anorexia nervosa. Whereas no report of which I am aware had previously linked systematic vomiting to emaciation, a trickle of such cases now appears, to turn into a flood in the 1880s. In the 1870s in Königsberg, Bernhard Naunyn, who treated nervous diseases as well as internal-medicine cases, commented on the number of young Polish Jewish women who would come to his clinic, "close to starvation, because they vomited up everything they ate, that is, they spit it up. He referred to these cases not as anorexia nervosa but as "childish neuroses of imagination."[43] The discussion in 1873 in London surrounding the establishment of a formal diagnosis of anorexia hysterica reminded Brudenell Carter, a London eye surgeon and authority on hysteria, of an emaciated female patient he had seen who "always thought of putrid cat-pudding when pressed to eat; thus food caused her to vomit." Finally frightened at her own weight loss, she "gave in, confessed how she had caused the dislike for food, began to eat, and recovered."[44] This represents one of the earliest cases of excessive weight loss from psychogenic vomiting.

Possibly because the new diagnosis of anorexia nervosa had made such an impact when announced in the 1870s, the 1880s saw in England numerous reports of vomiting leading to emaciation, though few made specific reference to anorexia hysterica or anorexia nervosa. In the spring of 1882 John Bristowe, a neurologist at Saint Thomas's Hospital in London, treated "a distinctly hysterical young girl who had been constantly vomiting for about four months and who had consequently become extremely thin and weak."[45] In 1884 Clifford Allbutt, a well-known internist in Leeds, distinguished between "hysterical vomiting," an affliction of silly young women leading to fatness, and "gastric vomiting," a real but invisible affliction of the stomach nerves "leading straitly to emaciation." His cases of "gastric vomiting" sound much like what other writers might have called anorexia nervosa: In Miss X., seen in 1881, an initial "facial neuralgia" had given way to stomach pain and vomiting. "The vomiting had gained upon her, and now she vomits all her food. . . . She is emaciated, but all functions and organs seem normal. There is no evidence of hysteria." (By "hysteria" Allbutt understood a condition rendering the patient "of feeble purpose, of limited reason, of foolish impulse, of wanton humours, of irregular or depraved appetites" and so on.)[46]

Using the label "severe hysteria," a doctor in small-town England described in 1888 a woman of eighteen, a dressmaker, who suffered from persistent vomiting, "nothing being retained, not even cold water; and when food was not taken frothy mucus was being regurgitated in large quantities all day long." The patient was "nothing but a bag of skin and bones." The doctor took her into his own home and, with the aid of daily two-hour massages, restored her to health. "During the last twelve months," he said, "about a dozen cases in all of severe hysteria, neurasthenia, and chronic dyspepsia have come under my personal care."[47]

Evident in many accounts of patients whose earnest vomiting emaciates them is their great impressionability. Here is another Miss X., aged twenty-nine when young Dr. Hale White of Guy's Hospital saw her for "hysterical vomiting and aphonia" for the first time in 1883. He put her into a private clinic for an "isolation cure." "At first the vomiting was very frequent; plain milk was returned, and she lost seventeen pounds in twenty days. Even enemata [nutritive enemas] were not retained, till one day the nurse accidentally said this was very strange, for only paralyzed patients returned enemata, and this one certainly was not paralyzed; after that remark all the enemata were retained." She was discharged cured but relapsed three years later, this time pursuing her vomiting so energetically as to become, after seven months in another private clinic, "a mere skeleton, vomiting everything she took, even plain water." White restored her in six weeks with massage and the other details of a firmly conducted rest cure.[48] The very impressionability of these patients may explain this sudden trend to emaciation. It is not inconceivable that such young women as Miss X. had by 1883 heard of the new disease anorexia nervosa, and realized that, to qualify for it, they must engage in vomiting far more relentlessly than ever before, using a quite familiar neurotic symptom in a new way in order to achieve substantial emaciation.

In other countries as well, vomiting became known in the 1880s as a route to emaciation for young women. It was at the spa of Marienbad (now Mariánské Lásznê) in Bohemia that Heinrich Kisch, among the most famous spa physicians of his day, saw numerous cases of "uterine dyspepsia," stomach problems attributed to the uterus. In 1888, for example, Kisch reported the case of Frau N., a twenty-eight-year-old woman married to a merchant, who had experienced "intense dyspeptic complaints" ever since the birth of her last child three years earlier. The waters of Carlsbad (now Karlovy Vary) and Ems had demonstrated themselves powerless against this malady, noted Kisch. Now she would try Marienbad: "The patient always vomits a short time after eating and disembarrasses herself more or less of whatever she has consumed. As a result she is now extremely emaciated [*ausserordentlich heruntergekommen*], and this formerly so lively and cheerful woman has now become tired of life." Kisch first fitted her with a vaginal pessary, on the grounds that a backward-tilting uterus might be causing a reflex neurosis, and then gave her a six-week course of the Marienbad waters, after which she gained twelve pounds.[49]

It was such a case that launched the career of medical-natur-
opath Max Bircher-Benner in Zurich. In 1895, four years out of
medical school, he was called to a female patient with a chronic
stomach complaint who had already been seen by a number of
physicians:

I treated her with all the remedies I had learned and consulted
the relevant textbooks. The X ray had not yet been discovered.
Her stomach was extremely enlarged and atonic. The food remained sitting in it, and when it filled up, it was emptied
through vomiting. The woman was emaciated and very weak.
She could no longer get out of bed. I ordered the kind of diet I
had been taught, washed out her stomach early every morning,
evacuating the numerous food debris. Weeks-long treatment of
this nature brought no improvement. To the contrary. I was at
my wits' end. I considered the case hopeless.

Then Bircher-Benner conceived the notion of giving her a raw
vegetable diet, and with her recovery his career as a naturopath
was launched.[50]

In the twentieth century this kind of chronic vomiting and emaciation would finally be reckoned to the disorder anorexia nervosa.
In the years after 1900, vomiting remained a constant though
minor theme in the self-starvation of young women. For example,
of 117 cases of anorexia nervosa seen at the Mayo Clinic in
Rochester, Minnesota, over the period 1917 to 1929, vomiting occurred in 56 percent. Twenty percent were characterized by the
combination of stomach pain and vomiting.[51]

William Houston recalled in 1936 "Miss Nannie Peters,"
twenty-one, a farmer's daughter, and the eldest of ten children,
who had been "a heavy girl, weighing 127 pounds [58 kilograms].
She then began having discomfort after eating, heaviness, fulness,
belching, constipation. From regurgitation of food she passed to
active vomiting." By the time Houston saw Miss Peters, her
weight had dropped 34 percent. Houston told an intern in the
hospital about the case. The intern replied, "There have been
three cases here [at the university hospital in Augusta] recently,
very much like this."[52] In rural Georgia in the 1920s and 1930s,
vomiting to achieve emaciation was quite a familiar phenomenon.

Of a sample of fifty-nine women with anorexia nervosa (and no history of bulimia) seen in Toronto in the 1980s, 24 percent had a history of vomiting to achieve emaciation.[53] It is clear that the symptom of psychogenic vomiting, already quite common before the emergence of anorexia nervosa as a formal diagnosis, became bent to the needs of this new disease after the 1870s.[54]

Loss of Appetite and the Launching of Anorexia Nervosa

The principal means of self-starvation in modern times has been claiming that one simply is not hungry. It is an irrefutable argument, for the statement that one has no appetite cannot be disproved. Loss of appetite, relatively unusual in the eighteenth century, flourished in the nineteenth long before the rise of anorexia nervosa as an official disease and would persist alongside it—without necessarily receiving the label—well into the twentieth. What is the meaning of this core psychosomatic symptom of loss of appetite?

In a premodern society of scarcity, loss of appetite in the absence of organic disease claimed little credibility as a symptom. The unconscious always attempts to produce physical symptoms that will be taken as evidence of real disease, and in an era where most of the population did not get enough to eat, loss of appetite would have been interpreted as madness or evidence of demonic possession. Outside the theater of the fasting girls, carrying on as objects of local celebrity by not eating "for years," the psychogenic refusal to eat was not common before 1800. In the nineteenth century dramatic changes in the basic conditions of life began. Industrial growth, a revolution in agriculture, the import of foodstuffs from overseas in the holds of iron ships, rising per capita incomes—all contributed to increasing calorie intake, at least for the middle classes. But this was a middle class that was rapidly growing in numbers. The refusal of food now ceased to be evidence of insanity but instead was taken as a possible consequence of a new kind of disease, nervous disease. The principal nervous disease for young women was hysteria. And nineteenth-century physicians increasingly encountered the phenomenon of hysterical young women who would not eat. Thomas Laycock said in 1840 of anorexia, "In no chronic disease is this symptom so constant and so strongly marked as in hysteria. . . . Women generally love notoriety, and to excite approbation, wonder, or admiration." Laycock assimilated his food-refusing patients to the "fasting women" of yore but noted how common approximations of the phenomenon had become in his own time. "Nothing is more true than that a hysterical girl will live and look fat on an incredibly small quantity of food, and that exclusively vegetable."[55] Briquet commented in 1859 on loss of appetite in hysteria: "The digestive functions are often abolished, the appetite generally weak or capricious. . . . It may even happen that hysterics take up eating one kind of food alone, sugar for example or jam."[56] In 1860 Max Leidesdorf said, after discussing food refusal in depressives, "Hysterical girls and women as well do without food occasionally for more or less long periods. Yet in such cases abstinence is never complete . . . ," and the patients recovered soon.[57]

Around midcentury the frequency accelerates of reports of hysterical patients whose abstinence did lead to emaciation.[58] In 1860 Louis-Victor Marcé described "hysterical" young women in his private Paris clinic whose loss of appetite had caused stark physical changes. He had recently seen, for example, a girl of fourteen from the South of France who seven months previously had been taken with "a profound distate for food. . . . Her anorexia steadily increased. The patient took every day as little nourishment as possible, a few spoonfuls of soup perhaps, and even they were swallowed only with extreme repugnance. The patient would stare at her plate for an hour before deciding to swallow them. When Marcé first saw her in June 1858, she had only begun to grow thin. Away from her family, she did better. But then in October she returned to her family and relapsed, "experiencing the same disgust, refusing food, and contenting herself each day with a cup of café au lait and three or four grams of bread. A trip to Nice, the exhortations of the family—all were to no avail. When she returned anew to Marcé's clinic in March 1859, "her emaciation was extreme, and the appearance of her body was such that she could not go out without attracting attention."[59] Now "hysterical" food refusal was leading to genuine emaciation.

In 1873 anorexia nervosa was discovered as a disease category, although it was, in reality, just an extreme form of the kind of food refusal that had manifested itself throughout the nineteenth century in the form of stomach pain, vomiting, and lack of appetite. But it was seized on by physicians as an exact scientific description of a hitherto vague clinical package of symptoms. It was also grasped by patients anxious to justify their lack of appetite in terms of a legitimate nervous disease. (One remembers that hysteria, neurasthenia, neuroses, and the like were considered to be invisible but real afflictions of the nerves.) In 1873 Ernest-Charles Lasègue, professor of clinical medicine at the Necker Hospital in Paris, formalized the diagnosis of "hysterical anorexia."[60] This label elicited some uneasiness, because a few anorexia cases were male (and many patients did not display what were becoming known as the Charcotian "stigmata" of hysteria, the anesthesias, convulsions, and a sensation of a lump in the throat). Thus a year later the English internist William Gull proposed the term "anorexia nervosa."[61]

The typical victim of hysterical anorexia, Lasègue said, was a young woman fifteen to twenty who had just suffered an emotional shock. She might at first feel some discomfort around her stomach after eating and resolve to "diminish her food." "At the end of some weeks there is no longer a supposed temporary repugnance, but a refusal of food that may be indefinitely prolonged. The disease is now declared." She eats less and less, suppressing one article of food after another and discontinuing entire meals. But months may pass without her general health seeming impaired; indeed she feels more energetic than ever before. Lasègue noted her mental state, despite all this bounding about, as one of quietude. "Not only does she not sigh for recovery, but she is not ill-pleased with her condition, notwithstanding all the unpleasantness it is attended with." Sooner or later her menses stop, and such importance did the nineteenth-century medical mind attach to menstruation that Lasègue thought this event ushered in the third and final stage of the disease: emaciation, which would continue until she finally came to her senses. He had never seen a patient die.[62]

Lasègue's 1873 paper, and the publicity surrounding the discussion at the Medical Society of London later that year, now forged a kind of template for self-starvation, disseminating a model of how the patient was to behave and the doctor to respond. The way had been cleared for turning a poorly circumscribed collection of symptoms revolving around food refusal into a clear-cut "disease." In this form it was launched into the twentieth century, to guide generations of young women through psychosomatic illness behavior.

One Symptom Among Many

Is anorexia nervosa an independent disease entity or just one symptom among many that the unconscious selects for reasons of its own and then discards? One would not expect to find mumps, polio, and cancer simultaneously in the same patient, all three being distinctive disease entities. Similarly, if anorexia nervosa represented a disease of its own, one would not expect to find it in the same person at the same time as other more or less independent psychiatric diseases, such as manic-depressive illness or Tourettism. If, on the other hand, anorexia nervosa represents merely one symptom among many available for the expression of psychic distress, one would expect to find the unconscious mind doing some "mixing and matching," choosing a colorful variety of symptoms at the same time. Historically the latter is true: Self-starvation was often found amid an entire market basket of various forms of somatization.

This association between self-starvation and larger patterns of neurosis goes back to the earliest reports. In August 1787 a woman of thirty-five came to see Dr. Charles Naudeau, a young physician in Saint-Etienne. Arising from bed one day, she had experienced a sudden attack of pain around the stomach, falling then into "such a state of languor as to lose all appetite. . . . Her repugnance for liquid and solid food was so extreme that she fell into a state of inanition extending to loss of consciousness [syncope]." As she became weaker and weaker, Naudeau was finally called. Spying an attack of "vapours," he gave appropriate medications and she recovered.[63] Naudeau's patient had, in other words, embedded her food refusal in the fashionable maladies of the late eighteenth century: cataleptic-style vapours.

In the cauldron of suggestion of the Salpêtrière at the end of the nineteenth century, self-starvation twinned itself with every fashionable symptom conceivable. "Mme X.," a woman of twenty-nine, seen in the 1880s in the outpatient service of the hospital, had been troubled with a "nervous anorexia" of a number of years' duration, also with "ovarie," causing a general "hyperexcitability," and with the belief that her hair gave off "electricity" and that a "luminous crepitation" radiated from her clothes. Her physician, Charles Féré, caught up in the modish beliefs of the day about magnetism and metallotherapy, believed he had seen the sparks too. "Mme X. continues to take insufficient nourishment," noted Féré. "She is very thin, highly anemic, and subject to edematous swelling of the legs [a clinical sign of advanced malnutrition]." If Mme X. had fallen into the hands of a Lasègue or a Gull, her principal diagnosis would undoubtedly have been "anorexia nervosa." Féré wanted to call it "electrical neurosis."[64]

Paul Sollier's clinic was a magnet in the 1890s for young women who believed themselves to be in second states of various kinds. Many of them were engaged in self-starvation as well. In October 1893 Sollier admitted Marceline K., twenty-nine. "She has been sent to me with hysterical anorexia. She has had no appetite for the last nine months and has been vomiting after each meal for a number of years." Previously doctors had nourished her with a feeding tube. "The vomiting has recently increased with such intensity that she is in a state of great emaciation." Among her other complaints were "complete insomnia" for years, and fits, each one followed by a contracture of all four limbs. But the contractures also occurred independently of the fits. What is of greatest interest, however, is that she believed herself in some kind of dissociative state, detached from reality. "For three years she has been bored with everything and everybody." She had a short attention span and paid no attention to what she was doing. She experienced frequent absence states, staring off into space. "I couldn't care less," she would often say. She declared herself frequently confused about what was going on, experiencing life "as though in a dream," and had largely forgotten her life before admission to

Sollier's "Villa Montsouris." The reporting of such dreamlike states was highly common in those years.

On admission Sollier gave her a physical examination, discovering the standard signs of Charcotian hysteria, including anesthesia on the left side of her body, constriction of both visual fields, and anesthesia in the pharynx. Both ovaries were hysterogenic, unleashing fits of hysteria on the spot, as were numerous points elsewhere on her body. A "hyperesthetic" point on the skin above her stomach could initiate vomiting. She had continual headaches.

Two months after her arrival, Sollier began to hypnotize her, pressing with fingers against her eyeballs. Although she had never been hypnotized, she went immediately into a trance. In the trance Sollier asked her if "she felt truly awake during the day."

She replied, "I haven't really felt awake for a long time. I don't see anything natural around me."

The next day she remained in this hypnotic trance. Sollier blew against her eyeballs and ordered her to wake up. She then produced a classic where-am-I? story. "She opens her eyes and looks at me with astonishment. She asks me where she is, who I am, what she's doing here. She thinks it is 1890 and has no memory of what has occurred in the intervening period." Over the next two months, using this kind of treatment, Sollier abolished her symptoms, including the anorexia, and she was discharged well.[65]

Sollier considered Marceline yet another instance of what Charcot had called "vigilambulism," going through life in a second state, or permanently hypnotized. Her case is relevant here because, whatever interior reasons she had for becoming symptomatic, she had selected her symptoms as though in a supermarket: choosing all that was medically fashionable in the 1890s as evidence of real illness. In this manner she had selected not only "hysterogenic zones" (an invention of Charcot's) and contractures of her limbs but "anorexia nervosa" as well. It would be absurd to argue that she was somehow the victim of a real disease called anorexia nervosa.

Jules Janet was Pierre's younger brother, an intern at the Pitié Hospital with an interest in hypnotism. In 1887 a fellow intern asked him to see a woman in her early twenties with a long history of hysterical anesthesias, contractures, and the like. Around a year and a half previously she had suddenly developed

> an anorexia which became steadily more intense and which turned into an absolute dysphagia [inability to swallow]. Even the sight of a glass of water or a spoonful of bouillon touched off efforts at vomiting and spasmodic contractures lasting for several minutes.
> For the last fifteen months, she has been fed with a tube, but as she vomits shortly afterwards almost everything fed to her, she inevitably has become emaciated, losing all her strength. She is no longer able to urinate, and must be catheterized twice daily. She has become paralyzed, so extreme is her emaciation.

It was in this state that in April 1887 she entered the service of Charcot's pupil Edouard Brissaud at the Pitié, where, two months later, Jules Janet was summoned to try to hypnotize her.

Over the next year and a half Janet battled bravely against an ever-rising tide of symptoms. No sooner was one of her symptoms conquered than a new one appeared or a former one would spring back to life. Her dysphagia waxed and waned, and she remained skeletal. What is of interest in this case is the tide of suggestion in which both Janet and his young patient bathed: the fashionable paralyses, the indulgence of fifteen months of tube-feeding. And as a final touch, in addition to her compendium of physical symptoms, the young woman developed a double personality. One personality would go about "awake," the other asleep under hypnosis. Janet concluded, "I ended up creating in this woman a double existence absolutely analogous to the case of Dr. Azam's Félida [a notorious double-personality case]. My patient is an artificial Félida whose two personalities I can regulate at will."[66] Double personalities, as a variant of second states, were then all the rage.

Perhaps a physician less interested than Janet in hypnosis and second states would have dubbed the case anorexia nervosa. Such focusing on her eating behavior might have suppressed her other symptoms, given that the unconscious mind is likely to produce the symptoms that the doctor will find most interesting or most legitimate. Fifty years later her case undoubtedly would have been called anorexia nervosa, illustrating the extent to which the choice of symptom is culturally and medically shaped.

Jules Janet's much more famous brother Pierre was, after his own graduation in medicine in 1893, more interested in phobias and panic disorders than in hysteria. In his subsequent clinical work at the Salpêtrière, Pierre Janet tried to shape all the cases of food refusal he encountered into the form of "abulia," a supposed weakness of "vital cerebral centers" that left the mind unable to cope, subjecting it to brainstorms of compulsion and obsession. Of the seventeen cases involving some kind of food refusal that Janet presented in his Tuesday lectures around 1900, several had a definite tinge of phobia or compulsion. A twenty-one-year-old woman, for example, preoccupied with choking, was so anxious as to be incapable of swallowing her food. (Unfortunately all her contortions about swallowing could not be demonstrated to the audience, "because you," she said, "are doctors." She could do anything requested in the presence of doctors, believing herself safe in their presence.)[67] Another patient, a woman of thirty-eight, had developed an obsessive concern about facial hair. To avoid the possibility of an encounter with her neighbors, whom she believed to be highly critical, she remained indoors: "How do you expect someone to deal with such fearful neighbors if one has a mustache?" Janet asked rhetorically. Then Janet helped cure her of this notion with some psychic exercises, at which point she stopped eating. By the time we lose sight of her, she had lost a good deal of weight.[68] Obviously she had exchanged one neurotic symptom for another. We are merely dealing with different forms of somatization, different symptoms selected from the pool depending on circumstances.

Because of the intensity of the climate of suggestion at the Salpêtrière, the nature of anorexia nervosa as one symptom among many is very visible. But in many other settings as well, self-starvation was allied to an efflorescence of other nervous symptoms. Weir Mitchell in Philadelphia specialized in society women who were bed cases. Self-starvation was often a theme in this kind of classical valetudinarian. Sometime in the 1870s Miss L., a twenty-eight-year-old Connecticut woman, developed pain in the scalp, the back of the head, and the spine, "after having suffered a long and severe strain on her emotions and sympathies." Her clinicians treated her by blistering her spine. The blisters then became infected. She had "a furious outbreak of weeping, general convulsions, and incessant local spasms of the extremities." She began taking hours-long walks and, apparently around the same time, "began to eat less and less, and at last [several months later] ceased to eat at all." Her body became racked by hiccups and spasms. For twenty-seven days she took in nothing, rectal feeding having been abandoned because it caused spasms: "Twice her physicians were called in to see her die."

Instead she started eating again, underwent a long period of fits and convulsions, and decided to go to Europe. That winter in Liverpool "she had variable degrees of anorexia, and the usual miserable variety of hysterical disorders." In Paris she was again close to death from self-starvation. She returned to New York and once again flirted with death from emaciation, "rallying" at the last minute. "From this time she remained in bed for nine months, eating little and irregularly, a wretched invalid, not very thin, but not fat, with occasional spasms, great nervousness, distressed by light, by sounds, by any company which was not quite agreeable, forever alarming her friends by threatenings of a repetition of her former troubles." Weir Mitchell cured her with his rest cure, which involved isolating patients from family and society until they recovered.[69]

In other patients it was paralysis, a fashionable late-nineteenth-century symptom, that alternated with anorexia. Freud's patient "Emmy von N." manifested anorexia and hysterical paralysis, both of which symptoms Freud attributed to "abulia."[70] In September 1881 John Bristowe admitted a "delicate-looking" fourteen-year-old girl to Saint Thomas's Hospital in London, who had been suffering for two years "from an hysterical affection of the right hip." She improved under treatment and was discharged three months later. In May 1882 she was readmitted. "It appeared that, soon after she left the hospital, she began to vomit after food, and before long, after everything she took, the sickness coming on immediately so that she rapidly lost flesh and strength. Although the hip-affection remained, it formed a less prominent subject of complaint than it had done previously."[71] Only in the early twentieth century as paralysis ceased being stylish, would anorexia and paralysis become unhooked, anorexia to continue alone.

Symptoms referable to the ovaries gripped the minds of many doctors and patients in the nineteenth century. It is therefore not unsurprising to see anorexia associated with imagined ovarian complaints. William Goodell, a prominent Philadelphia gynecologist whom Weir Mitchell would often consult before starting a patient on a rest cure, received from Mitchell one day "an unmarried lady of twenty-seven" who experienced severe suffering surrounding the menses. "She had violent headaches, great emaciation—weighing sixty-seven pounds only—and exhibited mental disturbances which threatened insanity. . . . After due deliberation," Goodell decided to remove her ovaries. "Menstruation did not return and she became wonderfully better, so much so as to astonish her friends, who were all ignorant of the nature of the operation. . . . Not long ago her physician informed me that 'she deemed herself perfectly well, and had told him that he need never call again as a physician, but as a friend.' " This last phrase "as a friend" illustrates the close emotional tie between doctor and patient that ultimately gave these nineteenth-century physicians such tremendous authority. Under her doctor's influence, she believed that her appetite had been diminished by her ovaries, and once those troublesome organs were removed, the appetite would revert to form.[72]

Published evidence of the intermingling of anorexia nervosa with other fashionable symptoms concerns mainly young women from urban centers. Surely rural people in small towns were less fashion driven in their choice of symptom, their eating behavior less vulnerable to the illness-of-the-month syndrome? Not necessarily. A Manitoba farm girl could plausibly—in her own mind—combine anorexia nervosa with fits. One of eleven siblings and of a family living "in straitened circumstances," she experienced a six-week bout of fits at the age of sixteen, following a prolonged period of constipation. She would have "four or five a day, and more at night, which started with twitching in the limbs and grinding of the teeth, after which the mouth frothed, the eyes rolled up and remained open and set. In this state she would lie sometimes for three hours." Then, as the fits subsided, "her appetite gradually left her, and she got so thin that about October 1st, 1890, eighteen months after the fits, she could not stand, and spent four weeks in bed, weighing, her parents say, forty-two pounds [nineteen kilograms]." A Winnipeg physician instructed her to undergo a modified rest cure at home; she gained seven pounds, "and in a short time could walk three and a half miles alone." Three years later she was fine.[73] Her choice of fits is interesting because of the backward-looking nature of the symptom, recalling hundreds of years of twitching and writhing on the continent of Europe. The urban middle classes of the twentieth century would select more modern symptoms to go alongside self-starvation, symptoms centering upon the derangement of the personality.[74] It was no long suitable for this new disease to display simultaneously other forms of somatization.

Culture and Fat

Ever since the turn of the century, many authorities have ascribed anorexia nervosa to an intense fear of obesity. In the 1960s psychiatrist Hilde Bruch found that anorexic patients had disturbed body images, seeing themselves as obese all the while growing thinner and thinner.[75] These two psychological phenomena—fear of fat and disturbed body image—have since become part of the definition of the disorder. Self-starvation does not currently qualify as "anorexia nervosa" unless accompanied by a distorted vision of one's body and an intense fear of overweight. The definition of anorexia nervosa devised by the American Psychiatric Association in 1987 declared: "The essential features of this disorder are: refusal to maintain body weight over a minimal normal weight for age and height; intense fear of gaining weight or becoming fat, even though underweight; a distorted body image; and amenorrhea (in females)."[76]

What started out as self-starvation has accordingly become "a disorder of body image." Is the true core of self-starvation in fact a delusional sense that one, though skeletal, is still "too fat"? Or are these concerns about overweight and body image culturally imposed outriders to the symptom of food refusal, adjoined by a pathologically weight-conscious society? If they are, they cannot be considered intrinsic components of a disease called anorexia nervosa.

The self-starvation of nineteenth-century Europe resembles current definitions of anorexia nervosa in every way except concerns about overweight or self-image.[77] Although cases of self-starvation that would qualify as anorexia nervosa go back to the 1820s and even before, only in the 1870s does fear of overweight begin to alarm the population as a whole.[78] Not until the late nineteenth century do patients with anorexia nervosa begin to mention fear of overweight to their doctors. Charcot himself encountered an early instance at some point before his death in 1893. As Pierre Janet later told the story: "The following observation of Charcot is famous: while undressing a patient of this kind, he found that she wore on her skin, fastened very tightly around her waist, a rose-coloured ribbon. He obtained the following confidence; the ribbon was a measure which the waist was not to exceed. 'I prefer dying of hunger to becoming as big as mamma.' "[79] Sollier, discussing in 1891 "psychological causes" of hysterical anorexia, referred among others to "the desire to reduce one's waist size."[80] Around this time another Salpetrian, Gabriel Wallet, encountered the case of Mlle. V., whose anorexia had begun at the age of twelve after she entered a convent as a boarder. "It was then the idea occurred to her that she was too fat, after having seen schoolmates trying to slim by drinking vinegar and not eating their fill at table. Since that time she has continually tried to achieve this herself and eats very little, consuming everything that she thinks might be bad for her stomach."[81] These are among the earliest references in France to self-starvation in order to obtain socially desirable degrees of thinness. But by this time the number of anorexic young French women had grown greatly, without a hint in the previous medical literature of weight concerns among patients.

References to fear of fat began to appear in the 1880s in Central Europe. In August 1887, Fräulein F., sixteen, was admitted to the Maria Grün nervous clinic near Graz. Her maternal grandmother had suffered from "mental anorexia." When the patient had reached puberty a year ago, she found the growth of her breasts particularly irritating, and so began eating less and less, "studying books to see how one could become thin." Her parents implored her to eat, sent her on a short tour of Italy in the hopes of effecting an improvement, and when nothing availed, dispatched her to the Graz clinic. Her weight at the time was fifty-nine pounds (twenty-seven kilos). When clinic staff asked her why she did not want to eat, "she replied that eating was torture, for she always got stomach pain immediately afterwards. She admitted that she had been eating less and less out of fear of becoming fat. She would have best preferred drinking vinegar in order to become slimmer still."[82] On the subject of "anorexia nervosa" clinic director Anton Stichl wrote in 1892, "Fear of fatness is a not insignificant etiological moment, especially among girls. Girls generally believe and indeed are steeped in the view that only nymphlike figures appeal to men, and to attain these the girls resort to two means, overly tight-lacing and eating insufficiently."[83]

Sometime between 1889 and 1891, Fräulein D., an Austrian woman of around twenty-five, experienced "dyspepsia, anemia, and a menstrual depression of mood." Thereupon she developed a host of obsessive-compulsive traits, such as endless praying from a fear of "not praying properly" or "erotic compulsions" following an encounter with a man whom "she could not marry but could not forget." She also had a "fear of becoming fat, especially of getting overly large breasts." For these characteristics she was admitted to Wilhelm Svetlin's private nervous clinic in Vienna. In the clinic she was said to "measure her breasts constantly; she eats little, and always exactly the same foods, loves to take long walks."[84] Even though some other psychiatric problem such as depression or obsessive-compulsive disorder might have been involved as well, she ranks among the early Central European anorexia patients to motivate her fasting with concerns about fatness and her own sexuality.

In the 1890s the nerve doctors who catered to the middle class became increasingly aware how fearful their young patients were of fat. In his discussion of "hysterical anorexia" in 1894, Leopold Löwenfeld mentioned, among the numerous causes of the disorder, "fear of excessive body size."[85] In 1904 Viennese psychiatrist Emil Raimann—at the time at the university clinic but who had

considerable experience in dealing with sanatorium patients—
speculated about "the wish to remain thin" in "hysterical patients
who refuse food."[86] Likewise in 1904, Otto Binswanger, professor
of psychiatry at Jena, ascribed to anorexic young girls and women
"the vain preoccupation with becoming too fat and thus losing
their beauty. By suppressing natural feelings of hunger, food intake gradually becomes reduced, until finally the appetite in fact
vanishes and the ardently desired emaciation occurs in full measure."[87] It is clear that by the turn of the century—but only by
then—fear of fatness had become a significant theme in what
physicians for three decades had been calling anorexia nervosa.

Whether the body images of these young women were distorted
we cannot say. Yet among patients with anorexia nervosa during
the first half of the twentieth century, fear of fatness received ever-
more-prominent mention. "Lose weight, lose weight at any price!"
mocked Edgar Bérillon (a middle-aged psychiatrist) of the milieu
of young Parisian women in the decade before World War I. "That
seems to be the slogan adopted by the young anorexics. Any food
that might put on weight is rejected with horror. Physical activity,
dancing, walking, strenuous gymnastics that reduce fat, all have
become objects of a passion that comes to an end only when the
patient is no longer able to stand up."[88] As another middle-aged
Parisian physician who felt himself left behind by the times complained in 1909:

> Coquetry is often the cause of mental anorexia. A young girl
> with a bit of fleshiness [*ayant de l'embonpoint*]—something
> which it seems is tolerated very poorly, especially with today's
> styles—stops eating in order to lose weight. [The reason] is per-
> haps the children who have teased her by calling her "fat little
> momma" [*la grosse mère*]. At first these patients reduce the
> amount they eat, but soon they surpass their goal and take off
> too much, because truly, after some point in time, they are no
> longer capable of eating.[89]

On the basis of the few quantitative data available, only half or
fewer of all anorexia patients in the years between the two world
wars said they had weight concerns. In only four of the thirty-
three young women whom John Ryle, an internist at Guy's

Hospital in London, treated for anorexia nervosa between 1920 and 1936 did the teasing of school friends and the like play a role in the origin of the illness.[90] This does not mean that the other anorexic patients were not at some level concerned about their weight, merely that they said so neither to their parents (whom Ryle questioned) nor to Ryle himself. Of eight patients seen for anorexia nervosa in Toronto in the 1930s, only three expressed to their physicians on the internal medicine service of the Toronto General Hospital a sensitivity about overweight: One, a boy of thirteen, had been called by his playmates "Tubby" and "Fat," and two girls in their late teens had been teased as "fat."[91] Of four young women with "mental anorexia" in the psychiatric service of the University of Rome in the early 1940s, two felt overweight: a sixteen-year-old who "tries to sleep as little as possible for fear of putting on weight," and another sixteen-year-old whom class-mates had teased as "chubby [la grassottella]."[92] Of Jürg Zutt's six anorexia patients in Berlin during the years of World War II, three felt they were too fat; in addition, a fourth had objectively been, before the onset of illness, "conspicuously fat."[93] On the basis of these data it would be fair to claim that before World War II a sub-stantial proportion of individuals with anorexia nervosa were in-deed responding to real or imagined weight concerns. Yet explanations stressing "body image," "societal demands for slim-ming," and the like by no means provide a comprehensive account of the phenomenon.

In these first decades of the twentieth century we start find-ing accounts of young women whose slimming behavior was motivated primarily by a sense of sexual inadequacy, a fear of facing the sexual perils of adult life. Janet's patient "Nadia" had initiated her self-starvation at the age of ten, when her cousins started teasing her. She began to be afraid of her own feet, hands, hips, head, and hair. As puberty began around fifteen, she determined to remain slim so that men would not love her. She swore a number of elaborate pacts with herself about not taking food. Finally, a love affair with a musician, a much older man, relieved her from the pacts. The relief was short-lived, as the man died soon after. She blamed her breaking of the pacts for his death. Twenty-eight at the turn of the century, she had become a chronic neurotic whom it was still very hard to get to eat.[94]

The anorexic English patients of psychiatrist Grace Nicolle spoke quite frankly about their sexual fears. Nicolle concluded, "When an anorexic patient begins to confide her troubles, they are always associated with doubts of sexual potency. She does not have periods like other girls, she does not experience the sexual thrills that others describe, she feels unable to attract boys."

Miss M. said to Dr. Nicolle, "I did not worry much about my periods till mother said, 'I couldn't let anyone marry you unless that comes right.' I knew I didn't have the same sex feelings as other girls. I began to think I was a freak." Nicolle concluded, "The anorexic associates the plumpness of adolescence with her sense of sexual insufficiency and begins to try to remedy this obvious sign by dealing drastically with the fat."[95] In these years two organically oriented French clinicians in Marseilles, a neurologist and an endocrinologist, exactly the opposite of the psychologically sensitive Grace Nicolle, also found these deep sexual themes audible enough to pick up. On the basis of a number of interviews with anorexic patients they concluded "that a majority of cases come from a more or less pronouncedly psychopathic milieu and that their often unexpressed fear of fatness is most often linked to notions of a psychosexual nature. One knows how much a young woman is convinced that success in the competition for a marriage partner depends in large measure on 'staying trim' [*la 'ligne' corporelle*]."[96]

In these interwar years the first testimony from patients indicating a disorder of body image begins to surface, as opposed to a mere preoccupation with weight. In January 1931 Miss X., a twenty-one-year-old New York woman, attended a party "where she became interested in a medical student. At that time someone made a remark about her plumpness. She began to diet and reduced her weight from 128 to 110 pounds [58 to 50 kilograms] in six months." She was now carrying on a courtship with this medical student. His parents became alarmed at the weight loss, fearing that she might have tuberculosis. Her dieting became pathological and several psychiatric admissions commenced, beginning in October 1933 with the Presbyterian Hospital in New York. Four years later, after a turbulent course, she was admitted to the Payne Whitney Psychiatric Clinic. Now weighing 75 pounds (34 kilograms), she told the staff that, although "my relatives are in despair over me . . . I still feel that I look husky and stocky."[97] One notes that only six decades after anorexia nervosa had become a widespread phenomenon did this sort of testimony start to appear.

On balance it seems quite unrealistic to make disturbances of body image or an intense fear of overweight part of the definition of anorexia nervosa. Not only is it impossible to determine historically if many patients satisfied these criteria, but many other patients in the past seem not to have had these concerns at all. Yet their dieting behavior was just as destructive as that of today's patients with anorexia nervosa.

If anorexia nervosa became an illness of youth, it was not primarily because of the importance that slimness has for youngsters engaged for the first time in the mating dance. Indeed, if food refusal were merely a slimming strategy conceived for the "meat market," it would backfire as its victims become grotesquely emaciated. Food refusal became a disorder of the young for the role that it played *inside* the family rather than outside.

Middle-Class Life and Intimacy

Anorexia nervosa and the new motor symptoms of hysteria, such as paralysis, began around the same time in the nineteenth century. Their coincidence was related to new forms of family life in which "sensitive natures and solicitude flourish side by side," as one physician familiar with the germinal milieu of anorexia put it.[98] This intimate family with its breathless attachments hallmarked the nineteenth century. Both the modern family and anorexia nervosa appeared within the middle class. Both seem to have stemmed from the sentimental arrangements of that class. What was it about middle-class life that generated such pathological forms of behavior as self-starvation on the one hand and immobility and paralysis on the other?

Let us take our cue from the little family as its members come together at the table. If any icon stood for the intimacy and solidarity of the nineteenth-century bourgeois family, it was the dinner-table scene. Here they were truly *chez soi,* in the privacy of the family, the only intruders the servants, gliding back and forth with dishes. Various writers describe the dinner table with the anorexic patient present. Sometime in the 1870s, the parents of Mlle X., a sixteen-year-old girl from a "very honorable" small-town family in eastern France, noticed that she had started to become "a little more taciturn than usual and above all that she ate very little." They became upset and asked her what was wrong. "Oh, it's nothing," they decided. "She's not hungry, that's all. Why press her to eat?"

The parents waited and then consulted the family doctor, who prescribed bitters. "But her appetite failed to return, and her weight was dropping appreciably." She now definitely appeared ill, and was eating nothing:

> It was not that she disliked this or that dish. She accepted everything that was put on her plate, and touched it, but took only infinitesimal quantities. One can imagine what family life was turning into. Mealtimes soon became occasions of struggle and anxiety. The mother, the father, their eyes riveted upon the child, counted every mouthful, mentally weighing the few grams of nourishment she consumed, begging her, imploring her, ordering her. Nothing worked, and Mlle X. lost forty pounds of her body weight in two months.[99]

Similar scenes from hell at the table were reported from Italy. Of the above-mentioned young woman from Bologna whose food "would not go down," it was said: "Dinnertime was a real punishment for her and for the family, who would urge her to eat and order her to put the food in her mouth. . . . Sometimes she would say it was no longer possible, and break out in bitter sobbing."[100] Anorexia created a nightmare at the table—the supposed shrine of family harmony.

And the nightmare was interminable, for, unlike a dramatic spat, it could stretch on for months, focusing the entire household on the miserable sixteen-year-old toying with her food. Said a Paris physician in 1896:

[The family] multiply the delicacies of the table in the hope of awakening her appetite; the more their solicitude increases, the more her appetite diminishes. The patient disdainfully tastes the new dishes, and having thus shown her good will, considers herself under no further obligation. The family supplicate, they ask as a favor, as a sovereign proof of affection, that the patient submits to adding one single extra mouthful to the meal that she declared finished. . . . The anorexia becomes by degrees the only object of preoccupation and conversation. It forms thus a kind of atmosphere around the patient which envelops her, and from which she cannot escape at any hour of the day.[101]

At the center of this psychodrama was a young woman, perhaps an only child, and, in the opinion of the physicians of the day, terribly spoiled and coddled by her family. As Grace Nicolle said in 1938, "The majority of cases are to be found among the leisured or wealthy classes and among girls who have been spoiled and petted. . . . Spoiling is the fostering of narcissism." Dr. Nicolle's patient "Miss M." had been "brought up in the luxury of a white society employing native servants, was a little princess, and she expected a fairy-tale success."[102] In Paris before World War I, Bérillon had called anorexia nervosa "a disorder specific to spoiled children or only daughters."[103] And other clinicians over the years would echo these comments almost literally.[104] Said Paris psychiatrist Lionel Vidart in 1937, "Mental anorexia . . . is found in the great majority of cases among young women of fifteen to twenty, and quite specifically among only children, pampered and much the center of attention [*choyé et très entourné*]."[105] Thus the target group in self-starvation was middle-class young women, cherished by their families and held tightly in a web of intimacy unusual among that class before 1800 and equally unusual after the 1960s. But what was it about this singular emotional matrix that might have produced self-starvation?

One is struck by the presence of an intimacy so suffocating and intense that refusal to eat and to walk might both be somehow conceived as a revolt against it. Consider the tenacity of the family's grasp, even as the worst approached. To save the dying daughter, an isolation cure, or Weir Mitchell cure, might have to be contemplated that would remove the patient from the parental home and place her in a private nervous clinic, where, under the forbidding authority of a physician, she would be fed with a rubber tube.

The families hated this kind of "parentectomy."[106] As Henri Huchard, a neurologist at Tenon Hospital in Paris, noted in 1882, "Because the family [*l'entourage*] is the obstacle to recovery, the physician must insist formally, imperiously, upon the isolation of the patient in another venue."[107] In 1885 Charcot, an early advocate of isolation, remembered "a young girl of thirteen or fourteen from Angoulême who had put on considerable weight for five or six months and who, from that moment, systematically refused any nutrition." Her desperate father begged Charcot to come to Angoulême, but Charcot refused, saying, "Bring the child to Paris: put her in this or that hydrotherapy clinic; abandon her there, or at least pretend to do it, so that she will believe you have left the capital. Notify me, and I will take care of the rest." No response arrived for six weeks, until one day Charcot received at home a much agitated doctor from Angoulême who told him the parents were in Paris, the daughter installed in the clinic, and that she probably had only a few days to live.

"I asked him why I had not been told of the girl's arrival." He responded that the parents had avoided doing so because they were resolved not to be separated from their child.

So Charcot went to the clinic and found the horrible sight of the daughter in the last stages of starvation. "There truly were grounds for being very, very uneasy." He continued:

> I took the parents aside and, having given them a sharp rebuke, told them that in my opinion only one chance remained for their daughter: for them to remove, or seem to remove, themselves instantly. . . . Their consent was difficult to attain, despite all my remonstrations. The father above all could not understand that a doctor could ask a father to remove himself from his child in a moment of danger. The mother said as much too. But conviction drove me on. I was perhaps so eloquent that first the mother gave in and then the father grumblingly went along.

The daughter recovered immediately after the parents' departure.[108]

Once a patient had been admitted, clinic physicians did their utmost to minimize her contact with the toxic parents, a contact that—in the doctors' view—would ensure a relapse just as inevitably as the parents' overprotectiveness had brought on the illness in the first place. "The resumption of contact, ardently desired whether the treatment succeeds or fails, would be disastrous if it is premature," wrote Sollier in 1891:

> Absolute and steady progress must be well under way before even correspondence is authorized, to say nothing of visiting. A letter that arouses memories of the maternal home, which contains promises about the homecoming, consolations for disappointments that the patient has probably not even had, a letter that she reads and re-reads ceaselessly, showing her that the same indulgence, the same irrational tenderness awaits her as in the past, causes immediately a slowing of progress toward recovery.[109]

This evidence of the daughter's longing for home is not incompatible with the hypothesis of a revolt against the enmeshment of that home: The process of boundary-drawing is always ambivalent and fraught with anxiety.

Sometimes a case would end fatally because the isolation cure was never given a chance. The doctor was never able to persuade the parents to detach themselves from the daughter. Georges Gasne at the Salpêtrière described a judge, one of whose daughters was already dead of anorexia, the other dying. The judge refused to send the second daughter to a private nervous clinic because his wife insisted on keeping her at home. Finally, under Gasne's prodding, the judge broke his wife's resistance; the daughter recovered.[110]

Emphasizing that anorexia nervosa, if left untreated, could sooner or later end fatally, Noël Perron, a neurologist at the Salpêtrière, stressed the importance of securing familial consent for isolation. He wrote in 1936, "Permission for isolation as *the most important measure* must be obtained from the patient and above all from her family. But most often this indispensable measure is decided upon only after long negotiations. To succeed, the physician must obtain carte blanche from the family, in order to pursue the cure for a sufficient period, generally two or three months."[111] Perron described a world in which everyone—the parents, the friends, the family doctor—clutched the patient tightly to them, all opposing her removal. Perron said that the physician's task was not merely convincing the family, whose attitude toward neurology and psychiatry was "profound repugnance," of the diagnosis of anorexia nervosa. He must as well "convince the often hostile patient of the necessity of isolation, deal with the usually incomprehending family, whose responsibility for the genesis of the illness is generally undeniable, and convince the patient's medical entourage of the correctness of the diagnosis and the necessity of the isolation cure."[112] Given the stakes involved in refusing an isolation cure—a possible fatal outcome—the family's reluctance to part for several weeks with their beloved, emaciated daughter is evidence of profound emotional enmeshment. It is not implausible that the food refusal itself might somehow have arisen from this cauldron of attachment.

Other scholars have speculated about such nervous disorders as hysteria and anorexia as a "protofeminist" form of revolt against male authority and women's subordinate roles.[113] It seems likely that what was being revolted against was not the doctor's authority or a society dominated by males—still unchallenged absolutes for most women—but the family's. The parallel with hysterical paralysis is instructive. These paralyses came to an end in the years between the two world wars as a more dynamic image of women became fashionable. But anorexia nervosa did not disappear. Unlike the passive valetudinarian, the thin, compulsively pacing woman in autonomous control of her diet never became unfashionable.

The thought is irresistible that the person against whom the daughter's revolt was directed was the mother. Among the most troubled dyads in this sentimental family was that of the mother and the daughter. Some evidence highlights ambivalence in this relationship, more than in the daughter's relationship to the father, as a wellspring of anorexia nervosa. In the summer of

1858, for example, Marcé saw for the first time Mlle. A., a Parisian in her late teens whose weight was less than fifty-one pounds (twenty-three kilograms). Once in Marcé's clinic, Mlle. A. made considerable progress:

> To demonstrate the enduring nature of the convalescence it was then decided to sent Mlle. A. to her mother, whom she had not seen for a number of months. This experiment did not, unfortunately, have a happy outcome. At the end of two weeks the patient was worse. After each meal Mlle. A. would begin, in front of her mother, whose presence only made her more agitated, a mournful enumeration of the dishes she had just consumed, crying, screaming, striking her head against the wall.[114]

Another example: Béatrice G., a Parisian of sixteen, to all intents and purposes loved her mother dearly, attending her closely in 1898 as the mother lay in bed with pleurisy. One night as the mother apparently lost consciousness, the frightened Béatrice ran to summon a neighbor, then herself fainted, and upon awakening had a hysterical fit so violent that it took "five men to hold her." She cried and screamed that "she ha[d] always wanted to see her mother dead."

After Béatrice recovered from this fit, she noted that her legs were paralyzed. More convulsions and nervous accidents ensued. Eight days later she was admitted to the Salpêtrière, paralyzed and blind. Inside the hospital she recovered immediately and was returned to her mother, whereupon "Saint Guy's dance," a kind of slow-motion fit, began. Three days before Christmas she was removed from the household again and sent to the country. It was here that Béatrice exchanged the symptom of fits for that of anorexia.

In the countryside she ate and "digested" poorly. After each meal she would "twist and writhe about," claim to be suffocating, and sigh noisily. As these events were going on she returned to Paris for a visit. Over a period of days, knowing that Béatrice was constipated, the mother administered to her fifteen enemas. On the fifteenth Béatrice fell into a fainting fit, and from this point on her emaciation commenced. Béatrice returned to the countryside. Her anorexia grew worse. Her mother was summoned, and upon her arrival Béatrice produced "a horrible crisis with vomiting and diarrhea."

When Béatrice was brought back to the Salpêtrière, she weighed only twenty-five kilograms (fifty-five pounds) and exhibited a shocking picture of wasting. However she quickly began eating and regained her weight. Here the case ends.[115] Of the role of the toxic mother there can be no doubt.

With the passage of time physicians became more sensitive to the psychological issues involved, their assessments more nuanced. In 1931 Walter Langdon-Brown, an elderly consulting physician at Saint Bartholomew's Hospital in London with an interest in psychoanalysis, commented of anorexia nervosa, "On the psychical side, these young women admitted to having a fear of growing up and facing adult responsibilities in the world . . . an undue dependence on the father, and a distinct hostility to the mother."[116] John Ryle, too, was struck too by these mother-daughter themes. Ryle said in 1939 of anorexia nervosa, "Perpetuating factors include . . . the sense of power over the mother. . . . Although they may be 'devoted to each other' mother and daughter are frequently 'at loggerheads' or 'on each other's nerves.' . . . Home treatment is commonly unsatisfactory on account of the mother-daughter relationship."[117]

We are unable yet to map the full pathology of the mother-daughter relationship. We know only that ambivalence in this relationship crops up anecdotally in the historical literature on anorexia nervosa and that certain medical observers considered it an issue in the genesis of the disorder. This ambivalence seems to have helped trigger the refusing of food, perhaps because the mother was responsible for the table or because food itself has always been a symbol of caring.

Recent scholarship on the history of the family suggests that such ambivalence was historically new. The intensification of family ties in England in the second half of the eighteenth century, and elsewhere in the nineteenth, abolished the strictly defined emotional roles villagers and burghers had once taken on.[118] This intensification made it possible for emotional ties within the family to unfold across a wide spectrum of variations, some of them extremely passionate. Caught in adolescent crises about boundary-drawing, about the differentiation of their own individuality from the intrusiveness of other family members, some young women might well have seized on anorexia nervosa as a way of constructing a private space. Perhaps food rejection and paralysis both served to ward off others from their own budding personhood. That these food-denying young women might have felt ambivalent about shutting out loved ones goes without saying; it is an ambivalence that turns up in the records as the daughters weeping for home once they are sequestrated in a private clinic. The whole pathology of the mother-daughter relationship illustrates well how cultural factors matter in the making of psychosomatic symptoms.

Do Doctors Make Their Patients Sick?

Historically it makes good sense to link anorexia nervosa to these new familial psychodynamics because of the timing: The symptom and the family form go together. Do these historical insights apply today? Since World War II, the incidence of anorexia nervosa appears to have increased greatly.[119] Has this kind of pathological intimacy also risen?

The problem in generalizing historical conclusions to our own society is that this pressure-cooker family style has by and large disappeared. What clinicians today perceive as enmeshment is a pallid version of the sobbing mothers, clinging daughters, and overprotective fathers of the nineteenth century. Instead of the crucible dining room of yore, we find today the fragmented dinner table, the family members grazing from the refrigerator in isolation. In the place of exhaustingly intense affect we find a postmodern cooling of ties, the hiving-off of mothers and fathers to work and of children to school and the ministrations of family service professionals.[120] Anorexia nervosa arose in a social climate in which it was often considered bad form for a middle-class woman to leave the house unescorted. Today women are driving fire trucks, yet anorexia nervosa is commoner than ever.

Many observers stress the role of the media-driven hype surrounding dieting and slimness today. It is true that what came to be called the "Twiggy effect" does seem to have spread the contagion. The average weight of contestants in the Miss America Pageant, for example, declined an average of 0.17 kilograms (0.37 pounds) per year between 1959 and 1978. The bust size of the 240 monthly "Playmates" in *Playboy* magazine over that period dropped from around 92 to 89 centimeters (35.9 to 34.7 inches).[121] Even though women as a whole have been getting heavier,[122] the most prominent representatives of female beauty have incorporated the new gospel in their own bodies. The broadcasting to young women today of body images that would have struck nineteenth-century observers as unappealingly skinny has obviously privileged food refusal as a symptom choice.

But we are dealing with something more than the media-driven diffusion of new images that passive patients are somehow obliged to accept. To see women as "victims" of the media reduces them to automatons in the same way as nineteenth-century reflex theory once did. What, then, is the real explanation of the almost epidemic spread of anorexia nervosa today?

Accounting for events as they explode about our heads is always a tricky business, one historians are best advised to stay away from. Doubtless there are many contributory factors in the spread of anorexia nervosa today. Among them is the role of psychiatry itself. The spread of anorexia nervosa is partly an effect of iatrogenesis, meaning illness created by physicians.[123] Thus the anorexia industry ends up evoking the very phenomenon it was designed to combat.

Physicians themselves tread the stage in the complex interplay between culture and biology. Biology drives to the surface the need to become symptomatic. Culture gives particular forms of symptoms an internal logic. And medicine confers legitimacy on them. This is the problem today with anorexia nervosa. It has been validated as an expression of psychic unease in the most appealing way possible: by the development of a whole psychiatric subspecialty that caters to it.

The anorexia industry justifies its existence by the logic that anorexia nervosa constitutes a separate disease. Clinicians and historians of anorexia alike have contributed to this validation. In attempting to write its history or in constructing special eating-disorder units, both groups of researchers lose sight of the evanescent nature of symptom choice. Anorexia nervosa is not a separate disease at all, merely one symptom among many in the symptom pool. It is not some distinctive malady that lies buried in the world of nature, waiting like cancer to break through to the surface as soon as conditions are right, but an almost capricious choice of symptom made by the unconscious mind. The unconscious strives to produce that which is legitimate as opposed to that which is judged to be playacting, or illegitimate. Granting official disease status to the phenomenon of self-starvation has in effect legitimated it, making it a desirable object of choice for many young women seeking somatic expressions of their psychic dysphoria. Which symptom is selected is left entirely to the unconscious: If not anorexia, then something else. The task of the unconscious is merely to produce behavior that will entitle the individual to a respectful medical hearing.

The initial legitimation occurred in 1873. But only since the 1960s has the whole apparatus of adolescent psychiatry experienced its exponential growth, creating informational structures designed to carry to the heartland the message that food refusal is considered "an important new disease." In the burst of writing surrounding anorexia nervosa in the 1960s, it was, in fact, deemed an unprecedented phenomenon. Only later in the 1980s did researchers establish that anorexia had already been common during the nineteenth century. The anorexia patients who emerged in the 1960s and afterwards thus entered into an implicit conspiracy with their physicians, not unlike the implicit conspiracy surrounding ovarian hysteria in the nineteenth century. Both doctors and patients agreed that the problem was new and that it was medical. Under these fictions doctors and patients ended up colluding in the medicalizing of behavior that is basically artifactual. The doctors see their theories confirmed and their new eating-disorder empires validated, the patients receive the dignity of a "real" illness. The conclusion from these observations is that, for self-starvation to go away, it will somehow have to become demedicalized. Yet this is difficult when the penalty for playing out the drama of the symptom is death itself.

The whole saga of anorexia nervosa is a textbook example of how culture creates a disease, of how psychosomatic symptoms are induced in a population many of whose members are genetically predisposed to acquire some kind of disturbance of the mind-body relationship. But the victims are not merely selected randomly. They are recruited along highly specific cultural pathways: age, social class, and gender. For anorexia nervosa was a kind of illness behavior that originated among the middle classes and has remained almost entirely confined to young females. The disorder evidently has a genetic component as well. The genetic implication is that, if these young patients were not starving themselves they would be doing something else hurtful to their own conscious objectives of achieving a rational, orderly life. In the eighteenth century they were convulsing on the ground; in the nineteenth, bedbound; in the late twentieth, scurrying frenziedly along exercise tracks, nightmare visions of skin and bones. The cycle of psychosomatic illness is one that never stops.

CHAPTER

7

———

Cultural Shaping

WE KNOW NOW from the historical evidence that many psychosomatic symptoms are culturally shaped. But how does this happen? How does the surrounding world influence our minds so that we interpret normal bodily sensations as evidence of organic illness? The question has interested physicians and social scientists every since the word *hysteria* became popular in the eighteenth century. Yet few have asked expressly about the role of culture, as opposed to an individual's personal history of stress or unhappiness.

In an age that makes much of political correctness, either to value or scorn it, physical symptoms too may be deemed as medically or socially correct. Correct symptoms win for their bearer the coveted label of real organic disease, as opposed to hysteria or playacting. What constitutes correctness in illness differs among the various age groups, social classes and ethnic affiliations. Among individual members of these solidarities there will be many reasons for becoming symptomatic. But the symptoms the group as a whole chooses are influenced by collective notions of health, illness, and "good medicine." The cultural shaping of illness means simply the ability of the group to act upon the suggestibility of its individual members. Let us see how this process affected Vanessa L.

An Example from the 1990s

Vanessa L., a woman of twenty, was admitted to the Psycho-somatic Medicine Clinic of a large midcontinental city with a history of total body weakness. She claimed to be too tired to walk and was in a wheelchair. But she was not paralyzed, for if she wanted something badly enough, she was able to stand up from the wheelchair and get it. This paralyzing lassitude had come on about four months previously at the family's country home, after her brother's best friend had asked her out on a date.

The parents, seeing their daughter suddenly abed with fatigue, had become the mirror of solicitousness. At the time of Vanessa's admission to the clinic, the mother said, "Oh, she can't talk to you very long, doctor, because it'll tire her out." The whole family had vied to give Vanessa total care and attention. At home she had drifted into a bizarre cycle of sleep, going to bed every night at three and getting up at two the next afternoon. The mother would arise in the middle of the night to fix Vanessa meals, serving them to her in bed. In fact, at home Vanessa received all her meals in bed.

Vanessa's parents had pursued all over the city one doctor after another, and Vanessa had a huge "chart," which cost large sums in copying merely to duplicate for all the specialists. The family had been quite demanding of the GP and thus had run through a series of family doctors. The current family doctor, a young woman with just one year in practice, used to call every evening to see Vanessa. The family would make tapes of television specials about medicine and summon the doctor to see them.

Vanessa's medical history went back to about age sixteen, when she had mononucleosis. After the initial infection had passed, she nonetheless found herself getting tireder and tireder. She was plagued by headaches too. She had wanted to go away to college but, lacking the energy, enrolled in the local university instead. Yet she was unable to attend even these classes because she was so tired, and spent all her time at home, most of it in bed. Her frantic parents, on the verge of chartering a plane to fly her to the Mayo Clinic, then learned of this clinic. The clinic psychiatrist, a highly empathic woman who enjoyed pretending that she was a tough old salt, rubbed her hands at the prospect of the admission. "A real pathological mess," she said, grinning.

It was apparent that Vanessa lived in a subculture of illness. Family members related to one another primarily via their symptoms, and all had difficult-to-disprove neurological diagnoses. That the family might be overinvested in illness started to dawn even on them after Vanessa had been admitted: One evening the father said, "We seem to be the only family that comes down here every night to have dinner with the patient."

The father was convinced that Vanessa had a chronic Epstein-Barr virus infection (also known as "yuppie flu"), and demanded expensive brain and liver scans with magnetic resonance imaging. At one point the family bought a photocopying machine so that they could reproduce all the articles on "chronic EBV" and send them to the father's business friends all over the world, in case their wives happened to have the same symptoms. "You've never told us your assessment," the father said to the psychiatrist. The entire family seemed stone-deaf to the message that their daughter's problem was psychological. The psychiatrist told them time after time, and it never sank in. The father wanted to go over all the lab tests yet again.

For all its solicitousness, the family expected the children to turn out as high-performance adults. The brother, for example, was to inherit the family firm, because business is "no place for a woman." The parents expected big achievements as well of their tired daughter. For example, the clinic staff felt that vocational rehabilitation therapy might be appropriate, but the father disdained such workshops. "I want something more career oriented," he said. In family meetings he would ask, "When is she going to start doing something worthwhile?"

Vanessa defined her own self-worth entirely in terms of "productivity." The psychiatrist said, "If she's not the chief financial officer of a major corporation, she's nothing. The only success that counts in her family's eyes is career success." When in group sessions other patients told her how well she was coping, Vanessa dismissed them. "Only career counts," she said. Vanessa feared the psychiatrist would abandon her because she was not "interest-ing" enough, contrasting herself with one of the pyschiatrist's other patients, a female professor, whom Vanessa had seen going in and out of the psychiatrist's office with stacks of books.

Unfortunately the clinic staff, unable to step outside their own culture, fed into this monomania about success. The female staff members were all impatient, of course, that Vanessa seemed so uninterested in careers. Rosalie, the occupational therapist, just could not wait to get her hooks into Vanessa once the slightest suggestion of career interest appeared. But none did. "There's just nothing there," said the psychiatrist. Vanessa appeared to have no ambitions at all. During the clinical conference at which these re-marks were made, the patients outside were having a pizza party. Vanessa lay on the sofa in the common room, her back toward the merrymakers.

As the staff got to know Vanessa, it turned out she was secretly terrified about what she perceived as her own ordinariness. She told the psychiatrist that she needed her symptoms: "If I'm not sick, I've got nothing," she said, meaning she thought she had no achievements to offer, no accomplishments, nothing that she felt might give her any status in her parents' eyes. She could not imag-ine her parents loving her for her own sake. The clinic psycholo-gist tested her IQ and broke to her the news that she had only average intelligence and average socializing skills. In other words, Vanessa could not possibly become the dazzling golden girl for whom her family so longed. Vanessa received this news calmly but asked that her parents not be told.

Vanessa took a long time to get better. Even detaching her from the wheelchair turned out to be a major operation. She had agreed to start walking the fifteen yards from her room to meals if she could have "time to rest up" afterwards. She initially wanted five hours, but the staff bargained her down to three and a half. Later, even after Vanessa began to appear brighter and more energetic at the clinic, she would revert dramatically when her father visited. "She falls apart like a nineteenth-century grande hystérique and collapses onto the bed," said the psychiatrist in a reference to the florid hysteria of Charcot's day. It took almost a year for Vanessa to move out of the family home, resume college, and become, if not entirely well, no longer entirely disabled either.

Vanessa's case is interesting as a mixture of personal and cultural moments in the genesis of psychosomatic symptoms. Of course, there were personal features in her illness, characteristics that derived from her own life history, such as her anger over her brother's preferment in the family, her highly ambivalent attitude toward sex (at twenty she was still a virgin), and her desire to please her intrusive father by producing the kind of disability called for by his theories about Epstein-Barr infections.

But culture shaped Vanessa's illness behavior as well. If she brought forth this particular constellation of symptoms, it was also because of larger social forces molding her unconscious attitudes as to what represented appropriate "disease." She inhabited, for example, a familial culture of hypochondriasis. For the family to function smoothly, everybody had to relate to everybody else on the basis of illness—obscure neurological illness in this particular family—hence an efflorescence of such central-nervous symptoms as headaches and fatigue. Such familial hypochondriasis tends, as sociologist David Mechanic has suggested, to characterize middle-class Jewish families more than non-Jewish ones, and Vanessa was Jewish.[1]

In addition, Vanessa dwelt in a subculture of credulity about bizarre new diseases that medicine was supposedly discovering every day. When admitted to the clinic, she attributed her problems to a total-body yeast infection, or candidiasis. But Vanessa had a friend who ascribed similar problems to "neuromyasthenia." The wealthy parents of this friend had bought her a condo and paid as well for her own limousine and chauffeur. So Vanessa abandoned the yeast infection theory, started to eat bread again, and considered that she might have neuromyasthenia too. Another patient, who at the time of admission to the clinic subscribed to the theory that she had a total-body yeast infection, later switched to a belief that endometriosis was the cause of her problems. This patient asked clinic staff if the spread of endometrial tissue to her brain could explain her headaches. So Vanessa's milieu was simply awash in chatter about new diseases that might account for the chronic pain and fatigue many of these young female patients experienced. These new diseases all had one feature in common: They were incapacitating.

Finally, Vanessa belonged to a progressive urban milieu that harbored, in the backwash of the feminist movement, the expectation that women would be stars. Whereas in Victorian times women of the middle classes were expected to be shrinking violets, middle-class life today calls on women for dynamic success. The Victorian heroines of an earlier era, bedbound with paralysis, may have been registering discontent with overly limiting social roles. Middle-class women today, who, like Vanessa, become incapacitated with fatigue and weariness, may be resisting overly expansive roles, virtually limitless expectations of what they are to accomplish. What is surprising is that Vanessa had some insight into her motivation, for the great majority of patients with disabling fatigue have none at all and believe themselves to be victims of a mysterious virus.[2]

An Intellectual Context

The theory of cultural shaping is not the only one that sets out to account for the genesis of psychosomatic symptoms. It borrows heavily from two other traditions, each in itself incomplete, of explaining such illness. One tradition emphasizes psychogenesis, the origin of symptoms in the mind; the other stresses neurogenesis, or the origin of symptoms in the brain.

Psychogenesis means that symptoms arise from unconscious mental processes. If I am in pain, it is because my unconscious mind, for arbitrary reasons of its own, is thinking "pain." My conscious mind responds by perceiving pain somewhere in the periphery of the body: stomach pain even though the stomach is perfectly well, headaches even though I do not have migraine or a brain tumor. In the nineteenth century the equivalent was: If my legs do not work, it is because I have spinal irritation or (depending on my gender) because my ovaries need to be removed.

Although the tradition of psychogenesis was not the first to arise historically, it is the most influential within psychosomatic medicine today.

The psychogenesis tradition comes in three versions. One sees stress as the motor of psychosomatic symptoms. Ever since Hans Selye's work in the 1950s,[3] stress has become a kind of magic formula with which to explain psychic distress. If an individual becomes symptomatic, it can only be in response to adverse circumstances in his or her life that have created psychic pressures. Symptom formation represents a means of escaping these pressures. Stress does play a role, yet perhaps a quarter of individuals with severe psychosomatic illnesses deny being under stress and indeed seem to lead relatively placid lives.[4] Also, many people under stress remain symptom-free. So stress by no means offers a comprehensive explanation of why individuals become symptomatic.

Another version of the psychogenesis tradition is Freud's doctrine of psychoanalysis, a doctrine that today has widened into many streams of depth psychology. Psychoanalysis attributes psychosomatic symptoms to anomalies in early childhood socialization. These anomalies, such as traumatic experiences around separation from the mother or identification with the father, create intrapsychic conflicts that in turn become sources of anxiety. Physical symptoms that an individual develops later in life become a kind of sponge for soaking up this anxiety. These psychoanalytic doctrines were refined in the 1920s by the Berlin school of psychoanalysts, including Franz Alexander, and by such Viennese figures as Wilhelm Stekel and Felix Deutsch. By the late 1930s psychoanalytic interpretations had become so influential in North America that the very word *psychosomatic* implied some kind of psychoanalytic orientation on the user's part.[5] Although psychoanalytic precepts have gone somewhat out of fashion today, in many university clinics psychiatrists will still muse first about anxiety whenever they encounter somatizing patients.

A third tradition of psychogenesis goes back to the Nancy physician Hippolyte Bernheim in the 1880s, and was continued by Paul Dubois and Jules-Joseph Dejerine around the turn of the century. This tradition said that psychosomatic symptoms were produced by suggestion. Bernheim and his successors discovered that merely suggesting to individuals, through hypnotism or through a close doctor-patient relationship, that they should get better often sufficed to cure them of psychosomatic symptoms. It was also noted that patients could be suggested into illness through the inadvertent comments of a physician ("Hmmm. Funny heart sounds you've got there"), or by friends and family. This tradition of what Dubois called "rational persuasion" was then eclipsed in the 1920s by the psychoanalysts, and today the names of its members have been largely forgotten.[6]

The distinction between the Freudian tradition and the older, non-Freudian tradition of psychogenesis is important. Both patients and doctors seek guidance as to where we go from here, and these various traditions supply a point of departure. True believers in psychoanalysis will not have to look further for explanations of psychosomatic symptoms. Yet the entire Freudian tradition is now fading away—at least within medicine, and serious future discussion of the nature of psychogenesis cannot simply continue to depend on these weary pieties. Nor does it suffice, one hundred years later, simply to invoke the black box of "suggestion," as though we had not surpassed the stage hypnotists of the turn of the century. Yet non-Freudians have really gone little beyond asserting that suggestive phenomena are somehow at the root of the culture's ability to mold the unconscious mind. Nor does suggestion explain why some individuals are more vulnerable than others, except to say that they are more "suggestible," a circular argument.

The neurogenic tradition, the major alternative to the psychogenic, explains psychosomatic illness in terms of disturbances in the physical chemistry of the brain. Based on brain biology, it is a tradition that reaches back to the central-nervous paradigm of the late nineteenth century, having as intellectual ancestors such biological psychiatrists as Theodor Meynert in Vienna and Karl Wernicke in Breslau. Although this tradition has been much scorned by humanists, it has the advantage of emphasizing the reciprocal relationship between mind and brain. Its powerful recent successes with drug therapy, brain imaging, and molecular genetics have shifted the burden of disproof to its assailants. We now know that a whole range of psychic disturbances of thought and mood, such as manic-depressive illness, schizophrenia, and the like, have an underlying basis in brain biology. The mind's tendency to interpret physiological signals as illness may equally rest on brain events.

But reducing the complexity of mind to the biology of brain makes the neurogenic tradition rather simplistic and incomplete. Perhaps in psychosomatic illness the deep need to become symptomatic is somehow driven by brain events. Yet disruptions in neurotransmitters do not account for the choice of symptom, or for the timing and the duration of the illness.

What do these psychogenic and neurogenic perspectives add to our understanding of the cultural shaping of symptoms? Let us start by drawing a line. Below the line we put the causative factors in somatization, above the line the particular form, or presentation, of a given psychosomatic illness.[7] Below the line is the substructure, the driving forces; above the line is the superstructure, the social circumstances that mold the end products of those forces into culturally familiar forms.

What do we find below the line? What causes the impulse to psychosomatic illness? Here both of the mainline explanatory traditions stand us in good stead, and neither is to be preferred over the other, given the complexity of what actually drives people to become symptomatic. In the tradition of psychogenesis, stress can cause us to form symptoms: the unhappy marriage, the blocked promotion. As was suggested in chapter 3, a major reason why women are more symptomatic than men is that they tend to have unhappier lives, another form of stress. Thus stress-related psychogenesis plays a cardinal role in becoming symptomatic.

Some of the psychoanalytic doctrine about intrapsychic conflicts originating in early childhood is doubtless correct. There is some evidence that unhappy childhood experiences cause psychosomatic illness in later life. For example, of ninety-two patients who were chronic somatizers, studied in a big-city clinic for psychosomatic illness in the 1980s, nine had at some point in their illness trajectories been diagnosed with "fibrositis." Of these nine, five gave information about whether their childhoods had been unhappy or not. All five had had unhappy childhoods.[8] One might well speculate that an early-life history of grief helps contribute to the psychosomatic problem of fibrositis in adulthood.

Clearly, therefore, the insights achieved by generations of social scientists and humanists, working within the tradition of psychogenesis, come to our aid. This tradition adds much to our understanding of the practical role of somatization in coping with unhappiness. And it has much to say about the impact of trauma, sadness, and grief—about the shadow side of human life from which psychosomatic symptoms may represent an escape.

The second mainline tradition, the neurogenic, insists on genetics and disorders of brain chemistry as the main forces acting below the line in producing symptoms above. It is thoroughly conceivable that chronic somatization has a genetic component. The several decades of research achieved in this tradition may not be forgotten or brushed from the table with an exasperated gesture. Quite apart from genetics, other brain events can cause disturbances in the mind-body relationship. In depression the metabolism of amines is often disrupted, giving rise to the nonorganic pain sensations that depressed patients experience. A number of the hormones that control the bowels, such as cholecystokinin, also appear in the brain as neurotransmitters, and the speculation that some disruption of neurochemistry lies behind such disorders of the bowel-brain relationship as irritable bowel syndrome is irresistible.[9] In the analysis of what lurks below the line, neurogenic factors thus matter as well as psychogenic. The circumstances that tug individuals toward the unconscious decision to become symptomatic are quite eclectic, embracing both major traditions of psychogenesis and neurogenesis. Neither is privileged, and the interaction of both probably explains why we develop psychosomatic symptoms.

Neither tradition, however, explains the particular form of symptom arising out of these deep drives from below. Neither gives us a handle for understanding the symptoms that appear clinically before the physician's eyes or historically in the sources.

How do specific psychosomatic symptoms, so changeable from epoch to epoch, arise?

Here we turn to factors with which social historians feel more comfortable, such as social class, gender, age, and ethnicity in the forming of human behavior. These are the regular circumstances that permeate the lives of millions of dissimilar people, bringing system to the chaos of individuality. These systematic factors have much to do with determining the form of psychosomatic illness. They are the backbone of culture.

It is cultural shaping that molds the presentation of psychosomatic illness, that permits us to understand what is happening above the line. This kind of shaping clarifies why entire groups of individuals develop common symptoms, and why—as I demonstrated in my earlier book *From Paralysis to Fatigue*—these symptoms change in unison from one period to another.

The surrounding culture shapes symptoms by giving people notions of what constitutes legitimate and illegitimate disease. By playing on legitimacy—for the unconscious mind does not want to be made a fool of—the culture bestows acceptability on some forms of behavior and denies it to others. Yet individuals experience these symptoms not as "forms of behavior" but as what seems to them to be genuine organic disease. The cultural shaping thus happens to the unconscious and not the conscious mind.

History helps our understanding of these matters by pointing out how unaware people in the past generally were of the larger cultural forces that molded their most intimate perceptions. This unawareness persists even today. The presentation of psychosomatic illness is subject to modeling by forces of whose existence the individual has but the dimmest notion. Just as "economic man" has scant understanding of the greater currents in the world economy that sweep him or her along, so the "psychosomatic person" has little understanding of the larger forces impinging on his or her interpretation of bodily sensations. Yet these larger forces model the individual's cognitive orientation in such a way that bodily sensations that themselves are not the result of organic disease become amplified, or misinterpreted, as evidence of illness.

Social and Medical Correctness

The culture shapes symptoms in individuals by two processes. One relates to socially correct models of proper behavior that surround the individual at home and in the larger society; the other relates to medically correct models to which the medical profession adheres in diagnosis and treatment.

Socially correct models of how one is supposed to behave as a man or a woman are manifest in all times and places.[10] Nineteenth-century society mandated that women be essentially passive; late-twentieth-century society mandates that they be dynamic. Each kind of society harvests the pathological distortions of correctness that its models call forth. In the nineteenth century that meant paralysis and chronic neurosis; in the late twentieth, bizarre notions about disabling immunological conditions. In past times motor hysteria represented a grotesque funhouse distortion of proper passive womanhood. Today, eccentric and fixedly held beliefs about chronic fatigue, environmental disease, and multiple chemical sensitivities represent a way of dodging the socially correct dynamism now expected of all women—the anticipation that they will be superwomen, successfully managing two careers in a time when men have trouble enough coping with one.

These socially correct models preserve the continuity between pathogenesis and pathoplasticity, between the creation of symptoms below the line and the shaping of symptoms above. Underneath the surface lurk the basic causes that drive somatization forward, such as brain biology, external stress, and the like. But the presentation of symptoms above the line is shaped by larger cultural expectations of sex roles and social behavior, of ethnic group and of age group.

The second process by which the culture shapes the symptoms that individuals perceive is through the practice of medicine itself.[11] Often individuals develop symptoms that are medically correct—which is to say symptoms as the doctor expects to see them on the basis of theories that he or she has learned in medical school. Catalepsy, artificial somnambulism, Charcot-style hysteria: All are textbook examples of symptoms that arose because medicine declared that they must exist. It was medical suggestion that evoked the multiple personalities associated with animal magnetism and hypnotism. The overarching influence of a single physician, Jean-Martin Charcot, was responsible for the stylized fits and stigmata of Charcot-style hysteria.[12]

Here again our above-and-below-the-line model holds true. The individuals who permitted themselves cataleptic comas and the "impassioned poses" of *la grande hystérie* were probably those who in a later era would have developed anorexia nervosa and chronic fatigue. It was perhaps intolerable stress in their own lives or genetic predisposition that caused them to reach for symptoms in the first place. Yet the symptoms as such were dictated by the medical teachings of the day.

I have been discussing these two pathways to illness—the social and the medical—as though they were independent of each other. But they are not. What doctors believe often tends to be a function of larger societal beliefs and prejudices. The dominant medical ideas of the day, although apparently scientific in nature, are often shaped by the dominant cultural beliefs. Perhaps this is not so for such intensely scientific fundaments of medicine as immunology and molecular biology, but it is surely true of medical ideas about human behavior. Physicians cannot, any more than the rest of us, abstract themselves from the times in which they live.

Reflex theory, for example, claimed a scientific basis in the pseudoscientific doctrine of "irritation" and in the genuinely scientific notion of reflex arcs in the spine. Yet the popularity of reflex theory among physicians was probably a result of their pejorative beliefs about women—beliefs that male physicians held in common with other males of the nineteenth century. It seemed credible to them that women's minds would be manipulated by their "irritated" ovaries and their prolapsed uteri.

Psychoanalysis, to take another example, has always claimed for itself a scientific basis. Yet psychoanalytic theory also reflects larger, culturally sanctioned attitudes, in particular the view that the physicality of the body does not really affect the mind at all. This view characterized much of what the educated middle classes in the first half of the twentieth century held to be true about mind-body relations. It bespoke a confidence in the autonomy of the intellect, in the predominance of reason, and in the inevitability of progress. And this belief transfixed western culture right up until the Nazi seizure of power in 1933. Since then we have known again that men can become beasts, that we do not possess the autonomous control over our minds and actions that liberal, humanistic society anticipated before the most nightmarish events of the twentieth century began. And Freud's original confidence that the act of understanding one's unconscious conflicts would suffice for their mastery emerges in retrospect as an inadequate basis for therapy. The vicissitudes of psychoanalysis show how dependent apparently scientific views are on culture, and what consequences such theories can have for people's lives.

Medicine is a part of society. While psychosomatic illness, and the cultural forces that form it, will always be with us, it need not always be the case that medicine must collude with prejudice in holding out normative models of behavior. We cannot free ourselves, at least not without great insight, from a need to become symptomatic. But we can indeed cast aside medical ideas that are based on cultural bias rather than the rock-hard bed of science.

Insight is a noble aspiration. Yet patients seeking relief from psychosomatic illness may not obtain relevant insights from depth therapies that are oriented toward clarifying presumably causative events in their own pasts. It is to their cultures that they must look, to the ideas about correct behavior brandished at them by the members of their immediate age group, social class, ethnic affiliation, and gender. The root of their problems may not lie in themselves but in being too much in conformity with their peers' ideas about the social correctness of illness. If one's underlying problems are in fact sociological rather than psychological, there is a message of hope. While one can only with difficulty change one's psychology, understanding the ways in which others make us sick is within the reach of all.

Notes

WKW	*Wiener Klinische Wochenschrift*
WMP	*Wiener Medizinische Presse*
WMW	*Wiener Medizinische Wochenschrift*
ZBG	*Zentralblatt für Gynäkologie*

The names of publishers have been omitted for books published before 1945. Following convention, I have not given volume numbers for the three British medical weeklies but have used arabic numerals to indicate whether the article appeared in the first half of the year or the second.

CHAPTER 1
The Play of Biology and Culture

1. William Perfect, *Select Cases in the Different Species of Insanity* (Rochester, England, 1787), pp. 226–33.
2. Ewald Hecker, *Über das Verhältniss zwischen Nerven-und Geisteskrankheiten* (Kassel, 1881), pp. 7–8.
3. For a good account of these developments, see Ian R. Dowbiggin, *Inheriting Madness: Professionalization and Psychiatric Knowledge in Nineteenth-Century France* (Berkeley: University of California Press, 1991), pp. 54–75, 116–43. On the lives of these French psychiatrists see René Semelaigne, *Les Pionniers de la psychiatrie française*, 2 vols. (Paris, 1930–32), vol. 1, pp. 294–301 (Moreau), 342–51 (Morel).
4. Daniel Pick, *Faces of Degeneration: A European Disorder, c. 1848–1918* (Cambridge, England: Cambridge University Press, 1989), p. 99; Semelaigne, *Les Pionniers*, vol. 2, pp. 210–22 (Magnan).
5. See Paul Weindling, *Health, Race and German Politics Between National Unification and Nazism, 1870–1945* (Cambridge, England: Cambridge University Press, 1989); and Pauline Mazumdar, *Eugenics, Human Genetics and Human Failings: The Eugenics Society, Its Sources and Its Critics in Britain* (London: Routledge, 1992).
6. For an overview see Edward Shorter, *From Paralysis to Fatigue: A History of Psychosomatic Illness in the Modern Era* (New York: Free Press, 1992), pp. 208–20. Emil Kraepelin, the most influential German psychiatrist at the end of the century, accorded genetic influences a role in, while not making them the driving force of, mental illness. See, for example, his "Die Erscheinungsformen des Irreseins," *Zeitschrift für die gesamte Neurologie und Psychiatrie* 62 (1920), pp. 1–29; especially p. 11.
7. Frieda Fromm-Reichmann, "Notes on the Development of Treatment of Schizophrenics by Psychoanalytic Psychotherapy," *Psychiatry* 11 (1948), pp. 263–73; especially p. 265. On Fromm-Reichmann see Uwe Henrik Peters, *Psychiatrie im Exil: die Emigration der dynamischen Psychiatrie aus Deutschland, 1933–1939* (Düsseldorf: Kupka, 1992), pp. 173–88.
8. In 1959 Franz Kallmann, of the Department of Medical Genetics at Columbia University, warned: "The deeply rooted reluctance to recognize genically determined elements in the etiology of mental illness will inevitably have harmful consequences." "The Genetics of Mental Illness," in Silvano Arieti, ed., *American Handbook of*

Psychiatry, 3 vols. (New York: Basic Books, 1959–66), vol. 2, pp. 175–96; quote p. 191.

9. Penrose's initial report was not published at the time, although it circulated widely in mimeographed form and became the basis of a later article. See T. J. Crow, "A Note on 'Survey of Cases of Familial Mental Illness' by L. S. Penrose," *European Archives of Psychiatry and Clinical Neuroscience* 240 (1991), pp. 314–24.

10. On these developments see Pierre Deniker, "From Chlorpromazine to Tardive Dyskinesia (Brief History of the Neuroleptics)," *Psychiatry Journal of the University of Ottawa* 14 (1989), pp. 253– 59; Frank J. Ayd, Jr., "The Early History of Modern Psychopharmacology," *Neuropsychopharmacology* 5 (1991), pp. 71–84; Edward Shorter, *The Health Century* (New York: Doubleday, 1987), pp. 120–26.

11. Michael Lesch and William L. Nyhan, "A Familial Disorder of Uric Acid Metabolism and Central Nervous System Function," *American Journal of Medicine* 36 (1964), pp. 561–70.

12. See, for example, Kenneth K. Kidd and James L. Kennedy, "The Genetics of Affective Disorders," in Lennart Wetterberg, ed., *Genetics of Neuropsychiatric Diseases* (London: Macmillan, 1989), pp. 191–98, and T. J. Crow et al., "Clues to the Nature and Location of the Psychosis Gene: Is Schizophrenia Due to an Anomaly of the Cerebral Dominance Gene Located in the Pseudoautosomal Region of the Sex Chromosomes?" ibid., pp. 199–210. For a brief overview of the argumentation in favor of a "psychosis gene," see T. J. Crow, "The Search for the Psychosis Gene," *British Journal of Psychiatry* 158 (1991), pp. 611–14; see also Roland D. Ciaranello and Andrea L. Ciaranello, "Genetics of Major Psychiatric Disorders," *Annual Review of Medicine* 42 (1991), pp. 151–58.

13. Herbert Pardes et al., "Genetics and Psychiatry: Past Discoveries, Current Dilemmas, and Future Directions," *AJP* 146 (1989), p. 435–43; especially p. 436. See also Kay Redfield Jamison, *Touched with Fire: Manic Depressive Illness and the Artistic Temperament* (New York: Free Press, 1993).

14. Ming T. Tsuang et al., "The Genetics of Schizophrenia: Current Knowledge and Future Directions," *Schizophrenia Research* 4 (1991), pp. 157–71; especially p. 158, table 1.

15. Ibid., p. 436.

16. Raymond R. Crowe, "The Application of Genetic Methods in the Study of Disease Associations in Psychiatry," *Psychiatric Clinics of North America*, 13 (1990), pp. 585–95, especially p. 589; see also

David E. Comings and Brenda G. Comings, "The Genetics of Tourette Syndrome and its Relationship to Other Psychiatric Disorders," in Wetterberg, *Genetics*, pp. 179–89.

17. Hubert M. M. Van Tol et al., "Cloning of the Gene for a Human Dopamine D4 Receptor with High Affinity for the Antipsychotic Clozapine," *Nature* 250 (Apr. 18, 1991), pp. 610–14. Van Tol *et al.*, "Multiple Dopamine D4 Receptor Variants in the Human Population," ibid. 358 (July 9, 1992), pp. 149–52.

18. Roger Smith, in a review of Ian Dowbiggin's book *Inheriting Madness* (1991), in *Medical History* 36 (1992), p. 342.

19. "Wenn Sie auch den Kopf schütteln, Herr von Strümpell, so ist es doch wahr." Anecdote from manuscript diary of Clarence B. Farrar, then on leave at Heidelberg from the Sheppard Pratt Hospital near Baltimore, n.d. Diary in Farrar private archive, Toronto, Canada.

20. Pierre Briquet, *Traité clinique et thérapeutique de l'hystérie* (Paris, 1859), pp. 80–83. When Briquet returned to this subject much later in life, he introduced the concept of degeneration as an explanation. In a reanalysis of these data using chi-square as a test of significance, François Mai and Harold Merskey found the association between heredity and hysteria to be highly significant. "Briquet's *Treatise on Hysteria:* A Synopsis and Commentary," *Archives of General Psychiatry* 37 (1980), pp. 1401–5; especially p. 1402. See Pierre Briquet, "De la prédisposition à l'hystérie," *Bulletin de l'Académie de Médecine*, 2nd ser., 10 (1881), pp. 1135–53. He concluded, "La prédisposition par hérédité est un fait grave, c'est le début de la dégénération de la famille" (p. 1144).

21. Lennart Ljungberg, *Hysteria: A Clinical, Prognostic and Genetic Study* (Copenhagen: Munksgaard, 1957), pp. 111, 124.

22. Fulgence Raymond and Pierre Janet, *Les Obsessions et la psychasthénie*, 2 vols. (Paris, 1903), vol. 2, p. 491.

23. Paul Hartenberg, *Traitement des neurasthéniques* (Paris, 1912), pp. 326–29.

24. Walter C. Alvarez, *Nervousness, Indigestion and Pain* (New York, 1943), pp. 230–32.

25. Stephen Taylor, *Good General Practice: A Report of a Survey* (London: Oxford University Press, 1954), pp. 420–21.

26. James J. Purtell, *et al.*, "Observation on Clinical Aspects of Hysteria: A Quantitative Study of 50 Hysteria Patients and 156 Control Subjects," *JAMA* 146 (July 7, 1951), pp. 902–9.

27. Eliot Slater, "Hysteria 311," *Journal of Mental Science* 107 (1961), pp. 359–81.

28. Guze mentions some of these details in his "Studies in Hysteria," *Canadian Journal of Psychiatry* 28 (1983), pp. 434–37.

29 Oguz Arkonac and Samuel B. Guze, "A Family Study of Hysteria," *NEJM* 268 (Jan. 31, 1963), pp. 239–42.

30. Samuel B. Guze, "The Role of Follow-Up Studies: Their Contribution to Diagnostic Classification as Applied to Hysteria," *Seminars in Psychiatry* 2 (1970), pp. 392–402. Guze argued that, just as patients' fear and loathing of the term "leprosy" had led to the adoption of the eponym "Hansen's Disease," patients' dislike of the term "hysteria" suggested the use of an eponym such as "Briquet's Syndrome or Briquet's Disease" (p. 401). Of Briquet's 400 hysteria patients, 136 had experienced chronic illness, with headache, back pain, abdominal symptoms, *et cetera*, for years or lifelong. "Des hystéries de cette sorte ont pu durer toute la vie, ou tout au moins se prolonger jusqu'à un âge très avancé." Briquet, *Traité clinique*, p. 497.

31. C. Robert Cloninger and Samuel B. Guze, "Hysteria and Parental Psychiatric Illness," *Psychological Medicine* 5 (1975), pp. 27–31.

32. For a review, see C. Robert Cloninger, "Somatoform and Dissociative Disorders," chap. 9 in George Winokur and Paula Clayton, eds., *The Medical Basis of Psychiatry* (Philadelphia: Saunders, 1986), pp. 123–51.

33. See, for example, Wayne J. Katon et al., "Psychiatric Illness in Patients with Chronic Fatigue and Those with Rheumatoid Arthritis," *Journal of General Internal Medicine* 6 (1991), pp. 277–85. It was not merely that the fatigue patients were depressed or anxious because of their condition. Arthritis is also a depressing and anxiety-provoking disease, yet the arthritis patients had much less psychiatric illness than did the fatigue patients.

34. For a statistical demonstration of the impact of a childhood environment of illness and familial unhappiness on the development of chronic illness in adult life, see David Mechanic, "The Experience and Reporting of Common Physical Complaints," *Journal of Health and Social Behavior* 21 (1980), pp. 146–55. Mechanic writes, "I would hypothesize that the mother's personal problems, the child's early illnesses, and school absence are primarily important in that they create a family climate that directs the child's attention to internal states" (p. 150). Mechanic does not consider the possibility that part of the transmission of illness behavior from generation to generation may be genetic.

35. Wilhelm Erb, *Über die wachsende Nervosität unserer Zeit* (Heidelberg, 1893), p. 5.

36. D. C. Taylor, "Outlandish Factitious Illness," in T. J. David, ed., *Recent Advances in Paediatrics* 10 (1992), pp. 63–76; anecdote p. 67. The father also had a history of psychotic illness.

37. Cited in George Pickering, *Creative Malady* (London: Allen & Unwin, 1974), p. 75.

38. Janet Browne, "Spas and Sensibilities: Darwin at Malvern," in Roy Porter, ed., *The Medical History of Waters and Spas* (London: Wellcome Institute for the History of Medicine, 1990), pp. 102–13; quotes pp. 108–9.

39. Gwen Raverat, *Period Piece: A Cambridge Childhood* (London: Faber & Faber, 1952), pp. 119–23.

40. Darwin invoked "an hereditary taint." Browne, "Spas and Sensibilities" (1990), p. 111.

41. The foregoing is greatly indebted to Kenneth S. Kendler and Lindon J. Eaves, "Models for the Joint Effect of Genotype and Environment on Liability to Psychiatric Illness," *AJP* 143 (1986), pp. 279–89.

42. See the literature cited in David Reiss et al., "Genetics and Psychiatry: An Unheralded Window on the Environment," *AJP* 148 (1991), pp. 283–91.

43. See Peter McGuffin and Anita Thapar, "The Genetics of Personality Disorder," *BJP* 160 (1992), pp. 12–23.

44. Mistrust of physicians is rife in the subculture of such illnesses as chronic fatigue syndrome and fibrositis. See, for example, Laura Lee Duval, "Family Doctors: Are They or Aren't They Changing?" *Perspectives: The Magazine of the Myalgic Encephalomyelitis Association* (summer 1992), pp. 11–13. Psychiatric patients with persistent pain do tend to have resentful personalities. See Harold Merskey, "Psychiatric Patients with Persistent Pain," *Journal of Psychosomatic Research* 9 (1965), pp. 299–309; especially pp. 305–6. Whether such patients in fact give more credence to the media has not been studied.

45. There is a substantial medical literature on character disorder and psychosomatic illness. See, for example, Arthur J. Barsky, "Patients Who Amplify Bodily Sensations," *Annals of Internal Medicine* 91 (1979), pp. 63–70; especially p. 64; Howard S. Friedman and Stephanie Booth-Kewley, "The 'Disease-Prone Personality': A Meta-Analytic View of the Construct," *American Psychologist* 42 (1987), pp. 539–55. The latter authors reject the view that certain personalities are prone to specific diseases, such as asthma or coronary heart disease. "However, there may well exist a generic 'dis-

ease-prone personality' " (p. 551). Another study found, in a sub-group of patients with chronic fatigue syndrome, high levels of emotionality, social withdrawal, and impulsivity. Antony A. Blakely et al., "Psychiatric Symptoms, Personality and Ways of Coping in Chronic Fatigue Syndrome," *Psychological Medicine* 21 (1991), pp. 347–62.

CHAPTER 2
Chronic Illness in the Comfortable Classes

1. See, for example, Earl Lomon Koos, *The Health of Regionville: What the People Thought and Did About It* (New York: Columbia University Press, 1954), p. 32; here, for example, 57 percent of the upper-class people believed they should consult for "loss of appetite," as opposed to 20 percent of working-class people. Eighty percent of the upper class believed that "chronic fatigue" required medical attention, 19 percent of the lower. See also Samuel W. Bloom, *The Doctor and His Patient: A Sociological Interpretation* (New York: Russell Sage, 1963), pp. 109–11.

2. Benedict-Augustin Morel, "Du délire émotif," *Archives générales de médecine* 6, no. 7 (1866), pp. 385–402; quote p. 392.

3. Briquet, *Traité clinique*, p. 108.

4. Thomas Dixon Savill, *Lectures on Hysteria and Allied Vaso-Motor Conditions* (London, 1909), pp. 176–77.

5. Harold Merskey, *The Analysis of Hysteria* (London: Baillière Tindall, 1979), p. 120. The original report was Merskey, "The Characteristics of Persistent Pain in Psychological Illness," *Journal of Psychosomatic Research* 9 (1965), pp. 291–98.

6. Dewitt L. Crandell and Bruce P. Dohrenwend, "Some Relations Among Psychiatric Symptoms, Organic Illness, and Social Class," *AJP* 123 (1967), pp. 1527–38; quote p. 1536.

7. J. G. Stefansson et al., "Hysterical Neurosis, Conversion Type: Clinical and Epidemiological Considerations," *Acta Psychiatrica Scandinavica* 53 (1976), pp. 119–38; see table 3, p. 124.

8. Clifton K. Meador reports these images from the small Alabama town where he practiced in the 1930s and 1940s. Among the locals the term *invalid* referred to individuals who, "for whatever reason, elected to lead lives that were bound to being in continued ill health, however vaguely and poorly defined medically that might have been." "Invalids: The Male Counterpart," *Southern Medical Journal* 85 (1992), pp. 628–31; quote p. 628.

9. William Buchan, *Domestic Medicine, or a Treatise on the Prevention and Cure of Diseases,* 10th ed. (London, 1788; 1st ed., 1769), p. 467. Although the entity Buchan was describing would later be called "hypochondria," he himself understood "hypochondriac affections" to mean something different; see pp. 500–504.

10. James Sims, "Pathological Remarks upon Various Kinds of Alienation of Mind," *Memoirs of the Medical Society of London* 5 (1799), pp. 372–406; quotes pp. 392–97.

11. Charles Cowan, "Report of Private Medical Practice for 1840," *Journal of the [Royal] Statistical Society of London* 5 (1842) (ser. A [general]), pp. 81–86; quote p. 84.

12. William N. Macartney, *Fifty Years a Country Doctor* (New York, 1938), p. 500.

13. Joseph Schneider, *Versuch einer Topographie der Residenzstadt Fulda* (Fulda, 1806), p. 187.

14. Jules-Joseph Dejerine and Ernest Gauckler, *Les Manifestations fonctionnelles des psychonévroses* (Paris, 1911), p. vi.

15. Thomas Arthur Ross, "Observations on the Diagnosis and Treatment of Functional Nervous Disorder," *BMJ* 2 (Dec. 7, 1929), pp. 1041–44.

16. Aaron J. Rosanoff, "editor," *Manual of Psychiatry,* 5th ed. (New York, 1920), p. 317. When this textbook appeared in 1905 it was primarily a translation of Joseph Rogues de Fursac's *Manuel de psychiatrie* (Paris, 1903). However, Rosanoff added much of his own material in subsequent editions, including apparently this judgment, which was based on his contact with soldiers encountered in the Plattsburg hospital.

17. William Stanley Sykes, *A Manual of General Medical Practice* (London, 1927), pp. 14–16.

18. Anton Theobald Brück, *Das Bad Driburg, in seinen Heilwirkungen dargestellt, für practische Ärzte* (Osnabrück, Germany, 1844), pp. 131–32.

19. Paul Dubois, "A propos de la définition de l'hystérie," *Revue médicale de la Suisse romande* 31 (1911), pp. 391–97; quote p. 396.

20. Constance Friess and Marjory J. Nelson, "Psychoneurotics Five Years Later," *American Journal of the Medical Sciences* n.s., 203 (1942), pp. 539–58; quote p. 548. These data also show how shaky the diagnosis of "psychoneurosis" was at that time, for of the 200 patients on whom direct information was obtained, 8 percent were dead five years later and 5 percent were in mental hospitals (p. 548).

21. John Fry, "What Happens to Our Neurotic Patients?" *Practitioner* 185 (1960), pp. 85–89.

22. Brian Cooper, John Fry, and Graham Kalton, "A Longitudinal Study of Psychiatric Morbidity in a General Practice Population," *British Journal of Preventive Social Medicine* 23 (1969), pp. 210–17; see also Michael Shepherd, "The Prevalence and Distribution of Psychiatric Illness in General Practice," in a symposium on "The Medical Use of Psychotropic Drugs," *Journal of the Royal College of General Practitioners*, supplement no. 2, vol. 23 (June 1973), pp. 16–19; quote p. 16. Among follow-up studies of hospitalization for "hysteria," the patients are so diverse (including a number with major mental illnesses) that the usefulness of the original diagnosis appears quite problematic. See, for example, Dewey Z. Ziegler and Norman Paul, "On the Natural History of Hysteria in Women (A Follow-up Study Twenty Years After Hospitalization)," *Diseases of the Nervous System* 15 (1954), pp. 301–6. A. Barham Carter found a quite favorable prognosis for patients hospitalized for classic hysterical conversion symptoms, such as aphonia, paralysis, and tremor. Yet these do not represent the kind of chronic neurosis that is of interest in this chapter. "The Prognosis of Certain Hysterical Symptoms," *BMJ* 1 (June 18, 1949), pp. 1076–79.

23. Luc Ciompi, "Le Vieillissement des hystériques: étude catamnéstique," *L'Encéphale* 55 (1966), pp. 287–335, main findings pp. 295–306. Of the thirty-eight, two had "turned into" schizophrenia, two more into epilepsy, and twenty-one (55 percent) had lost their original symptoms entirely. On the subject of hysteria patients who lose their symptoms as they get older, the Breslau psychiatry professor Ludwig Hirt said in 1890, "In old age, at a time when the patients begin to become sexless, the hysterical phenomena fade. As the hair turns gray the disposition becomes calmer and more equable, and even egotistical, exacting, peevish women, who have tormented their families continually and who were extremely hard to manage, become yielding, amiable old ladies after the hysterical manifestations have once left them." Ludwig Hirt, *The Diseases of the Nervous System* (London, 1893; 1st German ed., 1890), p. 516.

24. *Fremdenliste Kurort Meran* 58 (Mar. 24, 1900), pp. 1, 3.

25. On the physical therapies employed at Merano see Oskar Josef Kuntner, "Impianti ed iniziative turistiche della città di cura di Merano dall'inizio e fino alla prima guerra mondiale" (Ph.D. diss. University of Padua, academic year 1975–76). Paul Heyse left a pic-

ture of social mores in Merano in the novella "Unheilbar," part of his *Meraner Novellen* (Berlin, 1864).

26. Hans H. Walser, ed., *August Forel: Briefe/Correspondance, 1864–1927* (Berne: Hans Huber, 1968), p. 330. In a personal communication, Walter Vandereycken has noted that this patient might have had a "trigeminal neuralgia"—often called tic douloureux—of the area of the face supplied by the trigeminal nerve. Yet this local complaint would not have accounted for his long-standing complaints in multiple organ systems.

27. Charles L. Dana, "The Partial Passing of Neurasthenia," *BMSJ* 150 (Mar. 31, 1904), pp. 339–44; quote p. 341.

28. Max Müller, *Erinnerungen: Erlebte Psychiatriegeschichte, 1920–1960* (Berlin: Springer, 1982), p. 182.

29. George Bernard Shaw, *The Doctor's Dilemma: A Tragedy* (Harmondsworth, England: Penguin, 1946; preface first published 1911), p. 22.

30. Charles Fayette Taylor, " 'Spinal Irritation'; or the Causes of Back Ache among American Women," *Medical Society of the State of New York—Transactions* (1864), pp. 126–49; quotes and cases pp. 131, 143–45.

31. Mary Putnam Jacobi, letter in response to Robert Edes's articles on "The New England Invalid," *BMSJ* 133 (Aug. 15, 1895), pp. 174–75; quote p. 175.

32. Samuel Wilks, "Lectures on Diseases of the Nervous System," *MTG* 1 (March 27, 1869), pp. 823–25; quote p. 823.

33. Edmond [et Jules] de Goncourt, *Journal: Mémoires de la vie littéraire, 1890–1891*, vol. 17 (Monte Carlo, Eds. de l'imprimerie nationale de Monaco, 1956), p. 137.

34. Jules Chéron, *Introduction à l'étude des lois générales de l'hypodermie* (Paris, 1893), pp. 233–34.

35. Jules Batuaud, *La Neurasthénie génitale féminine* (Paris, 1906), pp. 204–6.

36. Raymond and Janet, *Les Obsessions*, vol. 2, pp. 163–66; see also the case on pp. 184–86.

37. On the history of hysterical paralysis see Shorter, *From Paralysis to Fatigue*, pp. 95–128.

38. William S. Playfair, "Notes on the Systematic Treatment of Nerve Prostration and Hysteria Connected with Uterine Disease," *Lancet* 1 (June 11, 1881), pp. 949–50.

39. Quentin Bell, *Virginia Woolf: A Biography* (New York: Harcourt Brace Jovanovich, 1972), pp. 6–7.

40. On these aspects of her life, see Jeannette Marks, *The Family of the Barrett: A Colonial Romance* (New York, 1938), pp. 335, 471–76. Carol Lewis has given her the rather improbable diagnosis of "anorexia nervosa." "Elizabeth Barrett Browning's 'Family Disease': Anorexia Nervosa," *Journal of Marital and Family Therapy* 8 (1982), pp. 129–34. For a discussion of some of the issues in this case, see Walter Vandereycken, Ron Van Deth, and Rolf Meermann, *Hungerkünstler, Fastenwunder, Magersucht: eine Kulturgeschichte der Ess-Störungen* (Zülpich, Germany: Biermann, 1990), pp. 239–42.

41. See Jean Strouse, *Alice James: A Biography* (Boston: Houghton Mifflin, 1980), pp. 98, 122, 233, and passim.

42. Silas Weir Mitchell, *Lectures on Diseases of the Nervous System, Especially in Women* (London, 1881), pp. 218, 221.

43. Silas Weir Mitchell, *Doctor and Patient* (Philadelphia, 1901; 1st ed. 1887), pp. 126–27.

44. William Basil Neftel, "Über Atremie, nebst Bemerkungen über die Nervosität der Amerikaner," *Virchows Archiv für pathologische Anatomie* 91 (1883), pp. 464–91; cases pp. 464–71, 474–75.

45. Robert T. Edes, "The New England Invalid," *BMSJ* 133 (July 8, 1895), pp. 53–57; quotes pp. 54, 56. On and on rolled the diagnoses. For George Waterman, a Harvard neurologist, this bedboundness added up to "fatigue hyperesthesia." He said in 1909 that in the "psycho-neuroses, there is no one symptom so frequently encountered as that of fatigue." These were truly the hopeless and helpless, often in bed "for months or years without beneficial results." One of Waterman's female patients, on being coaxed to attempt some daily activity, told him, "Very well, I'll do it, but I know what will happen, and you must take the consequences." George A. Waterman, "The Treatment of Fatigue States," *Journal of Abnormal Psychology* 4 (1909), pp. 128–39; quotes pp. 128, 133.

46. John Pierrepont Codrington Foster, "Suggestive and Hypnotic Treatment of Neurasthenia," *Yale Medical Journal* 8 (1901), pp. 14–22; case pp. 18–19. These turn-of-the-century middle-class patients represent an eerie foreshadowing of the morose self-pity of today's chronic fatigue subculture. For example, in the cartoons that liven up the numerous newsletters of the chronic fatigue subculture, the emphasis is on the patients' helplessness rather than on coping. In one newsletter a strip entitled "ME and My Shadow" depicts the poor sufferer saying, "It's today for sure! . . . Today we're going to get right on top of this thing." In the next frame the sufferer has

been crushed by a gigantic block labeled "ME" and says from under, "Well . . . Perhaps tomorrow." *Keeping in Touch* 5 (Dec. 1990), p. 4. "ME," or myalgic encephalomyelitis, is the British equivalent of CFS.

47. Richard Alan John Asher, "The Dangers of Going to Bed," *BMJ* 2 (Dec. 13, 1947), pp. 967–68. In a tongue-in-cheek article, Clifton Meador traces the end of invalidism to the introduction of Medicare (health care for the elderly) in 1966. Invalid patients would now be intensively investigated: "Anything that could be seen was abnormal; anything that could not be seen did not exist. It soon became impossible to be nonspecifically sick. Now one had to be specifically sick and labeled, especially if Medicare was to provide coverage." "A Lament for Invalids," *JAMA* 265 (Mar. 20, 1991), pp. 1374–75; quote p. 1375.

48. If any procedure were singled out as the strategic turning point, it would be the Viennese surgeon Theodor Billroth's operation for stomach cancer, which he first performed January 29, 1881. See Owen H. Wangensteen and Sarah D. Wangensteen, *The Rise of Surgery from Empiric Craft to Scientific Discipline* (Minneapolis: University of Minnesota Press, 1978), p. 149.

49. A contemporary example: In 1983 two gastroenterologists noted how many patients with gastrointestinal symptoms had been misdiagnosed as having an intestinal obstruction by the first doctor they saw: "These cases include anorexia nervosa, the functional bowel syndrome, the superior mesenteric artery syndrome . . . and the neurogenic bladder. Usually an intestinal obstruction will have been sufficiently strongly suggested that operation will have been done, no lesion being found the first time. Since the syndrome is characteristically a relapsing or recurring one, reoperation is then frequently the case in a search for obstructing adhesions from the first operation. Thus, cases often present a 'battlefield abdomen,' one covered with scars from multiple operations." James Christensen and Sinn Anuras, "Intestinal Pseudoobstruction: Clinical Features," in William Y. Chey, ed., *Functional Disorders of the Digestive Tract* (New York: Raven, 1983), pp. 219–30; quote p. 220.

50. Royal P. Watkins, "Chronic Appendicitis," *NEJM* 207 (Aug. 25, 1932), pp. 335–38; quote p. 336. According to Leslie T. Morton, *A Medical Bibliography (Garrison and Morton)*, 4th ed. (London: Gower, 1983), p. 480, ref. no. 3562, "chronic appendicitis" was first described in 1827 by François Mélier.

51. Chester M. Jones, in discussion of Watkins, *NEJM* (1932), p. 339.

52. Clarence A. McWilliams, "Reflex Disturbances due to Chronic Appendicitis," *Medical Record* 86 (Dec. 26, 1914), pp. 1077–79.

53. Ibid.

54. See, for example, Shorter, *From Paralysis to Fatigue*, pp. 76–79, on operations on the ovaries.

55. Julius Mannaberg, "Die chronische Appendizitis," *WMW* 73 (Sept. 8, 1923), pp. 1606–8; quote p. 1608.

56. Robert Hutchison, "An Address on the Chronic Abdomen," *BMJ* 1 (Apr. 21, 1923), pp. 667–69. Of fifty patients with a diagnosis of spastic colon and mucous colitis seen by John Ryle at Guy's Hospital in the 1920s, eighteen had already been subject to appendectomy (and only three had had acute appendicitis). Ryle deplored these appendectomies "for a so-called 'grumbling appendix.' . . . We still see too many scarred abdomens with persistence of symptoms, too many 're-operations' and operations undertaken for pain." John A. Ryle, "An Address on Chronic Spasmodic Affections of the Colon," *Lancet* 2 (Dec. 1, 1928), pp. 1115–19.

57. Edward Young, in discussion of Watkins, *NEJM* (Aug. 25, 1932), p. 340.

58. Walter C. Alvarez, *Incurable Physician: An Autobiography* (Englewood Cliffs, N.J.: Prentice Hall, 1963), p. 16.

59. Gladys V. Swackhamer, *Choice and Change of Doctors: A Study of the Consumer of Medical Services* (New York, 1939), pp. 35–36.

60. Frank J. Hathaway, "The So-Called Chronic Appendix," *Practitioner* 117 (1926), pp. 240–51; quote p. 240.

61. John Berton Carnett, "Pain and Tenderness of the Abdominal Wall," *JAMA* 102 (Feb. 3, 1934), pp. 345–348; quote p. 347.

62. Cited in Clarence B. Farrar, "The Four Doctors," *Proceedings of the Seventh Annual Psychiatric Institute, Held September 16, 1959* Princeton: New Jersey Neuro Psychiatric Institute, 1959), pp. 105–16; quote p. 110.

63. Walter C. Alvarez, "When Should One Operate for 'Chronic Appendicitis'?" *JAMA* 114 (Apr. 6, 1940), pp. 1301–6.

64. Charles L. Bonifield, in discussion of Edwin Walker, "A Further Protest Against the Routine Use of Purgatives," *AJO* 64 (1911), p. 755.

65. John Janvier Black, *Forty Years in the Medical Profession, 1858–1898* (Philadelphia, 1900), pp. 194, 196.

66. William Arbuthnot Lane, "A Lecture on Chronic Obstruction of the Caecum and Ascending Colon," *Lancet* 1 (Jan. 17, 1903), pp. 153–155.

67. Élie Metchnikoff [Mechnikov], *The Nature of Man: Studies in Optimistic Philosophy,* Eng. trans. (London, 1903; 1st French ed. 1903); chapter 4 contained sections on "appendicitis and its gravity," and on the "uselessness of the caeceum and of the large intestine." Lane must have been particularly impressed by the line, "As one result of the astonishing progress of surgery, it has been found possible to excise certain parts of the gut, and particularly the large intestine" (p. 70). Also: "The large intestine is the reservoir of the waste of the digestive processes, and this waste stagnates long enough to putrefy. The products of putrefaction are harmful . . . In cases of constipation, a common complaint, certain products are absorbed by the organism and produce poisoning, often of a serious nature" (p. 73). The author also argued that the stomach was an organ "that the human body would do well to be rid of" (p. 74).

68. William Arbuthnot Lane, "An Effectual Means of Dealing with the Conditions of Chronic Obstruction of the Large Bowel Resulting from the Adhesions Which Develop in Consequence of Chronic Constipation," *Lancet* 1 (Jan. 2, 1904), pp. 19–20.

69. Ibid. See also D'Arcy Power, *Lives of the Fellows of the Royal College of Surgeons of London, 1930–1951* (London: RCS, 1953), p. 466.

70. William Arbuthnot Lane, *Operative Treatment of Chronic Constipation* (London, 1904).

71. William Arbuthnot Lane, "Remarks on the Results of the Operative Treatment of Chronic Constipation," *BMJ* 1 (Jan. 18, 1908), pp. 126–30.

72. T. B. Layton, *Sir William Arbuthnot Lane, Bt.* (Edinburgh: Livingstone, 1956), pp. 91–93 on Metchnikoff's influence; pp. 94–103 on the controversy.

73. Hutchison, *BMJ* (1923), p. 668.

74. Else Neustadt-Steinfeld, "Über einen Fall von doppelseitiger hysterischer Amaurose," *PNW* 28 (Sept. 18, 1926), pp. 421–24; quote p. 423.

75. A major boost to the doctrine of "focal infection," whence autointoxication was thought to proceed, was Frank Billings's lecture in 1915 at Stanford University, *Focal Infection: The Lane Medical Lectures* (New York, 1916). Although Billings dissociated himself from some of his colleagues' operative excesses, he did not denounce the operation and helped popularize the doctrine within the profession; see pp. 3, 10.

76. Joseph Mathews, in discussion of Walker, *AJO* (1911), p. 752.

77. William Gray Schauffler, "The Treatment of Chronic Nervous

Conditions," *Journal of the Medical Society of New Jersey* 3 (1907), pp. 197–203; quote p. 197.

78. Summary of a paper by Francis Xavier Dercum, "Hysteria with Many Operations," and of ensuing discussion, *JNMD* 49 (1919), p. 324.

79. The term is Karl Menninger's. See his "Polysurgery and Polysurgical Addiction," *Psychoanalytic Quarterly* 3 (1934), pp. 173–99; especially p. 176.

80. John W. Macy and Edgar V. Allen, "A Justification of the Diagnosis of Chronic Nervous Exhaustion," *Annals of Internal Medicine* 7 (1934), pp. 861–67; quote p. 863.

81. William R. Houston, *The Art of Treatment* (New York, 1936), p. 410.

82. Helen Flanders Dunbar, *Emotions and Bodily Changes* (New York, 1935), p. 350.

83. Elisabeth Roudinesco, *La Bataille de cent ans: histoire de la psychanalyse en France, vol. 2, 1925–1985* (Paris: Seuil, 1976), pp. 36–37.

CHAPTER 3
Women at Risk

1. Walter R. Gove and Jeanette F. Tudor, "Adult Sex Roles and Mental Illness," *American Journal of Sociology* 78 (1973), pp. 812–35; table 8, p. 826.

2. A. H. Watts et al., "Survey of Mental Illness in General Practice," *BMJ* 2 (Nov. 28, 1964), pp. 1351–58; table 4, p. 1352. The data also included patients referred to psychiatrists by the family doctor. An earlier survey in 1955–56 found even greater disparities between the genders. See data on "hysterical" and "asthenic" reactions, broken down by gender and age group, in Research Committee of the Council of the College of General Practitioners, *Morbidity Statistics from General Practice, vol. III (Disease in General Practice)* London: HMSO, 1962; General Register Office, Studies on Medical and Population Subjects, no. 14, p. 39.

3. Donna Stewart, "Unusual Presentations of Psychiatric Disease," *Medicine North America* 37 (1989), pp. 6718–21; quote p. 6718.

4. Judith M. Bardwick, *Psychology of Women: a Study of Bio-Cultural Conflicts* (New York: Harper & Row, 1971), p. 70.

5. Carroll Smith-Rosenberg, "The Hysterical Woman: Sex Roles and Role Conflict in 19th-Century America," *Social Research* 39 (1972), pp. 652–78; quote pp. 653–54.

6. Hilary Allen, "Psychiatry and the Construction of the Feminine," in Peter Miller and Nikolas Rose, *The Power of Psychiatry* (Cambridge, England: Polity Press, 1986), pp. 85–110; quote p. 86. "Embarrassment tending towards denial and compassion tending towards indignation: out of these two tendencies there has emerged a feminist analysis of psychiatry whose main thrust has been towards the demonstration of a patriarchal complicity in the apparent mental morbidity of women, and whose main conceptual schema comprises an elaborate interlinking of women's mental troubles with the social imposition of a debilitating norm of femininity" (p. 86). I find unconvincing Elaine Showalter's explanation of hysteria in nineteenth-century England as an implicit, latent form of what would later become explicit and active feminist protest. Once one gets away from the ailing matriarchal figures, the patients appear simply too powerless, downtrodden, and unhappy to be plausible as protofeminists. Showalter, *The Female Malady: Women, Madness, and English Culture, 1830–1980* (New York: Pantheon, 1985), for example, p. 147. There is also the problem that, although the lives of women become transformed in the twentieth century, "hysteria" does not go away.

7. Beulah K. Cypress, *Office Visits by Women* (United States Department of Health Education and Welfare, publication no. [PHS] 80-1976; Vital and Health Statistics, Data from the National Health Survey, series 13, no. 45), p. 14; rates estimated from figure 12. For women in all other age groups higher rates of neurosis were reported as well.

8. Gove and Tudor, "Adult Sex Roles," table 8, p. 826.

9. National Center for Health Statistics, *Vital and Health Statistics: Current Estimates from the National Health Interview Survey, 1989* (Hyattsville, Md.: United States, Department of Health and Human Services, 1990; series 10: data from the National Health Survey, no. 176), pp. 85–86. Data for population under forty-five years of age.

10. National Center for Health Statistics, *Health, United States, 1991* (Hyattsville, Md.: Public Health Service, 1992), p. 140; table 17.

11. Briquet, *Traité clinique*, pp. 47–50.

12. Charles Odier, "Le Signe de cinq heures," *Revue Médicale de la suisse romande* 46 (1926), pp. 389–403.

13. Bruce Rounsaville et al., "Briquet's Syndrome in a Man," *JNMD* 167 (1979), pp. 364–67.

14. James W. Pennebaker, *The Psychology of Physical Symptoms* (New York: Springer, 1982), pp. 9–10, 136–38, 149.

15. Charles Putnam Symonds, "Two Cases of Hysterical Paraplegia," *Guy's Hospital Gazette* 42 (1928), pp. 323–28; case pp. 325–27.

16. Edward Shorter, *A History of Women's Bodies* (New York: Basic Books, 1982; reprint, with a new preface by the author, *Women's Bodies: A Social History of Women's Encounter with Health, Ill-Health, and Medicine* [New Brunswick, N.J.: Transaction Publishers, 1991]), see pp. 227–54.

17. Ibid., p. 238.

18. Michael Macdonald, *Mystical Bedlam: Madness, Anxiety, and Healing in Seventeenth-Century England* (London: Cambridge University Press, 1981), pp. 39, 243–45.

19. Georg Wilhelm Christoph Consbruch, *Medicinische Ephemeriden, nebst einer medicinischen Topographie der Grafschaft Ravensberg* (Chemnitz, 1793), p. 56.

20. Étienne-Jean Georget, *De la physiologie du système nerveux... recherches sur les maladies nerveuses,* 2 vols. (Paris, 1821), vol. 1, pp. 331–32.

21. Raoul LeRoy d'Étiolles, *Des paralysies des membres inférieurs,* 2 vols. (Paris, 1856–57), vol. 1, pp. 248–50.

22. Franz Windscheid, "Die Beziehungen zwischen Gynäkologie and Neurologie," *ZBG* 20 (May 30, 1896), pp. 569–84; quote pp. 571–72.

23. Cornelius William Suckling, "Exhaustion Paralysis," *Lancet* 1 (Mar. 23, 1889), pp. 573–574; case p. 573.

24. Hughes Maret, *Mémoire dans lequel on cherche à déterminer quelle influence les moeurs des François ont sur leur santé* (Amiens, 1772), p. 90.

25. Edme-Pierre Chauvot de Beauchêne, *De l'influence des affections de l'âme dans les maladies nerveuses des femmes,* new ed. (Amsterdam, 1783; 1st ed. 1781), p. 6.

26. Méglin, "Topographie médicale à Guebwiller [1786]," manuscript in the Paris Académie de médecine, shelf no. SRM 175.

27. François Emmanuel Foderé, *Voyage aux Alpes maritimes,* 2 vols. (Paris, 1821), vol. 2, pp. 246–47.

28. Louis Caradec, *Topographie médico-hygiènique du département du Finistère* (Brest, 1860), pp. 67–68.

29. Franz Strohmayr, *Versuch einer physisch-medicinischen Topographie... St. Pölten* (Vienna, 1813), p. 246. "Nervenkrankheiten. Diese machen einen ansehnlichen Theil der Peingung und des Wehklagens, vorzüglich unter unserer distinguirten Klasse von Menschen aus. Nervenschwäche, Krämpfungen und quälende Mutterzustände sind die täglichen Seufzer und Jammersprache des schönen Geschlechts." For similar remarks see Dietrich Wilhelm

Heinrich Busch, *Das Geschlechtsleben des Weibes,* 5 vols., 1839–44, vol. 2 (Leipzig, 1840), pp. 324–25.

30. Joseph Amann, *Über den Einfluss der weiblichen Geschlechtskrankheiten auf das Nervensystem* (Erlangen, 1868), p. 93.

31. Felix Preissner, "Die Abteilung für Nervenkranke des Krankenhauses der Landesversicherungsanstalt Schlesien in Breslau," *PNW* 27 (Dec. 26, 1925), pp. 533–37; quote p. 533.

32. John Evans Riadore, *A Treatise on Irritation of the Spinal Nerves . . .* (London, 1843), p. 13.

33. Walter Johnson, *An Essay on the Diseases of Young Women* (London, 1849), p. 55. He said it was not unknown among the poor as well.

34. Stephen Taylor, "The Suburban Neurosis," *Lancet* 1 (Mar. 26, 1938), pp. 759–61.

35. I have in mind such intellectual heirs of Michel Foucault as Klaus Dörner, *Bürger und Irre: Zur Sozialgeschichte und Wissenschaftssoziologie der Psychiatrie* (Frankfurt: Europäische Verlagsanstalt, 1969; Eng. trans. *Madmen and the Bourgeoisie,* Oxford: Blackwell, 1981). See for example his section "Hysterie und Identität des Bürgers" (pp. 38–45). Dörner situates "hysteria" in the commercial middle classes: "Die Hysterie zeigt dem Individuum wie der Gesellschaft an, dass es nun möglich, aber auch notwendig ist, reflexiv sich selbst zu behandeln, die Stabilität der Bewegungen selbst zu regulieren" (p. 45)

36. It seems to be true that valetudinarianism presents itself first as a middle-class symptom before symptoms of chronic fatigue spread throughout society in the twentieth century. Similarly, motor hysteria recedes first among the middle classes, last among the working classes and peasantry. On these differences in timing see Shorter, *From Paralysis to Fatigue,* pp. 267–73, and Edward Shorter, "Chronic Fatigue in Historical Perspective," in Ciba Foundation, ed., *Chronic Fatigue Syndrome* (Chichester, Eng.: Wiley, 1993), pp. 6–22.

37. Quoted from Smellie's record of the case, in Robert William Johnstone, *William Smellie: The Master of British Midwifery* (Edinburgh: Livingstone, 1952), p. 12.

38. Jacques Lisfranc, *Clinique chirurgicale de l'hôpital de la Pitié,* 2 vols. (Paris, 1842), vol. 2, pp. 585–87.

39. Julius von Gomperz, *Jugend-Erinnerungen,* 2nd ed. (Vienna, 1903; 1st ed. 1901), pp. 60–62.

40. Briquet, *Traité clinique,* p. 185.

41. J. Munk, "Über wirkliche und simulirte Katalepsie," *WMP* 21 (May 23, 1880), pp. 678–80; case pp. 679–80.

42. Julius Grinker, "Nervous Cases for the General Practitioner," *Chicago Medical Recorder* 27 (1905), pp. 788–96; case pp. 790–91.

43. George S. Stevenson, "Why Patients Consult the Gastro-Enterologist," *JAMA* 94 (Feb. 1, 1930), pp. 333–37; case p. 333.

44. Maurice Macario, "De la paralysie hystérique," *Annales médico-psychologiques* 3 (1844), pp. 62–82; case p. 68.

45. Charles Negrier, *Recueil de faits pour servir à l'histoire des ovaires et des affections hystériques de la femme* (Angers, 1858), pp. 125–26.

46. The background of this discussion is my book, *The Making of the Modern Family* (New York: Basic Books, 1975).

47. Briquet, *Traité Clinique*, p. 513.

48. Ibid., p. 191.

49. Fulgence Raymond and Pierre Janet, *Les Obsessions*, vol. 2, pp. 335–37.

50. Joseph-Marie-Alfred Beni-Barde, *La Neurasthénie: les vrais et les faux neurasthéniques* (Paris, 1908), pp. 328–38. I have shorn some of the detail from the case, including accounts of conflicts with in-laws. Beni-Barde was called Alfred.

51. Adolf Müller, *Beiträge zur einer hessischen Medizingeschichte des 15–18. Jahrhunderts* (Darmstadt, 1929), p. 19.

52. Silas Weir Mitchell, *Doctor and Patient* (Philadelphia, 1901; first ed. 1887), p. 117.

53. Julian de Ajuriaguerra, "Le Problème de l'hystérie," *L'Encéphale* 40 (1951), pp. 50–87; especially p. 76.

54. For a vivid portrait of a wealthy, ailing matriarch as a "hysterical fury," see Peter Swales's account of the life of Freud's early patient Anna von Lieben (née von Todesco) in "Freud, His Teacher, and the Birth of Psychoanalysis," in Paul Stepansky, ed., *Freud: Appraisals and Reappraisals, Contributions to Freud Studies*, vol. 1 (Hillsdale, N.J.: Analytic Press, 1986), pp. 3–82. Swales argues that Anna von Lieben, who as "Frau Cäcilie M." figured in Freud and Breuer's *Studies in Hysteria*, best corresponded of the women in that book to the notion of a "hysterical fury," a notion on which Viennese dramatist Hugo von Hofmannsthal drew for his play *Elektra* (p. 73, n. 59).

55. Anthony Hutton Clarke, "The Dominant Matriarch Syndrome," *BJP* 113 (1967), pp. 1069–71.

56. Paul Schilder, "The Concept of Hysteria," *AJP* 95 (1939), pp. 1389–1413; quote p. 1405.

57. Meador, "Invalids"; quote p. 628.

58. Ibid.

59. Gilbert Ballet, "Le Sommeil provoqué par l'occlusion des oreilles et des yeux chez les individus affectés d'anesthésie hystérique généralisée," *Prog. méd.* 20 (June 25, 1892), pp. 497–501.

60. See Eric J. Dingwall, *Abnormal Hypnotic Phenomena: A Survey of Nineteenth-Century Cases,* vol. 1, *France* (London: J. A. Churchill, 1967).

61. Francis E. Anstie, *Neuralgia and the Diseases that Resemble It* (New York, 1882; first published London, 1871), pp. 208–10.

62. Hugo Gugl and Anton Stichl, *Neuropathologische Studien* (Stuttgart, 1892), p. 23.

63. Paul Dubois, *The Psychic Treatment of Nervous Disorders,* 6th ed. (New York, 1909; first French ed. 1904), pp. 380–85.

64. Louis R. Caplan and Theodore Nadelson, "The Oklahoma Complex: A Common Form of Conversion Hysteria," *Archives of Internal Medicine* 140 (1980), pp. 185–86.

65. See, for example, Henry B. M. Murphy, *Comparative Psychiatry: The International and Intercultural Distribution of Mental Illness* (New York: Springer, 1982), pp. 254–59.

66. Robert Peirce, *The History and Memoirs of the Bath* (London, 1713), p. 187.

67. George Steiner writes, "No man or woman but has felt, during a lifetime, the strong subtle barriers which sexual identity interposes in communication. At the heart of intimacy, there above all perhaps, differences of linguistic reflex intervene." *After Babel: Aspects of Language and Translation* (New York: Oxford University Press, 1975), p. 41.

68. For example, Carol Gilligan writes, "In their portrayal of relationships, women replace the bias of men toward separation with a representation of the interdependence of self and other, both in love and in work." By emphasizing "relationships of care" rather than individual achievement, "women depict ongoing attachment as the path that leads to maturity." Further: "In the different voice of women lies the truth of an ethic of care, the tie between relationship and responsibility, and the origins of aggression in the failure of connection." *In a Different Voice: Psychological Theory and Women's Development* (Cambridge, Mass.: Harvard University Press, 1982), pp. 170, 173. See also Mary Field Belenky, *Women's Ways of Knowing: The Development of Self, Voice, and Mind* (New York: Basic Books, 1986). Although such writers carefully avoid such words as *biological,* the implication in their work is that these characteristics

may be attributed to women in all times and places. Thus the characteristics would be biologically determined.

CHAPTER 4
Ethnic Components

1. Arthur Kleinman, *Social Origins of Distress and Disease: Depression, Neurasthenia, and Pain in Modern China* (New Haven: Yale University Press, 1986), p. 145.
2. See Julian Leff, *Psychiatry around the Globe: A Transcultural View* (New York: Dekker, 1981), pp. 42–53, "The Language of Emotion."
3. A study of ninety-two chronically somatizing inpatients found that, of those who were depressed, 69 percent were rated as having no or very low insight; of the nondepressed, 92 percent. See Edward Shorter et al., "Inpatient Treatment of Persistent Somatization," *Psychosomatics* 33 (1992), pp. 295–301; especially p. 298.
4. M. Yap, "Mental Diseases Peculiar to Certain Cultures: A Survey of Comparative Psychiatry," *Journal of Mental Science* 97 (1951), pp. 313–27; quote p. 318.
5. See Charles I. Fitzsimmons, "*Susto:* An Epidemiological Study of Stress Adaptation" (Ph.D. diss., University of Texas at Austin, 1974), pp. 55–77.
6. Kleinman, *Social Origins of Distress,* pp. 53–55, 93–95; also Arthur Kleinman, "Depression, Somatization and the 'New Cross-Cultural Psychiatry,' " *Social Science and Medicine* 11 (1977), pp. 3–10.
7. Irving Kenneth Zola, "Culture and Symptoms—An Analysis of Patients' Presenting Complaints," *American Sociological Review* 31 (1966), pp. 615–30.
8. See Richard M. Goodman, *Genetic Disorders Among the Jewish People* (Baltimore: Johns Hopkins University Press, 1979), pp. 115–123. Although pockets of Ashkenazic Jews in various areas of Eastern Europe did constitute a fairly identifiable racial group, Jews as a whole do not. Jews tend to share the genes of the non-Jews in whose midst they live rather than exhibit universal genetic characteristics common to all Jews. Thus there would be no "Jewish" hereditary tendency toward anything, certainly not to "hysteria" or to psychosomatic illness. See Raphael Patai and Jennifer Patai Wing, *The Myth of the Jewish Race* (New York: Scribner's, 1975).
9. See Boris M. Levinson, "Cognitive Style of Eastern European Jewish Males," *Perceptual and Motor Skills* 45 (1977), pp. 279–83.

Levinson describes the style as characterized by "high verbal and low spatial analysis ability" and continues: "It is hypothesized that the mechanism through which genetic factors produce their effect is the differential development of the cerebral hemispheres [namely, the left hemisphere]" (p. 281). Zecharia Dor-Shav [Dershowitz], however, proposes an environmental explanation of the difference: "The Jewish cultural environment as expressed in early childhood experience may affect the organization of the brain in a manner leading to lesser lateralization. Jewish culture—being a highly verbal culture—may lead to a relatively earlier male development of the left hemisphere capacity." See "Cognitive Ability, Biological Psychology, and Psychological Differentiation: An Application from Jewish Sub-culture," in John Berry and P. Schmitz, eds., *Theory of Psychological Differentiation: An Appreciation of Witkin's Influence on Psychology* (forthcoming).

10. See Steven Beller, *Vienna and the Jews, 1867–1938: A Cultural History* (Cambridge, England: Cambridge University Press, 1989), p. 42 and passim.

11. For facts about Nunberg's life, I am indebted to his daughter Melanie Sischy, living in Toronto. Nunberg mentioned little personal detail in his biography, *Memoirs, Recollections, Ideas, Reflections* (New York: Psychoanalytic Research and Development Fund, 1969). There is some additional biographical information in Herbert A. Strauss and Werner Röder, eds., *International Biographical Dictionary of Central European Emigrés 1933–1945* (Munich: Saur, 1983), vol. 2, p. 868. For Nunberg's given name at birth I am grateful to the archives of Zurich University, where Nunberg graduated in medicine in 1910.

12. Frederick Parkes Weber casebooks, Contemporary Medical Archives Centre, Wellcome Institute for the History of Medicine, vol. 1913–; case begins p. 128.

13. See, for example, Steven E. Aschheim, *Brothers and Strangers: The East European Jew in German and German Jewish Consciousness, 1800–1923* (Madison: University of Wisconsin Press, 1982); Sander L. Gilman, *Jewish Self-Hatred: Anti-Semitism and the Hidden Language of the Jews* (Baltimore: Johns Hopkins University Press, 1986); Trude Maurer, *Ostjuden in Deutschland, 1918–1933* (Hamburg: Hans Christians Verlag, 1986).

14. For example, in the city of Liebàja (Libau) in Latvia in the years 1834–82, Jewish families had an infant mortality rate of 22.8 per 100 live births, as opposed to a native Latvian one of 37.5 per 100 (the

infant mortality of the resident German community was 31.4 per 100). Ewald Kaspar, *Biostatistik der Stadt Libau und ihrer Landgemeinde in den Jahren 1834–1882* (Dorpat [Tartu]: med. diss., 1883), p. 99.

15. For a selection of anti-Semitic opinions about Jews and "nervous disease" see Michael Tschoetschel, *Die Diskussion über die Häufigkeit von Krankheiten bei den Juden bis 1920* (Mainz: med. diss., 1990), pp. 289–23. On nervous disease in the eighteenth century see Shorter, *From Paralysis to Fatigue*, pp. 14–24.

16. Anton Müller, *Die Irren-Anstalt in dem königlichen Julius-Hospitale zu Würzburg* (Würzburg, 1824), p. 177.

17. [Francis Bond Head], *Bubbles from the Brunnens of Nassau by an Old Man* (London, 1834), p. 36. Forty-three at the time, Head lived another forty-odd years. He was a nonphysician.

18. See Shorter, *From Paralysis to Fatigue*, pp. 201–32.

19. Ludwig Hirt, *The Diseases of the Nervous System* (London, 1893; 1st German ed. 1890), pp. 520–21.

20. Valentin von Holst, *Erfahrungen aus einer vierzigjährigen neurologischen Praxis* (Stuttgart, 1903), p. 58.

21. Harald Siebert, "Die Psychosen und Neurosen bei der Bevölkerung Kurlands," *Allgemeine Zeitschrift für Psychiatrie* 73 (1917), pp. 493–535; quote p. 525.

22. Well known is Erb's judgment that "Semites are by birth a neurotically predisposed race, among whom an incorrigible desire for gain, a life-style that has been imposed on them for centuries, and inbreeding and intermarriage have caused nervosity to develop to a quite astonishing degree." *Über die wachsende Nervosität*, p. 19.

23. [Jean-Martin Charcot], *Leçons du mardi à la Salpêtrière: Policlinique, 1888–1889* (Paris, 1889), lecture of Oct. 23, 1888, p. 11.

24. "De la Pathologie des Juifs," *Prog. méd.* 19 (Sept. 19, 1891), pp. 209–10; quote p. 210. The editorial was probably written by Désiré-Magloire Bourneville, the editor of the journal.

25. [Charcot], *Leçons du mardi 1888–89*, lecture of Feb. 19, 1889, p. 353.

26. Cited in Toby Gelfand, "Charcot's Response to Freud's Rebellion," *Journal of the History of Ideas* 50 (1989), pp. 293–307; quote p. 302.

27. Henry Meige, "Le Juif errant à la Salpêtrière," *Revue de l'hypnotisme* 8 (1894), pp. 146–50; quote p. 148.

28. Raymond and Janet, *Les Obsessions*, vol. 2, p. 34; see also pp. 513–17 for a Jewish patient who had what Janet considered an almost psychotic obsession about persecution.

29. Alfred T. Schofield, *Behind the Brass Plate: Life's Little Stories* (London, 1928), p. 106.
30. Cecil F. Beadles, "The Insane Jew," *Journal of Mental Science* 46 (1900), pp. 731–37; quote pp. 732–33.
31. Ibid., p. 736.
32. Smith Ely Jelliffe, "Dispensary Work in Nervous and Mental Diseases," *JNMD* 33 (1906), pp. 234–41; quote p. 237. Jelliffe did not, however, think Jews especially prone to hysteria, for he added six years later of the Post-Graduate Hospital and Dispensary, "There were 21, four men and 17 women, diagnosed as suffering from hysteria [of a total of 670 patients in 1911]. This is a comparatively small number, when it is recalled that fully one-half of the dispensary population is recruited from among simple Hebrew people." "Nervous and Mental Disease Dispensary Work," *Post-Graduate* 27 (1912), pp. 467–82, 593–607; quote p. 593.
33. Philip Coombs Knapp, "The Alleged Increase of Nervous Diseases," *BMSJ* 164 (Mar. 23, 1911), pp. 419–420; quote p. 20.
34. Walter C. Alvarez, *Nervousness, Indigestion and Pain*, pp. 170, 187–88, 197–98, 282.
35. Elcan Isaac Wolf, *Von den Krankheiten der Juden* (Mannheim, 1777), pp. 12–13. "Der unaufhörlich nagende Kummer, das beständige Nachsinnen auf den täglichen Lebensunterhalt, das marternde Schröckbild der in Zukunft durch das Alter abnehmenden Lebenskräfte, der Verlust des Reichthumes bei absterbenden Kapitalien ungültiger Wechsel, die endlich zu erschwingen sehr schwer fallenden Auflagen und Beiträge, sind jene Plagen, und unserm Geschlechte besonders eigene Leidenschaften, welchen den Nerven unendlich nachtheilig sind; und es ist auch deswegen nicht zu bewundern, dass man bei uns so viel Nervenhipochondrien wahrnimmt, welche nach und nach in eine Tiefsinnigkeit und schwarze Galle ausarten."
36. Leopold Löwenfeld, *Pathologie und Therapie der Neurasthenie und Hysterie* (Wiesbaden, 1894), p. 45.
37. Heinrich Singer, *Allgemeine und spezielle Krankheitslehre der Juden* (Leipzig, 1904), p. 85.
38. Max Sichel, "Die psychischen Erkrankungen der Juden in Kriegs- und Friedenszeiten," *Monatsschrift für Psychiatrie und Neurologie* 55 (1923), pp. 207–28; quote p. 218. The phrasing of the sentence indirectly attributes the *bon mot* to some unnamed individual; though I have seen other references to Fulgence Raymond as its originator, I have not located it in his writings.

39. Sander Gilman writes; "For Jewish scientists, whose orientation was Western (no matter what their actual geographical locus), these qualities [such as "Jewish" flat feet and intermittent claudication] were a sign of the atavistic nature of the Eastern Jews and served as a boundary between Western Jews and the degenerated Jews in the East." "The Jewish Body: A 'Footnote,' " *Bulletin of the History of Medicine* 64 (1990), pp. 588–602; quote p. 602. In this form Gilman's argument is virtually impossible to prove wrong. Not only, he says, were all Western Jews automatically biased against the East, but the Eastern Jews who had studied medicine were also biased against their countrymen. Thus, according to Gilman, a medical education perforce inclined one toward derogatory views of the *Ostjuden*. Gilman has also written on historical stereotypes of the "Madness of Jews," see his volume of essays, *Difference and Pathology: Stereotypes of Sexuality, Race, and Madness* (Ithaca: Cornell University Press, 1985), chap. 6, pp. 150–162.

40. Martin Engländer, *Die auffallend häufigen Krankheitserscheinungen der jüdischen Rasse* (Vienna, 1902), pp. 17–21. Information on Engländer's birthplace from the Rigorosen-Protokoll-Bücher of the Universitätsarchiv of Vienna. Born in 1878, he was thirty-four in 1902.

41. Arthur Stern, *In bewegter Zeit: Erinnerungen und Gedanken eines jüdischen Nervenarztes, Berlin–Jerusalem* (Jerusalem: Verlag Rubin Mass, 1968), p. 57. Stern had worked in Oppenheim's clinic in Berlin before World War I.

42. Salomon Behrendt and Salomon August Rosenthal, "Israelitische Heil- und Pflege-Anstalt für Nerven- und Gemütskranke Sayn bei Coblenz," in Johannes Bresler, ed., *Deutsche Heil- und Pflegeanstalten für Psychischkranke in Wort und Bild*, 2 vols. (Halle/S., 1910–12), vol. 2, pp. 426–433, quote p. 432.

43. Rafael Becker, *Die Nervosität bei den Juden* (Zurich, 1919), pp. 12, 23–24.

44. Hermann Oppenheim, "Zur Psychopathologie und Nosologie der russisch-jüdischen Bevölkerung," *Journal für Psychologie und Neurologie* 13 (1908), pp. 1–9; quote p. 4. On the subject of higher rates of admission of Jews to psychiatric hospitals, Arnold Kutzinski, a Berlin psychiatrist who emigrated to Palestine in 1936, said, "Jews are more prone to bring their patients into institutions because of their keener desire to provide treatment, also to keep knowledge of the disease secret from the neighbors." "The Psychopathological Problems of the Jews," *Hebrew Medical Journal* 2 (1949), pp. 166–72; quote p. 171.

45. Quoted in Stern, *In bewegter Zeit,* p. 121, "Die Neurasthenie ver-
    längert das Leben."
46. Georges Wulfing, *Contribution à l'étude de la pathologie nerveuse et
    mentale chez les Anciens Hébreux et dans la Race juive* (Paris: med. the-
    sis, 1907), pp. 61–62.
47. Henri Stern, "The Aftermath of Belsen," in Henry B. M. Murphy,
    ed., *Flight and Resettlement* (Lucerne: UNESCO, 1955), pp. 64–75;
    quote p. 73. Originally published as "Observations sur la psycholo-
    gie collective dans les camps des personnes déplacées," *Psyché* 3
    (1948), translated and abridged by Murphy. After Murphy himself
    had spent a year in the postwar period inspecting Belsen and other
    camps for the International Relief Organization, he said, "Some sur-
    gical wards were disproportionately full of Jewish patients, not peo-
    ple suffering from the aftereffects of physical or nutritional
    mistreatment in the concentration camps, but people who were
    seeking operations which they did not need and whom the surgeons
    could not understand." Murphy misinterpreted this behavior as "the
    desire for punishment or mutilation among the Jewish concentration
    camp survivors." It represented, in fact, merely a continuation of the
    East European tradition of hypochondriasis and veneration of mod-
    ern medicine. Murphy, "Lines of Personal Development," in *Careers
    in Transcultural Psychiatry, Career Directions,* vol. 4, no. 2 (East
    Hanover, N.J.: D.J. Publications, 1974), pp. 15–25; quote p. 20. I
    am grateful to Raymond Prince for bringing this reference to my at-
    tention.
48. Maurice Fishberg, "The Comparative Pathology of the Jews," *New
    York Medical Journal* 73 (Mar. 30, April 6, 1901), pp. 537–43,
    576–81; quotes pp. 543, 576.
49. Abraham Myerson, "The 'Nervousness' of the Jew," *Mental Hygiene*
    4 (1920), pp. 65–72; quote p. 66.
50. Hyman Morrison, "A Study of Fifty-One Cases of Debility in Jewish
    Patients," *BMSJ* 157 (Dec. 19, 1907), pp. 816–19.
51. Toby Cohn, "Nervenkrankheiten bei Juden," *Zeitschrift für
    Demographie und Statistik der Juden,* NF 3 (1926), pp. 73–86; quote
    p. 81.
52. On U.S. medical culture in the first half of the twentieth century,
    see Edward Shorter, *Bedside Manners: The Troubled History of
    Doctors and Patients* (New York: Simon & Schuster, 1985),
    pp. 107–39, 213.
53. Oppenheim, *Journal für Psychologie,* p. 4. Berlin psychiatrist Toby
    Cohn referred to the "grössere Konsultationsfreudigkeit der

Ostjuden" (the Eastern Jews' heightened willingness to seek consultations), *Demographie Juden* (1926), p. 74.

54. Paul Rosenstein, *Narben bleiben zurück: Die Lebenserinnerungen des grossen jüdischen Chirurgen* (Bad Wörishofen: Kindler, 1954), p. 73.

55. Emil Kraepelin, *Lebenserinnerungen* (Berlin: Springer, 1983), p. 48.

56. Johannes Heinrich Schultz, *Lebensbilderbuch eines Nervenarztes: Jahrzehnte in Dankbarkeit* (Stuttgart: Thieme, 1964), pp. 64–65.

57. Emile Bratz, *Humor in der Neurologie und Psychiatrie* (Berlin, 1930), p. 11.

58. Friedrich Torberg, *Die Erben der Tante Jolesch* (Munich: DTV, 1981), pp. 84–85.

59. Adolf Strümpell, *Aus dem Leben eines deutschen Klinikers: Erinnerungen und Beobachtungen* (Leipzig, 1925), p. 232.

60. Ibid., p. 243.

61. Bernhard Naunyn, *Erinnerungen, Gedanken und Meinungen* (Munich, 1925), p. 294.

62. Elias Canetti, *Die gerettete Zunge: Geschichte einer Jugend* (Munich: Hanser, 1977), p. 36. I assume that Canetti was referring to Adolf Lorenz, Hermann Schlesinger, Johann Schnitzler, Isidor Neumann, Markus Hajek, and Josef Halban. But there were a number of famous Neumanns and Schlesingers, and the family could have had any of them in mind.

63. Ernst von Leyden, *Lebenserinnerungen* (Stuttgart, 1910), pp. 100–101.

64. Naunyn, *Erinnerungen,* pp. 296–97.

65. Stern, "Aftermath Belsen" (1948), p. 73.

66. Strümpell, *Leben deutschen Klinikers,* pp. 231–32.

67. See Otto Braus, *Akademische Erinnerungen eines alten Arztes an Berlins klinische Grössen* (Leipzig, 1901), p. 108.

68. See Rolf Winau, *Medizin in Berlin* (Berlin: de Gruyter, 1987), p. 325.

69. See Dagmar Hartung–von Doetinchem and Rolf Winau, eds., *Zerstörte Fortschritte: das jüdische Krankenhaus in Berlin, 1756–1989* (Berlin: Eds. Hentrich, 1989), p. 27; Regine Lockot, *Erinnern und Durcharbeiten: Zur Geschichte der Psychoanalyse und Psychotherapie im Nationalsozialismus* (Frankfurt/M.: Fischer, 1985), p. 172; Stephan Leibfried and Florian Tennstedt, *Berufsverbote und Sozialpolitik 1933: Die Auswirkungen der nationalsozialistischen Machtergreifung auf die Krankenkassenverwaltung und die Kassenärzte* Arbeitspapiere des Forchungsschwerpunktes Reproduktionsrisiken, no. 2, (Bremen: Universität Bremen, 1981), p. 74.

70. Alfred Grotjahn, *Erlebtes und Erstrebtes: Erinnerungen eines sozialistischen Arztes* (Berlin, 1932), pp. 75–76.

71. As Paul Julius Möbius wrote in a letter to Forel of Nov. 21, 1891, in Hans H. Walser, ed., *August Forel: Briefe/Correspondance, 1864–1927* (Berne: Hans Huber, 1968), p. 264.

72. As Georg Jürgens described his own anti-Semitic views, as well as those of the professor of internal medicine Friedrich Kraus, around the time of World War I. Jürgens, *Arzt und Wissenschaft: Erkenntnisse eines Lebens* (Hanover: Schmorl, 1949), pp. 74–75.

73. From the years after World War I, Arthur Stern remembered Richard Cassirer, Kurt Goldstein, Kurt Löwenstein, and Paul Schuster. *In bewegter Zeit*, p. 50.

74. Jürg Zutt et al., eds., *Karl Bonhoeffer zum hundertsten Geburtstag am 31. März 1968* (Berlin: Springer, 1969), p. 84. This volume contains Bonhoeffer's manuscript autobiography, written around 1941.

75. Oppenheim, *Journal für Psychologie*, p. 4.

76. From Goldscheider's answer to a questionnaire Cohn had circulated, quoted in Cohn, *Demographie Juden*, p. 75.

77. See David Mechanic, "Religion, Religiosity, and Illness Behavior: The Special Case of the Jews," *Human Organization* 22 (1963), pp. 202–8. Mechanic concluded that "Jewish populations exhibit higher illness behavior than Protestant and Catholic populations, especially at the higher-class levels" (p. 207).

78. Several surveys have shown that manic-depressive illness in particular clusters in Jewish women of East European origin. For a review see Edward Shorter, "Women and Jews in a Private Nervous Clinic in Late Nineteenth-Century Vienna," *Medical History* 33 (1989), pp. 149–83; especially pp. 181–82.

CHAPTER 5
The Cultural Face of Melancholy

1. Archives of Holloway Sanatorium Hospital, Wellcome Institute for the History of Medicine, London, ms. 5162, p. 45. "Dec. 16, Patient left today," represents the only information we have about Herbert C.'s clinical course as a "voluntary boarder" at the asylum.

2. See Stanley W. Jackson, *Melancholia and Depression: From Hippocratic Times to Modern Times* (New Haven, Conn.: Yale University Press, 1986).

3. Hagop S. Akiskal, "A Developmental Perspective on Recurrent

Mood Disorders: A Review of Studies in Man," *Psychopharmacology Bulletin* 22 (1986), pp. 579–86; especially p. 583.

4. On the basis of rates for men and women, given in seven studies containing data on "point prevalence per 100 [population at risk] of depressive symptoms," cited in Jeffrey H. Boyd and Myrna M. Weissman, "Epidemiology of Affective Disorders," *Archives of General Psychiatry* 38 (1981), pp. 1039–46; table 1, p. 1041.

5. Ibid.

6. George W. Comstock and Knud J. Helsing, "Symptoms of Depression in Two Communities," *Psychological Medicine* 6 (1976), pp. 551–63; 20.1 percent of the whites, 17.6 percent of the blacks, table 3, p. 557.

7. Tómas Helgason, "Frequency of Depressive States within Geographically Delimited Population Groups," *Acta Psychiatrica Scandinavica,* suppl. 162, vol. 37 (1961), pp. 81–90; see table 5, p. 88.

8. For references see Boyd and Weissman, "Epidemiology of Affective Disorders," table 5, "Point Prevalences per 100 for Nonbipolar Depression," p. 1042.

9. For reviews of the literature on somatization in primary care and its depressive component, see Zbigniew J. Lipowski, "Somatization and Depression," *Psychosomatics* 31 (1990), pp. 13–21; and Donna E. Stewart, "Emotional Disorders Misdiagnosed as Physical Illness: Einvironmental Hypersensitivity, Candidiasis Hypersensitivity, and Chronic Fatigue Syndrome," *International Journal of Mental Health* 19 (1990), pp. 56–68;

10. Edward George Earle Lytton (first Baron Bulwer-Lytton), *Confessions of a Water-Patient* (London, 1845), pp. 14–15, 18, 26, 52.

11. Kleinman, *Social Origins of Distress,* especially pp. 44–50 on how only certain cultures process dysphoria as "depression."

12. This is one insight of Michel Foucault's that I believe to be quite correct: "In the anxiety of the second half of the eighteenth century, the fear of madness grew at the same time as the dread of unreason: and thereby the two forms of obsession, leaning upon each other, continued to reinforce each other." Michael Foucault, *Madness and Civilization: A History of Insanity in the Age of Reason,* Eng. trans. (New York: Random House, 1965; 1st French ed. 1961), p. 171. But I think the cause of this growing fear of madness was not, as Foucault suggests, "the great confinement," but a horror of familial inheritance of madness based upon wildly exaggerated statements of genetic risk.

13. Markus Schär, *Seelennöte der Untertanen: Selbstmord, Melancholie und Religion im Alten Zürich, 1500–1800* (Zurich: Chronos, 1985), p. 15.

14. For an overview of the large psychiatric literature on cross-cultural variations in depression, see Henry B. M. Murphy, *Comparative Psychiatry: The International and Intercultural Distribution of Mental Illness* (New York: Springer, 1982), pp. 115–46.

15. See Jackson, *Melancholia and Depression,* pp. 30–31, for Hippocratic references.

16. Barbara H. Traister made available these quotes from Forman's record of treating Robert Burton. "New Evidence about Burton's Melancholy?" *Renaissance Quarterly* 29 (1976), pp. 66–70; quotes p. 67.

17. Floyd Dell and Paul Jordan-Smith, eds., *The Anatomy of Melancholy by Robert Burton* (New York, 1927); quotes pp. 323, 325, 328, 331, 333.

18. Thomas Sydenham, "Letter to Dr. Cole" [1682], in R. G. Latham, ed., *The Works of Thomas Sydenham, M.D.,* 2 vols. (London, 1848–50), vol. 2, pp. 26–118; quote p. 94.

19. Vanessa S. Doe, ed., *The Diary of James Clegg of Chapel en le Frith, 1708–1755* (Matlock: Derbyshire Record Society, 1978), vol. 2, part 1, p. 255.

20. For an energetic though quite unsystematic view of the evidence, see Roy Porter, *Mind-Forg'd Manacles: A History of Madness in England from the Restoration to the Regency* (Cambridge, Mass.: Harvard University Press, 1987); especially pp. 241–46 on patients' voices.

21. John Purcell, *A Treatise of Vapours,* 2nd ed. (London, 1707; 1st ed. 1702), pp. 13, 170.

22. Richard Blackmore, *A Treatise of the Spleen and Vapours, or Hypochondriacal and Hysterical Affections* (London, 1725), pp. 26–27. For later analyses, see, for example, Hagop S. Akiskal and Gopinath Mallya, "Criteria for the 'Soft' Bipolar Spectrum: Treatment Implications," *Psychopharmacology Bulletin* 23 (1987), pp. 68–73.

23. James Sims, "Pathological Remarks upon Various Kinds of Alienation of Mind," *Memoirs of the Medical Society of London* 5 (1799), pp. 372–406; quotes pp. 378–81.

24. Shorter, *From Paralysis to Fatigue,* pp. 233–66.

25. See, for example, the advertisement for the "Sanatorium for Patients with Nervous Illnesses and Diseases of the Circulatory System in Friedrichroda/Thüringen": "The mentally ill [*Geisteskranke*] are absolutely excluded," the institution insisted. Paul Berger, *Führer durch*

die Privat-Heilanstalten Deutschlands, Österreichs und der Schweiz (Berlin, 1889), pp. 81–82.

26. Landes-Irren-Anstalt Kierling-Gugging, Archives, discharge number 1903/149.

27. For an overview of the diagnosis of hypochondria, see Esther Fischer-Homberger, *Hypochondrie: Melancholie bis Neurose: Krankheiten und Zustandsbilder* (Berne: Huber, 1970).

28. James Rymer, *A Tract Upon Indigestion and the Hypochondriac Disease*, 2nd ed. (London, 1785; 1st ed., 1784), p. 5–7.

29. Jean-Baptiste Louyer-Villermay, *Recherches historiques et médicales sur l'hypochondrie, isolée . . . de l'hystérie et de la mélancholie* (Paris, 1802), pp. 106–9.

30. John Evans Riadore, *Introductory Lectures to a Course on Nervous Irritation, Spinal Affections. . . .* (London, 1835), p. 60.

31. Max Leidesdorf, *Lehrbuch der psychischen Krankheiten*, 2nd ed. (Erlangen, 1865; 1st ed. 1860), pp. 151–56, paraphrase from p. 154.

32. See, for example, Ian Dowbiggin, *Inheriting Madness: Professionalization and Psychiatric Knowledge in Nineteenth-Century France* (Berkeley: University of California Press, 1991).

33. Karl Kahlbaum, *Die Gruppierung der psychischen Krankheiten und die Eintheilung der Seelenstörungen* (Danzig, 1863). Kahlbaum proposed "dysthymia meläna," or what other authors had called "dysthymia atra," more or less as a synonym for "melancholia." Dysthymia lacked the imputed causal association with "black bile" of the term *melancholia.* "Melancholia [*dysthymia atra*] is in my opinion not a distinctive disease entity but a complex of symptoms seen in various conditions and diseases—even organic diseases—a complex of symptoms that is usually so well demarcated and consistent that it probably requires a designation of its own" (pp. 97–100). On the development of Kahlbaum's thinking see Clemens Neisser, "Karl Ludwig Kahlbaum, 1828–1899," in Theodor Kirchhoff, ed., *Deutsche Irrenärzte*, 2 vols. (Berlin, 1921–24), vol. 2, pp. 87–96; especially pp. 94–95.

34. Theodor Tiling, "Über Dysthymia und die offenen Curanstalten," *Jahrbuch für Psychiatrie* 3 (1879), pp 171–86; especially pp. 173–74.

35. See, for example, Shorter, "Private Clinics in Central Europe, 1850–1933," *Social History of Medicine* 3 (1990), pp. 159–95.

36. Hirt, *Diseases of the Nervous System*, pp. 499–500.

37. Maurice de Fleury, *Manuel pour l'étude des maladies du système nerveux* (Paris, 1904), pp. 838–40.

38. Heinrich Averbeck, "Die akute Neurasthenie," *Deutsche Medizinal-Zeitung* 7 (April 1, 5, 8, 12, 15, 1886), pp. 293–96, 301–5, 313–15, 325–28, 337–40; quotes pp. 301, 325.

39. Hugo Gugl, "Die Grenzformen schwerer cerebraler Neurasthenie," in Gugl and Stichl, *Neuropathologische Studien,* pp. 124–151; especially pp. 135–38, 151.

40. G. Renaudin, "Du rôle de la virginité dans l'étiologie de la neurasthénie," *Archives médico-chirurgicales de province* 6 (1911), pp. 527–32.

41. Hartenberg, *Traitement des neurasthéniques.* He ruled out depression in cases in which the patients showed signs of "nervous irritability," such as "exaggerated emotivity and insomnia" (p. 8). Insomnia, at least, would be considered evidence of depression today.

42. I have not been able to consult Heinroth's *Lehrbuch der Störungen des Seelenlebens* (1818) and rely here on Michael Schmidt-Degenhard, *Melancholie und Depression: Zur Problemgeschichte der depressiven Erkrankungen seit Beginn des 19. Jahrhunderts* (Stuttgart: Kohlhammer, 1983), pp. 26–29. In Heinroth's later *Lehrbuch der Seelengesundheitskunde, Erster Theil: Theorie und Lehre von der Leibespflege* (Leipzig, 1823), the concept of depression is taken as self-understood, as for example, p. 590: "unsere psychischen Stimmungen überhaupt, die Exaltation oder Depression unseres Gemüths . . ."

43. Louis-Jean-François Delasiauve, "Du diagnostic différentiel de la lypémanie," *Annales médico-psychologiques* 3 (1856), pp. 380–442. I have not seen this, and depend here upon German E. Berrios, "Melancholia and Depression During the 19th Century: A Conceptual History," *BJP* 153 (1988), pp. 298–304; especially p. 300.

44. Emil Kraepelin, *Psychiatrie: Ein Lehrbuch für Studirende und Ärzte,* 5th ed. (Leipzig, 1896). Although the table of contents uses the phrase "simple depression," categorized under "depressive forms" (p. xiii), Kraepelin avoided such a clear delineation in the text: "Finally we turn to one last group of cases in which the clinical picture presents only simple inner agitation without the delusion of having sinned" (p.650). If relapsing, Kraepelin referred to this form as "periodic depressive states" (p. 652). On the evolution of Kraepelin's views about depression, see Schmidt-Degenhard, *Melancholie und Depression,* pp. 88–89.

45. Adolf Meyer, in discussion, "Society Proceedings: New York Neurological Society, November 1, 1904," *JNMD* 32 (1905); com-

ments pp. 114–15. On Meyer's general views about mood disorders, see Jackson, *Melancholia*, pp. 195–202.

46. Walter Cimbal, "Vegetative Äquivalente der Depressionszustände," *Deutsche Zeitschrift für Nervenheilkunde* 107 (1929), pp. 36–41; quote p. 36: "A mood swing may be considered depressive only if to the feelings of dysphoria are added feelings of physical weakness and lack of well-being, of the inability to resist or achieve anything." On the continuance of this tradition, see R. Lemke, "Über die vegetative Depression," *Psychiatrie, Neurologie und medizinische Psychologie* 1 (1949), pp. 161–66. On Cimbal's later career, see Geoffrey Cocks, *Psychotherapy in the Third Reich: The Göring Institute* (New York: Oxford University Press, 1985), p. 17 and passim.

47. Z. J. Lipowski, "Somatization: A Borderland Between Medicine and Psychiatry," *Canadian Medical Association Journal* 135 (1986), pp. 609–14; quote pp. 611–12.

48. Richard von Krafft-Ebing, *Die Melancholie* (Erlangen, 1874), pp. 8–9.

49. Wellcome ms. 5157, Holloway Sanatorium Hospital, case no. 427, 1889. The identity of the staff physician is unclear.

50. Landes-Irren-Anstalt Kierling-Gugging, Archives, discharge no. 1901/296. Her official diagnosis was "melancholia in transition to secondary dementia."

51. The t-test of proportions is 1.087.

52. Andreas von Orelli, "Der Wandel des Inhaltes der depressiven Ideen bei der reinen Melancholie," *Schweizer Archiv für Neurologie und Psychiatrie* 73 (1954), pp. 217–87; data pp. 228–29. For men the rise was from 17 percent in the first period to 27 percent in the last.

53. John M. Eagles, "Delusional Depressive In-Patients, 1892 to 1982," *BJP* 143 (1983), pp. 558–63; especially p. 560. It declined to 19 percent by 1981–82. To be sure, three other studies show no change in the frequency of delusions about disease among depressed people. Yet no study demonstrates a long-term decline. At the university psychiatric clinic in Heidelberg, 40 percent of "cyclothymics" expressed "delusional hypochondria" in 1886, 25 percent in 1916, and 44 percent in 1946. Heinrich Kranz, "Das Thema des Wahns im Wandel der Zeit," *Fortschritte der Neurologie und Psychiatrie* 23 (1955), pp. 58–72; especially p. 61. Among depressed patients at the Niedernhart asylum near Linz in the period 1903–48, the percentage voicing "hypochondriacal complaints" remained at about 30. Hermann Lenz, *Vergleichende Psychiatrie: eine Studie über die Beziehung von Kultur, Soziologie und Psychopathologie* (Vienna:

Maudrich, 1964), p. 28. At the university psychiatry clinic in Helsinki, the percent of psychotically depressed patients having "some" hypochondriacal concerns remained steady at about 28 percent over the years 1880 to 1969. It is true that those with "severe hypochondriacal symptoms" declined from 15 percent to 1 percent. Those with "some" were a considerably more numerous group. P. Niskanen and Kalle Achté, "Disease Pictures of Depressive Psychoses in the Decades 1880–89, 1900–09, 1930–39 and 1960–69," *Psychiatria Fennica* (1972), pp. 95–101; especially p. 97.

54. Purcell, *A Treatise of Vapours,* p. 170.

55. Georget, *De la physiologie du système nerveux,* vol. 2, p. 282.

56. Beni-Barde, *La Neurasthénie,* pp. 68–72. Pierre-Charles-Édouard Potain died in 1901 and so this intriguing surgical reference could not have been to colectomy for neurosis, which became popular only after 1904.

57. Maurice Krishaber, *De la névropathie cérébro-cardiaque* (Paris, 1873), pp. 32–38.

58. Shorter, *Paralysis to Fatigue,* pp. 175–81.

59. André Blouquier de Claret, "Une cause curieuse de dépression mélancolique chez une hystérique," *Montpellier médical* 44 (1922), pp. 568–70.

60. Shorter, *From Paralysis to Fatigue,* pp. 157–59.

61. Raymond and Janet, *Les Obsessions,* vol. 2, pp. 492–95. Janet's own categories for the analysis of this case, needless to say, were completely different. For a second evidently depressed young woman who also "sees everything for the first time," see pp. 34–35.

62. Leidesdorf, *Lehrbuch,* pp. 158–59.

63. Mary A. Hill, *Charlotte Perkins Gilman: The Making of a Radical Feminist, 1860–1896* (Philadelphia: Temple University Press, 1980), pp. 148–49.

64. Case from the Svetlin Heilanstalt, Wien III; chart preserved in the Psychiatrisches Krankenhaus der Stadt Wien. I am grateful to Professor Eberhard Gabriel for giving me access to this material.

65. Parkes Weber Papers, Wellcome Institute for the History of Medicine, Contemporary Medical Archives Centre, London, vol. 1907–9, p. 200.

66. Shorter, *From Paralysis to Fatigue,* pp. 301–13.

67. Gary S. Taerk et al., "Depression in Patients with Neuromyasthenia (Benign Myalgic Encephalomyelitis) [chronic fatigue]," *International Journal of Psychiatry in Medicine* 17 (1987), pp. 49–56.

68. Simon Wessely and R. Powell, " 'Postviral' Fatigue with Neuro-

muscular and Affective Disorders," *Journal of Neurology, Neuro-surgery and Psychiatry* 52 (1989), pp. 940–48; especially p. 946.

69. On the genetics of depression, see the literature cited in chapter 1. On its biochemistry, it is interesting that one group of researchers, finding a close relationship between endometriosis (a gynecological disease in which tissue resembling that of the lining of the uterus oc-curs elsewhere in the pelvic cavity) and manic-depressive illness, speculated that both might be caused by disruption of the same hor-mones and neurotransmitters. Dorothy Otnow Lewis et al., "Bipolar Mood Disorder and Endometriosis: Preliminary Findings," *AJP* 144 (1987), pp. 1588–91.

70. See George Winokur, "Unipolar Depression," in George Winokur and Paula Clayton, eds., *The Medical Basis of Psychiatry* (Philadelphia: Saunders, 1986), pp. 60–79; especially pp. 70–71.

CHAPTER 6
Youth and Psychosomatic Illness

1. National Center for Health Statistics, *Current Estimates from the National Health Interview Survey, United States, 1987* (Hyattsville, Md.: DHHS Pub. No. [PHS] 88-1595, 1988), p. 86, table 58. The surplus for elderly women is smaller only because younger women are plagued more by irritable bowels. The rate of "spastic colon" is 1.1 per one thousand persons for men under 45, 6.1 for men sixty-five to seventy-four; 6.7 for women under forty-five, 13.9 for women sixty-five to seventy-four.

2. See Shorter, *From Paralysis to Fatigue*, pp. 95–128.

3. Buchan, *Domestic Medicine*, p. 151.

4. John Russell Reynolds, ed., *A System of Medicine*, 5 vols. (London, 1866–79), vol. 2 (1872), pp. 83–84. Reynolds wrote the chapter "Hysteria" (pp. 82–107).

5. Löwenfeld, *Pathologie und Therapie*, p. 40.

6. Hector Landouzy, *Traité complet de l'hystérie* (Paris, 1846), p. 184. It is unclear whether Landouzy had seen all these patients personally or whether he obtained some cases from their charts or from the lit-erature.

7. Briquet, "De la prédisposition à l'hystérie," p. 1138.

8. François-Louis-Isidor Valleix, *Traité des névralgies ou affections douloureuses* (Paris, 1841), p. 692. After age thirty men were more in predominance. It is unclear exactly how the statistical base of 286 cases was compiled.

9. Edward Shorter et al., "Inpatient Treatment of Persistent Soma-tization," *Psychosomatics* 33 (1992), pp. 295–301; especially p. 297.
10. A survey taken in 1961 of fifteen thousand patients in a number of general practices in London found that the incidence of new cases of psychiatric morbidity rose sharply from ages fifteen to thirty, declining thereafter. Many of these cases would turn into lifelong illness, for the number of chronic cases among both males and females rose sharply from ages fifteen to forty, plateauing for older age groups. In this study psychosomatic conditions amounted to 30 percent of all psychiatric illness. Michael Shepherd et al., "Minor Mental Illness in London: Some Aspects of a General Practice Survey," *BMJ* 2 (Nov. 28, 1964), pp. 1359–63; see figs. 2 and 3, p. 1361.
11. Houston, *The Art of Treatment,* p. 414.
12. See Frederick H. Lowy, "Foreword: Anorexia Nervosa: A Paradigm for Mind-Body Interdependence?" in Padraig L. Darby et al., eds., *Anorexia Nervosa: Recent Developments in Research* (New York: Alan R. Liss, 1983), pp. xii–xv. "Anorexia nervosa is often regarded as the quintessential psychosomatic disorder" (p. xiii).
13. L. K. George Hsu, "The Gender Gap in Eating Disorders: Why Are the Eating Disorders More Common Among Women"? *Clinical Psychology Review* 9 (1989), pp. 393–407.
14. Higher estimates of fatality often stem from specialized clinics that treat the severest cases. For the figure of one in ten I am indebted to Walter Vandereycken of Louvain University, with his great clinical experience and knowledge of the literature.
15. E. S. Gershon, "Anorexia Nervosa and Major Affective Disorders Associated in Families: A Preliminary Report," Samuel B. Guze et al., eds., *Childhood Psychopathology and Development* (New York: Raven Press, 1983), pp. 279–84.
16. A. J. Holland et al., "Anorexia Nervosa: Evidence for a Genetic Basis," *Journal of Psychosomatic Research* 32 (1988), pp. 561–71; quote p. 568. "Eggs" refers to monozygotes and dizygotes. See also Andrew Winokur et al., "Primary Affective Disorder in Relatives of Patients with Anorexia Nervosa," *AJP* 137 (1980), pp. 695–98, which found anorexia occurring twice as frequently in families with a history of depression as in the population as a whole; see also James I. Hudson et al., "Family History Study of Anorexia Nervosa and Bulimia," *BJP* 142 (1983), pp. 133–38, which established that anorexics have about the same frequency of affective disorder in their backgrounds as do patients with manic-depressive illness

("bipolar disorder"). By contrast, in schizophrenics and patients with borderline personality disorder, family histories of mental illness were less common.

17. On the culture-specific nature of eating disorders, see Raymond Prince, "The Concept of Culture-Bound Syndromes: Anorexia Nervosa and Brain Fag," *Social Science and Medicine* 21 (1985), pp. 197–203; Joan Jacobs Brumberg, *Fasting Girls: the Emergence of Anorexia Nervosa as a Modern Disease* (Cambridge, Mass.: Harvard University Press, 1988); Vincenzo F. DiNicola, "Anorexia Nervosa: a Culture-Bound Syndrome," in *Psychiatry: A World Perspective . . . Proceedings of the VIII World Congress of Psychiatry, Athens, 12–19 October 1989*, vol. 4 (Amsterdam: Excerpta Medica, 1990), pp. 201–6; also Vincenzo F. DiNicola, "Anorexia Multiforme: Self-Starvation in Historical and Cultural Context," *Transcultural Psychiatric Research Review* 27 (1990), pp. 165–96, 245–86. One authority notes: "Eating disorders are unusual and unique among psychiatric disorders in that . . . they appear to be culturally determined." James E. Mitchell, "The Treatment of Eating Disorders," *Psychosomatics* 31 (1990), pp. 1–3; quote p. 1. On the question of whether anorexia nervosa is found outside Western, white culture, see the review of the literature in Tilmann Habermas, *Heisshunger: historische Bedingungen der Bulimia nervosa* (Frankfurt/M.: Fischer, 1990), pp. 235–36, n. 12.

18. For a review of the literature on "fasting maidens," as well as an assessment of what pre-1850 behaviors legitimately constituted early instances of anorexia nervosa, see Vandereycken, Van Deth, and Meermann, *Hungerkünstler, Fastenwunder, Magersucht:* especially chap. 4. Fady Hajal proposes a possible case of anorexia nervosa from the early Middle Ages, "Psychological Treatment of Anorexia: A Case from the Ninth Century," *Journal of the History of Medicine,* 37 (1982), pp. 325–28.

19. Kelly Bemis writes, "Anorectic patients generally have no wish to recover from the disabling and demanding disorder that possesses them—or are at least profoundly ambivalent at the prospect. . . . Indeed, anorectic patients may take *pride* in the fact that their weight is *not* normal, treasuring the sense of 'specialness' that this seems to confer, and often want therapists to remove their other distressing symptoms without interfering with their chosen weight [italics Bemis's]. "A Comparison of Functional Relationships in Anorexia Nervosa and Phobia," in Darby, *Anorexia Nervosa,* p. 407.

20. American Psychiatric Association, *Diagnostic and Statistical Manual*

of Mental Disorders: DSM-III-R, 3rd rev. ed. (Washington, D.C.: APA, 1987), p. 67.

21. Ron van Deth and Walter Vandereycken, "Was Nervous Consumption a Precursor of Anorexia Nervosa?" *Journal of the History of Medicine and Allied Sciences* 46 (1991), pp. 3–19; especially p. 6. They also propose "denial of illness" as an additional criterion.

22. The high frequency of self-starvation among psychiatric patients generally was evident at Oxford's Littlemore Asylum, where in the years 1877 to 1880, 38 percent of the 207 newly admitted patients had been refusing food at the time of admission. "Many were emaciated, forced feeding had to be used extensively." William L. Parry-Jones, "Archival Exploration of Anorexia Nervosa," *Journal of Psychiatric Research* 19 (1985), pp. 95–100; quote p. 97.

23. It is revealing that "Nadia," an anorexic patient of Janet's, wanted to become thin so as to be unappealing. She began a program of self-starvation because, as she said, "Men like big women. I want always to remain extremely thin." Raymond and Janet, *Les Obsessions,* vol. 2, case no. 166, pp. 368–73; quote p. 370.

24. See Shorter, *From Paralysis to Fatigue,* pp. 120–25.

25. Salomon Stiebel, *Kleine Beiträge zur Heilwissenschaft* (Frankfurt/M., 1823), pp. 1–8.

26. For further instances of anorexic patients chosing the fashionable symptoms of the day, see the reports in Albert Willem van Renterghem and Frederik van Eeden, *Clinique de psycho-thérapie suggestive fondée à Amsterdam le 16 août 1887 . . .* (Brussels, 1889); especially case no. 6, pp. 64–65.

27. Giovanni Brugnoli, "Sull'anoressia," *Accademia delle scienze del Istituto di Bologna. Memorie* 6 (1875), pp. 351–61; cases pp. 352–57.

28. Frederic Carpenter Skey, *Hysteria* (New York, 1867), pp. 85–87.

29. Weir Mitchell, *Lectures* p. 203.

30. The same phenomenon occurred between the 1920s and 1950s, as patients with psychogenic anorexia received the organic endocrinological diagnosis "Simmonds' disease," whose pathology is the destruction of the anterior part of the pituitary gland. Morris Simmonds, "Über Hypophysisschwund mit tödlichem Ausgang," *DMW* 40 (Feb. 12, 1914), pp. 322–23.

31. See the discussion of "Gastrodynia neuralgica" in Moritz Heinrich Romberg, *Lehrbuch der Nervenkrankheiten des Menschen,* vol. 1, pt. 1 (Berlin, 1840), pp. 103–5. The disorder occurred more commonly in women, Romberg said. The appetite, however, remained normal.

32. Louis-Victor Marcé, "Note sur une forme de délire hypochondriaque consécutive aux dyspepsies et charactérisée principalement par le refus d'aliments," *Annales médico-psychologiques* 6 (1860), pp. 15–28; quotes pp. 15–16.

33. Ernst von Leyden, "Über periodisches Erbrechen (gastrische Krisen) nebst Bemerkungen über nervöse Magenaffectionen," *Zeitschrift für klinische Medizin* 4 (1882) pp. 605–15.

34. Ottomar Rosenbach, "Die Emotionsdyspepsie," *BKW* 34 (Jan. 25, 1897), pp. 70–75; especially p. 73.

35. Moritz Rosenthal, *Zur Diagnose und Therapie der Magenkrankheiten, insbesondere der Neurosen des Magens* (Vienna, 1883), pp. 12–13.

36. On chlorosis and hyperemesis hysterica as possible forerunners of anorexia nervosa, see I. S. L. Loudun, "Chlorosis, Anaemia, and Anorexia Nervosa," *BMJ* 281 (Dec. 20, 1980), pp. 1669–75; F. Reimer, "Anorexia nervosa: die Chlorose der 80er Jahre?" *Fundamenta Psychiatrica* 2 (1988), pp. 53–54. "Hyperemesis" means continued vomiting.

37. Thomas Laycock, *A Treatise on the Nervous Diseases of Women* (London, 1840), p. 258.

38. d'Étiolles, *Des paralysies*, vol. 1, p. 259.

39. John W. Ogle, "Clinical Lecture on a Case of Hysteria . . . and Persistent Vomiting," *BMJ* 2 (July 16, 1870), pp. 57–60; details pp. 57–58. She secretly sneaked food, giving the case an element of simulation, yet it was vomiting that she selected as a symptom.

40. A. Amann, *Über den Einfluss*, pp. 17, 21.

41. Wilks, "Lectures on Diseases of the Nervous System," p. 824.

42. Mitchell, *Diseases of the Nervous System*, p. 204.

43. Naunyn, *Erinnerungen*, p. 353. "Kindische Imaginationsneurosen." Other patients would appear "paralyzed," meaning, said Naunyn, that "they imagined themselves to be paralyzed." Many of the vomiters and the paralyzed "brought along excessively indulgent relatives, most dangerous being the mother." Naunyn cured them by isolating them from their relatives in his clinic.

44. Robert Brudenell Carter, in discussion at Clinical Society of London meeting of Oct. 24, *BMJ* 2 (Nov. 1, 1873), p. 528.

45. John Syer Bristowe, "Clinical Remarks on the Functional Vomiting of Hysteria," *Practitioner* 30 (1883), pp. 161–174; case p. 162.

46. Thomas Clifford Allbutt, *On Visceral Neuroses* (Philadelphia, 1884), pp. 21, 46, 49.

47. Edward G. Dutton, "A Severe Case of Hysteria, Cured by Massage, Seclusion, and Overfeeding," *Lancet* 1 (June 9, 1888), pp. 1128–29.

48. William Hale White, "Clinical Lecture on a Case of Severe Hysteria Treated by Massage, Isolation, and Overfeeding," *BMJ* 2 (July 30, 1887), pp. 232–33.

49. Enoch Heinrich Kisch, "Dyspepsia uterina," *BKW* 20 (Apr. 30, 1883), pp. 263–67; case p. 267.

50. Max Bircher-Benner, *Vom Werden des neuen Arztes: Erkenntnisse und Bekenntnisse* (Dresden, 1938), p. 41.

51. John M. Berkman, "Anorexia Nervosa, Anorexia, Inanition, and Low Basal Metabolic Rate," *American Journal of the Medical Sciences* 180 (1930), pp. 411–24; data p. 416.

52. Houston, *The Art of Treatment*, pp. 406–7.

53. David M. Garner et al., "The Validity of the Distinction Between Bulimia With and Without Anorexia Nervosa," *AJP* 142 (1985), pp. 581–87; table 2, p. 584. Of the fifty-nine women who alternated bingeing and self-starvation, 80 percent had a history of vomiting.

54. Vomiting has maintained its popularity across the years more than I suggested in an earlier article. Edward Shorter, "The First Great Increase in Anorexia Nervosa," *Journal of Social History* 21 (1987), pp. 69–96.

55. Laycock, *Nervous Diseases of Women* (1840), p. 257.

56. Briquet, *Traité clinique*, p. 520.

57. Leidesdorf, *Lehrbuch*, p. 177.

58. Among early possible instances of anorexia nervosa is the character Ottilie in Johann Wolfgang von Goethe's novel *Wahlverwandt-schaften (Elective Affinities)* (1809). See S. Bhanji et al., "Goethe's Ottilie: an Early 19th Century Description of Anorexia Nervosa," *Journal of the Royal Society of Medicine* 83 (1990), pp. 581–85; yet it is likelier that the qualities Goethe gives his character are more those of depression, a diagnosis that excludes anorexia nervosa.

59. Marcé, "Note sur une forme de délire," pp. 25–26.

60. Ernest-Charles Lasègue, "De l'anorexie hystérique," *Archives générales de médecine* 21 (Apr. 1873), pp. 385–403; translated in abridged form, into English as "On Hysterical Anorexia," *MTG* 2 (Sept. 6, 27, 1873), pp. 265–66, 367–69.

61. William Gull, "Anorexia Nervosa (Apepsia Hysterica, Anorexia Hysterica)," *Transactions of the Clinical Society of London* 7 (1874), pp. 22–28. At the October 24, 1873, meeting of the Clinical Society, Gull had actually given a paper on anorexia, but had called it at the time "Anorexia Hysterica (Apepsia Hysterica)." Summary of paper in *BMJ* 2 (Nov. 1, 1873), pp. 527–28. In a talk on medical diagnosis of a rather general nature in 1868, Gull had made reference to

self-starvation, and on this basis later claimed for himself the priority in describing the "new disease." He had written, "At present our diagnosis [of abdominal disease] is mostly one of inference, from our knowledge of the liability of the several organs to particular lesions; thus we avoid the error of supposing the presence of mesenteric disease in young women emaciated to the last degree through hysteric apepsia, by our knowledge of the latter affection, and by the absence of tubercular disease elsewhere." William W. Gull, "The Address in Medicine," *Lancet* 2 (Aug. 8, 1868), pp. 171–76; quote p. 175. Such a paltry mention could not possibly represent the first description of an independent disease entity, were anorexia nervosa to constitute such an entity. On quarrels about the priority in naming the disorder, see Walter Vandereycken and Ron Van Deth, "Who Was the First to Describe Anorexia Nervosa: Gull or Lasègue?" *Psychological Medicine* 19 (1989), pp. 837–45.

62. Lasègue, quotes from the English translation in *MTG*.

63. Charles Naudeau, "Observation sur une maladie nerveuse, accompagnée d'un dégoût extraordinaire pour les alimens," *Journal de médecine, chirurgie, pharmacie* (July 1789), pp. 197–200.

64. Charles Féré, "Névrose électrique," *Prog. méd* 12 (July 5, 1884), pp. 540–41.

65. Paul Sollier, *Genése et nature de l'hystérie*, 2 vols. (Paris, 1897), vol. 2, pp. 20–25.

66. Jules Janet, "Un Cas d'hystérie grave," *Revue de l'hypnotisme* 3 (1889), pp. 339–42. For background on the double-personality vogue see Shorter, *From Paralysis to Fatigue*, pp. 159–65.

67. Raymond and Janet, *Obsessions*, vol. 2; case 68, pp. 162–63.

68. Ibid.; case 162, pp. 360–61.

69. Weir Mitchell, *Diseases of the Nervous System*, pp. 209–13.

70. Josef Breuer and Sigmund Freud, *Studies on Hysteria* (1895), Eng. trans. (Harmondsworth: Penguin, 1974), p. 150.

71. Bristowe, *Practitioner*, pp. 169–70.

72. William Goodell, "The Extirpation of the Ovaries for Some of the Disorders of Menstrual Life," *BMSJ* 100 (June 19, 1879), pp. 841–48; case pp. 842–43.

73. Thomas Beath, "Extreme Emaciation in Hysteria, with Notes of a Case," *Canadian Journal of Medicine and Surgery* 7 (1900), pp. 95–98.

74. "Borderline personality disorder" in particular has become a beloved diagnosis of both doctors and patients. Intrinsic personality disturbances may well accompany the phenomenon of self-starvation, yet

everyone—physician and patient alike—knows the prescribed "de-controlled" manner in which a "borderline" is supposed to act. See for example, Richard A. Gordon, "A Sociocultural Interpretation of the Current Epidemic of Eating Disorders," in Barton J. Blinder et al., eds., *The Eating Disorders: Medical and Psychological Bases of Diagnosis and Treatment* (New York: PMA, 1988), p. 156. For an example of the literature see Randy A. Sansone et al., "The Prevalence of Borderline Personality Symptomatology Among Women With Eating Disorders," *Journal of Clinical Psychology* 45 (1989), pp. 603–10.

75. Hilde Bruch, "Perceptual and Conceptual Disturbances in Anorexia Nervosa," *Psychosomatic Medicine* 24 (1962), pp. 187–94.

76. *DSM-III-R,* p. 65. The phrase "significant weight loss," present in the diagnostic guide published in 1980, was removed from the 1987 version. American Psychiatric Association, *Diagnostic and Statistical Manual of Mental Disorders,* 3rd ed. (Washington: APA, 1980), p. 67.

77. Here I diverge from Tillmann Habermas, who argues that weight concerns have always existed, yet only recently did doctors notice them: "It is plausible that weight concerns have been present in anorexia nervosa from its beginning on but have been overlooked by most German and British medical men." Further: "It seems probable that the variations in how often weight concerns have been registered in anorexic patients are not due to historical developments in the nature of anorexia nervosa but to developments of diagnostic thinking." Habermas, "The Psychiatric History of Anorexia Nervosa and Bulimia Nervosa: Weight Concerns and Bulimic Symptoms in Early Case Reports," *International Journal of Eating Disorders* 8 (1989), pp. 259–73; quotes p. 269. It stretches credulity to imagine that the many careful clinical accounts of self-starvation we have before 1873 somehow neglected to mention a major motivation such as slimming simply because physicians were "insensitive" to it.

78. On the increase of concern about weight, see Hillel Schwartz, *Never Satisfied: A Cultural History of Diets, Fantasies and Fat* (New York: Free Press, 1986), chap. 5, "The Regulated Body."

79. Pierre Janet, *The Major Symptoms of Hysteria: Fifteen Lectures Given in the Medical School of Harvard University* (1907; 2nd rev. ed. New York, 1929), p. 234.

80. Paul Sollier, "Anorexie hystérique," *Revue de médecine* 11 (1891), pp. 625–50; quote p. 629.

81. [Gabriel?] Wallet, "Deux cas d'anorexie hystérique," *Nouvelle icono-graphie de la Salpêtrière* 5 (1892), pp. 276–280, here p. 278. See also J. Girou, "Anorexie, suite d'arrêt volontaire de l'alimentation," *Revue neurologique* 13 (1905), pp. 144–45, on a girl of nineteen in Aurillac who suddenly started eating less and vomiting after meals after her friends had mocked her as "la plus forte d'elles toutes" during a wedding. She resumed eating only at the point of death.

82. Gugl and Stichl, *Neuropathologische Studien*, p. 66.

83. Ibid., pp. 54–55.

84. Hanns Kaan, *Der neurasthenische Angstaffect bei Zwangsvorstellungen und der primordiale Grübelzwang* (Vienna, 1892), p. 92. On this clinic and its patients, see Shorter, "Women and Jews in a Private Nervous Clinic," pp. 149–83. Kaan was at the clinic between 1889 and 1891. It is possible that he saw her at the university psychiatric clinic in Graz, where he had earlier been on staff.

85. Löwenfeld, *Pathologie und Therapie*, p. 442.

86. Emil Raimann, *Die hysterischen Geistesstörungen* (Leipzig, 1904), p. 173.

87. Otto Binswanger, *Die Hysterie* (Vienna, 1904), pp. 610–11. In discussing "Anorexia nervosa" he also called it "hysterische Anorexie."

88. Edgar Bérillon, "L'Anorexie des adolescents: particularités mentales et traitement psychologique," *Revue de l'hypnotisme* 24 (1909–10), pp. 46–49; quote p. 47.

89. Victor-Henri Hutinel, "L'Anorexie mentale," *Journal des practiciens* (June 5, 1909), pp. 352–60; quote p. 359.

90. John A. Ryle, "Anorexia nervosa," *Lancet* 2 (Oct. 17, 1936), pp. 893–899; quote p. 895.

91. Ray F. Farquharson and Herbert H. Hyland, "Anorexia Nervosa: a Metabolic Disorder of Psychologic Origin," *JAMA* 111 (Sept. 17, 1938), 1085–92.

92. Ferdinando Accornero, "L'Anoressia mentale," *Rivista Sperimentale di Freniatria* 67 (1943), pp. 447–489; cases pp. 463, 478.

93. Jürg Zutt, "Das psychiatrische Krankheitsbild der Pubertätsmagersucht" (1948), reprinted in Jürg Zutt, ed., *Auf dem Wege zu einer anthropologischen Psychiatrie: gesammelte Aufsätze* (Berlin: Springer, 1963), pp. 195–255; cases pp. 200, 220, 228, 233.

94. Raymond and Janet, *Les Obsessions*, vol. 2, pp. 368–73.

95. Grace Nicolle, "Pre-Psychotic Anorexia," *Proceedings of the Royal Society of Medicine* 32 (1938), pp. 153–62; quote p. 159.

96. Lucien Cornil and Mendel Schachter, "La Querelle de l'anorexie

mentale," *L'Encéphale* 34 (1939–41), pp. 371–90; quote pp. 372–73. In these interwar years a sense of physical disgust with one's own body was reported as well in connection with compulsive overeating, or bulimia. See Moshe Wulff, "Über einen interessanten oralen Symptomenkomplex und seine Beziehung zur Sucht," *Internationale Zeitschrift für Psychoanalyse* 18 (1932), pp. 281–302. All four of these bulimic patients reported themselves disgusted with their bodies as they gorged.

97. Henry B. Richardson, "Simmonds' Disease and Anorexia Nervosa," *Archives of Internal Medicine* 63 (1939), pp. 1–28; quote p. 15.

98. Ryle, "Anorexia Nervosa," p. 894.

99. [Adrien?] Rist, "Observation d'anorexie idiopathique," *Bulletin de la société médicale de la suisse romande* 12 (1878), pp. 59–64; quote p. 60.

100. Brugnoli, "Sull' Anoressia," pp. 353–54.

101. La Faure, "Hysterical Anorexia," *Massachusetts Medical Journal* 16 (1896), pp. 289–98; quote p. 296. The writer was listed as a Parisian "M.D."

102. Nicolle, "Pre-Psychotic Anorexia," p. 159.

103. Bérillon, "L'Anorexie des adolescents," p. 47.

104. André-Thomas said that, "L'anorexie mentale a une affinité marquée pour les enfants gâtés, pour les filles uniques." "L'Anorexie mentale," *La Clinique* 4 (Jan. 15, 1909), pp. 33–37; quote p. 35.

105. Lionel Vidart, "L'Anorexie mentale," *Gazette des hôpitaux* 110 (July 3, 1937), pp. 861–64; quote p. 861.

106. The expression comes from Walter Vandereycken and Rolf Meermann, *Anorexia Nervosa: A Clinician's Guide to Treatment* (Berlin: Walter de Gruyter, 1984), p. 151.

107. Henri Huchard, "Caractère, moeurs, état mental des hystériques," *Archives de neurologie* 3 (1882), pp. 187–211; quote p. 194.

108. Jean-Martin Charcot, "De l'isolement dans le traitement de l'hystérie," *Prog. méd.* 13 (Feb. 28, 1885), pp. 161–64; case pp. 162–63.

109. Sollier, "Anorexie hystérique," p. 650.

110. Georges Gasne, "Un Cas d'anorexie hystérique," *Nouvelle iconographie de la Salpêtrière* 13 (1900), pp. 51–56; especially p. 56.

111. Noël Perron, "Quelques considérations sur le traitement des anorexies mentales," *Bulletin général de thérapeutique* 187 (1936), pp. 390–93; quote p. 392.

112. Noël Perron, "Défense de l'anorexie mentale," *Paris médical* 2 (July 16, 1938), pp. 65–70; quotes pp. 65–66.

113. Showalter, *The Female Malady*. On anorexia, see pp. 127–29. The author asks: "Was hysteria—the 'daughter's disease'—a mode of protest for women deprived of other social or intellectual outlets or expressive options" (p. 147). Later she answers her question: "Hysteria and feminism do exist on a kind of continuum. . . . The availability of a women's movement in which the 'protofeminism' of hysterical protest could be articulated and put to work, offered a potent alternative to the self-destructive and self-enclosed strategies of hysteria, and a genuine form of resistance to the patriarchal order" (p. 161). The problem with this analysis is that "hysteria" does not go away: it merely shifts from the motor side of the nervous system to the sensory. And anorexia nervosa certainly does not vanish.

114. Marcé, "Note sur une forme de délire," pp. 21–25.

115. Gasne, "Un Cas d'anorexie hystérique," pp. 51–54.

116. Walter Langdon-Brown, "Anorexia Nervosa," *Medical Press and Circular,* 182 (Apr. 15, 1931), pp. 308–9; quote p. 309; summary of remarks.

117. John A. Ryle, "Discussion on Anorexia Nervosa," *Proceedings Royal Society of Medicine* 32 (1939), pp. 735–735; quote p. 736.

118. On this process at the summit of eighteenth-century English society, see Judith Schneid Lewis, *In the Family Way: Childbearing in the British Aristocracy, 1760–1860* (New Brunswick, N.J.: Rutgers University Press, 1986), chaps. 1–2. More generally see also Shorter, *The Making of the Modern Family.*

119. Although all studies do not point to an increase, it is now widely accepted that the statistical incidence of anorexia nervosa, especially among women fifteen to twenty-four, has in fact risen. A careful study of Rochester, Minnesota, from 1935 to 1984, based on cases for 166 females and 15 males, taken from screening more than thirteen thousand medical records, showed a sharp rise for younger women, stable rates for women over twenty-five. Alexander R. Lucas et al., "50-Year Trends in the Incidence of Anorexia Nervosa in Rochester, Minn.: A Population-Based Study," *AJP* 148 (1991), pp. 917–22. An epidemiological study in Switzerland for the period 1956 to 1975 also identified an increase. Jürg Willi and Samuel Grossmann, "Epidemiology of Anorexia Nervosa in a Defined Region of Switzerland," *AJP* 140 (1983), pp. 564–67. Paul Williams and Michael King failed, however, to find rising rates in England in the 1970s (as opposed to a simple increase in the numbers of women in the vulnerable age groups):

"The 'Epidemic' of Anorexia Nervosa: Another Medical Myth?" *Lancet* 1 (Jan. 24, 1987), pp. 205–7. Among elite groups of young women the prevalence currently is as high as 5 percent. See, for example, Gordon, *Anorexia,* p. 39. If the prevalence had been this high in London between the two world wars, surely such clinicians as John Ryle would have seen more than the already-not-inconsiderable number they encountered.

120. On the "postmodern" family, see Shorter, "Einige demographische Auswirkungen des postmodernen Familienlebens," *Zeitschrift für Bevölkerungswissenschaft* 15 (1989), pp. 221–33. The Milanese psychotherapist and anorexia scholar Mara Selvini-Palazzoli attempted in 1985 to integrate new societal demands for "slimness," imposed by the mass media, into the games that family members play with each other, thus linking cultural themes to family issues. "The feminine image that fashion has prescribed," she writes, "is that of a slender body." Therefore young women diet. "It is a short step from this to the discovery that a silent hunger strike is a powerful instrument of indictment of their parents." If girls indict their parents more than boys, it is "the result of the fact, the sexual revolution and feminism notwithstanding, that they continue to be more controlled by parents than boys." Mara Selvini-Palazzoli, "Anorexia Nervosa: A Syndrome of the Affluent Society," *Transcultural Psychiatric Research Review* 22 (1985), pp. 199–205; quote p. 203.

121. David M. Garner et al., "Cultural Expectations of Thinness in Women," *Psychological Reports* 47 (1980), pp. 483–91; data pp. 485–86.

122. See the evidence in Hsu, "The Gender Gaps," p. 395.

123. See Leslie Swartz, "Illness Negotiation: The Case of Eating Disorders," *Social Science and Medicine* 24 (1987), pp. 613–18. The author asks, "Can people be educated into eating disorders . . . ?" She further calls attention to the role of medical shaping, though she does not use that term: "[How the] patient views the clinician's interpretation of her problem must be informed by her knowledge about professional understanding of the disorder. . . . The process of clinical history-taking sets up a series of expectations in any patient's mind. . . . Having the symptoms of an eating disorder can easily become a way of being authentic as a patient. Giving up these symptoms may mean for the patient that she will no longer be worthy of the attention that people with the symptoms have enjoyed" (p. 617).

CHAPTER 7
Cultural Shaping

1. Mechanic, "Religion, Religiosity, and Illness Behavior," pp. 202–8.
2. For further information on patterns of somatization surrounding such trendy diagnoses as "chronic fatigue syndrome," "chronic EBV" and the like, see Shorter, *From Paralysis to Fatigue,* chap. 11.
3. Hans Selye, *The Physiology and Pathology of Exposure to Stress* (Montreal: Acta, 1950).
4. An unpublished finding of the study of ninety-two chronically somatizing patients at a clinic for psychosomatic illness in a large North American city, twenty-two of whom denied stress. For a description of this study see Shorter et al., "Inpatient Treatment of Persistent Somatization," pp. 295–301. To implicate stress as a cause, we would have to know how many people who *did not* develop a psychosomatic illness were under stress. The proportion might be even higher than among the ill patients.
5. An influential textbook was Edward Weiss and O. Spurgeon English, *Psychosomatic Medicine: The Clinical Application of Psychopathology to General Medical Problems* (Philadelphia, 1943).
6. For a recent review see Shorter, *From Paralysis to Fatigue,* pp. 246–48.
7. I have derived this metaphor of a "line" from the work of Berlin psychiatrist Karl Birnbaum in the 1920s and 1930s. *Soziologie der Neurosen: die nervösen Störungen in ihren Beziehungen zum Gemeinschafts- und Kulturleben* (Berlin, 1933; reprint from *Archiv für Psychiatrie und Nervenkrankheiten* 99 [1933] pp. 339–425); for example, pp. 13–14: "We may separate all that is relevant to our concerns into two groups: the one contains everything affecting the origins of a neurosis (both external and internal causes alike), in other words the sociopathogenetic factors [*sozialpathogenetische Zusammenhänge*]. The other group concerns everything affecting the presentation of a neurosis [*Gestaltung der Neurose*], namely the socioplastic factors [*sozialpathoplastische Zusammenhänge*]." Because of the timing of its publication, this seminal work by a Jewish psychiatrist ended up being largely overlooked. For some details on Birnbaum's life see P. M. Yap and L. Z. Vogel, "Karl Birnbaum's Concept of Pathoplasticity and its Relevance for Comparative Psychiatry" (Paper presented at the Annual Meeting of the Canadian Psychiatric Association, Halifax, Nova Scotia, June 1971). Birnbaum originally worked out these important distinctions be-

tween "Pathoplastik" and "Pathogenetik" in work on the psychoses during the 1920s. See his *Der Aufbau der Psychose: Grundzüge der psychiatrischen Strukturanalyse* (Berlin, 1923), especially the table on pp. 98–99; also Karl Birnbaum, "Der Aufbau der Psychose," in Oswald Bumke, ed., *Handbuch der Geisteskrankheiten,* vol. 5 (1) (Berlin, 1928), pp. 1–18.

8. All five were female and middle class, in a patient population that was split more or less evenly between males and females, and between middle and working classes. Eight of the forty-three patients who commented on their childhoods had happy ones. For a description of the research from which these findings are taken, see Shorter, "Inpatient Treatment of Persistent Somatization."

9. See for example Edward A. Walker et al., "Irritable Bowel Syndrome and Psychiatric Illness," *AJP* 147 (1990), pp. 565–72; especially p. 569.

10. On cultural modeling, see, for example, Nancy F. Cott, *The Bonds of Womanhood: "Woman's Sphere" in New England, 1780–1835* (New Haven, Conn.: Yale University Press, 1977).

11. For links between larger cultural representations and the diagnosis of psychiatric illness see the various essays by Andrew Scull, collected in his *Social Order/Mental Disorder: Anglo-American Psychiatry in Historical Perspective* (Berkeley: University of California Press, 1989). Among Porter's extensive writing on England, *Mind-Forg'd Manacles* might be mentioned.

12. These issues are explained in detail in Shorter, *From Paralysis to Fatigue,* passim, and alluded to here as a way of establishing a bridge between the two volumes.

Index